THE
NEW
MAN

THE NEW MAN

BECOMING A MAN
AFTER GOD'S HEART

DAN DORIANI

P.O. BOX 817 • PHILLIPSBURG • NEW JERSEY 08865-0817

First published by Crossway in 2001 under the title *The Life of a God-Made Man: Becoming a Man After God's Heart*

New edition published 2015 by P&R Publishing

Library of Congress Cataloging-in-Publication Data

Doriani, Daniel M., 1953-
[Life of a God-made man]
The new man : becoming a man after God's heart / Dan Doriani. -- New edition.
    pages cm
"First published by Crossway in 2001 under the title The Life of a God-Made Man: Becoming a Man After God's Heart."
Includes bibliographical references and index.
ISBN 978-1-59638-951-9 (pbk.) -- ISBN 978-1-59638-952-6 (ePub) -- ISBN 978-1-59638-953-3 (Mobi)
1. Christian men--Religious life. I. Title.
BV4528.2.D67 2015
248.8'42--dc23
                    2015004266

Contents

Preface

This book is a proposal and a protest. It protests all the books that reduce the Christian life to a string of techniques and how-to lists. It proposes instead that the course of the Christian is the course of his God. It protests all the lists of four steps for building lasting friendships, five techniques for raising obedient children, and seven methods of loving your wife. To avoid man-made lists, we will spend more time exploring Bible texts than typical men's books do. We will also focus on character over technique and law. God is remaking his children in his image. Therefore, it is our heritage and destiny to become more like the Father, the Son, and the Spirit. We are most true to ourselves when most like Christ.

That conviction shapes this book. Instead of starting with rules and guidelines for godly living, we will consider the nature of God first. For example:

- Godly husbands follow the pattern of sacrificial love set by Jesus. His love for his bride, the church, shows husbands how to love their wives.
- Good fathers are like God, our Father. His love, justice, faithfulness, and loving discipline set the pattern for godly fathers.
- Godly friends imitate God's friendship with Abraham and Moses, the friendship of Jesus and his disciples. Self-disclosure and helpful presence are the marks of his friendship with us, and ours with each other.
- Godly workers love to create because God the Creator made us in his image. We like to finish tasks because we resemble Jesus who exulted, "It is finished."

- Even in our play, we imitate the playfulness of God that we see in his world. His pattern of work and rest liberates us to rest and play.

There is more to godly masculinity than this, but nothing is more foundational. God created us in his image, and by his grace he restores us to that image day by day. For that reason, this book accents character over technique, being over doing.

This approach follows Jesus, who says, "Every good tree bears good fruit, but a bad tree bears bad fruit. A good tree cannot bear bad fruit, and a bad tree cannot bear good fruit" (Matt. 7:17–18). Jesus also says, "I am the vine; you are the branches. If a man remains in me and I in him, he will bear much fruit; apart from me you can do nothing" (John 15:5). Talk of inability offends men who have a high estimate of their strength. So be it. Progress cannot begin until we know ourselves, weaknesses included. We must know that love, sacrifice, and service are alien to our lazy and self-seeking souls. Left to ourselves, we have little desire to sacrifice. But Jesus renews people.

In the language of Scripture, Jesus gives us a new heart. We gain spiritual sensitivity and new interests. A Christian man still cares about his honor, and he cares about God's honor too. He loves his family, and loves the family of God as well. We each become, in the language of Scripture, a man after God's heart.

The phrase *a man after God's heart* captures the way a changed life radiates out from a renewed spirit. First Samuel 13:14 uses it to describe David before he became king, and it suits him well. He longed for nothing more than God's presence (Ps. 27:4–8). Zeal for God's house consumed him (Ps. 69:9). These passions transformed David. When a Philistine giant taunted God's people, David could not bear the insult to God's honor, and fought the giant in the Lord's strength (1 Sam. 17). When David became king, his first act was to bring the ark of God, the sign of God's presence, into his capital city (2 Sam. 6). As king he showed mercy and protected the weak, because he knew that *God* "has regard for the weak [and] delivers him in times of trouble" (Ps. 41:1–2; see also 2 Sam. 9). In the course of his affair with beautiful, reckless Bathsheba, David learned that he was weak too, a man who needed to *receive* mercy and deliverance, not just give it. But as a man after God's heart, he eventually confessed his sin. Making no excuses, he threw himself on God's mercy, and received it (2 Sam. 11–12).

Although David certainly knew and loved God's law, David was not essentially a law-driven man. He loved his God, and that directed his actions. Anyone who takes his sins and sinfulness seriously knows lists of duties will never be the prime guides for a believer.

Why then do we act as if we can hand out rules and methods and expect any Joe to follow them? Why do certain Christians sound as if we can solve every problem by spooning out the right techniques? Do they think proper instruction is the key to life? If it is, why are there so many self-help books? Wouldn't three or four be enough to cover our topics? Our cultures shape us more than we realize. I wonder: Do Christian leaders focus on techniques because science, technology, and business dominate our culture? Has our fascination with technological solutions to problems seeped into our theological bones? Have management models led us to think we can govern our relationships by following easy steps?

Jesus appears often enough in books for Christian men. Sadly, some use him as teacher more than our Savior. His actions are made to illustrate the principles of the book—the "how-to" of whatever a chapter requires. Meanwhile, if the grace of Jesus is mentioned, it is the grace that forgives, rather than the grace that transforms and sustains sinners.

Of course, a book on marriage, fatherhood, money, work, friendship, and play will make suggestions. I will not ground all of them in the character of God. Some explore the life of faith. Some address Christian discernment—the ability to see things God's way and act on it day by day. But the interest in God's character will remain. We become like that which we behold. Law neither motivates nor transforms, but grace does. When that grace changes us, it changes all.

A Word to the Wives

Women like to read men's books. This is a man's book, but women read more than men, who sometimes need their beloved to nudge them. I hope husbands and wives will jointly read the chapters on marriage and parenting. Since I wrote those chapters for mouth and ear, a couple might read them to each other, making this a read-aloud book.

Acknowledgments

Thank you, Debbie, for helping celebrate all our undeserved blessings and for your patience and mercy in my painfully slow movement toward maturity. It is a joy to have my daughter Sarah illustrate the chapter on play. Her sketches arise from happy memories. I dedicate this book to the godly men with whom I have explored these issues and lived together as we sought godly manhood over the last twelve years: Clay, Robbie, Lance, Eric 1 and 2, Tim, Jay Thomas, Marc, Mark, Randy, Norman, Frank, Allen, Todd, Josh, Bob 1 and 2, Gerry, Bill, Jimmy, Joe, Ted, and David.

| 1 |

A Man After God's Heart

Finding the Right Path

Some years ago, I tried downhill skiing for the first time. Each night I instructed a group of men and women in the Christian faith, and each day they instructed me on the slopes of a peak in the Austrian Alps. I fell down too many times to count, yet the men stuck by me. One gave formal lessons in the morning. Others skied gentler slopes at slower speeds in the afternoon, patiently teaching me their art. On the last run of the fourth afternoon, my companion, an athletic Dutchman, took me to the top of the mountain. "I think you'll like this trail," he said, as we hopped off the lift. We skied a short distance and stopped to peer down what seemed more like a cliff than a trail.

"That looks a little steep," I said, trying to sound calm.

"Well, yes," my friend replied. "This is where the downhill race starts when the World Cup comes to town."

"How fast do they go?" I wondered.

"About 140 kilometers per hour."

I stared downhill and calculated, "That's over 85 miles an hour."

My friend understood. "It's OK," he assured me. "They go straight down. We'll ski from side to side, across the mountain. Look, I'll go first. Follow in my tracks and you will be fine." I trusted him (and I had no choice), so when he launched, I followed, skiing in his tracks. I crashed on the first turn and slid down the first, steepest slope. After that, I found that his tracks were good, because they allowed me to ski slowly enough to stay upright (usually) as my skis followed his. Farther down, we found milder paths and skied side by side as we enjoyed the mountain's magnificent vistas.

The Christian life is like my journey down the mountain. We have to follow the trail, but we're not good enough. Left to our own devices, we fall down over and over. Indeed, left to ourselves, we die. But we are not on our own. Someone is willing to help us find the right path. Ultimately, that Someone is God. At another level, our fellow Christians help us. They know the way down, they negotiated the path with skill, skied before us, and made a track we could follow.

The Bible describes the Christian life as a way or a path. Moses summoned the people of God to "walk in all his ways" (Deut. 11:22). Psalm 1 says, "The LORD watches over the way of the righteous" (Ps. 1:6, see also 18:36; 119:32–35). And Paul says Christians should "walk in the footsteps of the faith [of] our father Abraham" (Rom. 4:12). So the life of faith is active—a walk or journey in the right path. Indeed Scripture often compares the believer to a runner, even a racer (Ps. 119:32; Isa. 40:31; 1 Cor. 9:24–26; Heb. 12:1). Yet we must understand the journey correctly. We don't simply achieve success by our striving. We must beware of Christianity as simply as performance, or what we can call "Nike Christianity."

Following the Path of Performance; or Nike Christianity

Performance Christianity, or Nike Christianity, is a "just do it" approach to the Christian life.[1] Nike Christianity is a form of legalism. Since the term *legalism* is tossed around carelessly in some circles, we should distinguish four classes of legalist.

A class one legalist believes that he can *do* something to obtain salvation, to *earn* God's favor. The rich young man who

---

1. The motto has been in continuous use since 1988 as I write. Clearly it resonates with something in the Western psyche.

asked Jesus what he could do to inherit eternal life was a class one legalist (Matt. 19:16–22; Luke 18:18–23). Class two legalists require believers to submit to man-made commandments as if they were the law of God. Think of the Pharisees who attacked Jesus when he didn't follow their rules (Matt. 15:1–2). Class three legalists obey God and do good in order to gain or retain God's favor. Here we should think of the prosperity gospel, as well as all believers who think God's daily favor depends on their daily performance.

Class four legalists—Nike Christians—avoid the worst errors, but so accentuate obedience to God's law that other ideas shrivel up. They think of Christian living as little more than obedience to God's law. They reason, "God says we should tithe, so tithe. The Bible says we must pray, so pray. It says submit to leaders, witness, read Scripture, so we should submit, witness, and read. Just do it." Some Christian leaders unintentionally support Nike Christianity. One said, "The moral keynote of Christianity must be obedience." The Christian life is "submission to demands," so that "God calls and man obeys." They reason, "God has redeemed us at the cost of his Son's life. Now he demands our service in return. This is our duty." Class four legalists so dwell on God's law that they neglect the other aspects of the Christian life—the love of others, the nurture of character, the pursuit of noble but entirely optional projects, and more.

A great deal of Christian literature for men smacks of Nike Christianity. Books stress the need to repent and live better, according to the advice the book will dispense shortly. Nike Christian literature loves "how-to" lists. It offers five ways to form edifying friendship, six pointers for handling conflict, seven ways to exercise loving leadership, and eight techniques for more effective parenting.

Nike speakers set up their advice by reciting litanies of woes afflicting our culture. Next, they ask how we can break the downward spiral. They answer goes roughly like this: We break the cycle by getting men to assume their responsibilities. If anyone has failed, he needs to confess his sins to God. Then, O man, "Recommit yourself to your spiritual priorities. Get back on your feet, dust yourself off, and 'go and sin no more.'" In essence, their counsel goes like this:

- Some of you are doing bad things. You should stop! God wants you to do good things instead of bad things.
- Some of you are doing good things. Keep it up!
- Here is how to keep it up. You must plan to endure, taking these steps: Make a decision. Pray every morning. Commit yourself to God, 100 percent. Avoid temptation. Guard your mind, heart, and eyes. Seek a partner in accountability. Then you will stay on the right path.

The Problem with Nike Christianity

In one way, no one could object to this advice; those who dispense it certainly mean well. But the relentless stress on what men should *do* misses the most basic issue, the heart issue. Men fail to take the steps to "keep it up" because they don't *want* to keep it up. Prayer? Some men have no desire to be alone with God in prayer. They are bored or fearful. Commit 100 percent? We are double-minded, resisting God's authority one hour and embracing it the next. Accountability? Men *avoid* accountability because they prefer to answer to themselves alone. They don't want to guard the mind and/or the eye too closely. They *want* to indulge the eye's lusts for women and the mind's fantasies of dominance or wealth.

Most popular Christian books for men and women, most books about marriage and family, have a strong whiff of Nike Christianity. They are full of advice, but nearly devoid of grace. They speak often of what we should do for God, but little of what God has done for us. They often invoke the example of Jesus, but rarely discuss the *prior* love of Jesus that draws us to love him.

One day I was reading such a book in our family room as my wife sat nearby. The author was telling women how to act so their husbands would love them and long for their company: They must never nag. They must never greet their beleaguered heroes at the door with a litany of the day's problems. Rather they must always be welcoming, gentle, thankful, complimentary. Never criticize, complain, or get angry, the author said. Then your husband will love your very presence.

"Not a bad book," I thought. But as the obligations heaped up, I began to wonder what a real woman would say to this. So, selecting the lead sentences in fifteen or twenty sections, I read the gist of it to my wife. After five minutes or so, I paused, "What do you think?"

"It's good advice," she said thoughtfully, "But I felt over-whelmed and defeated after the first five ideas—and there were a dozen more." Exactly. What else can we say of books that say, in the final analysis, "Your husband [or your wife] will love you more if you never make a mistake"? They motivate with nothing but duty and guilt.

Please understand: it is good to submit to God's law and follow Jesus' example. The Savior is also our Sovereign and Lord (Jude 4). The Creator and Redeemer has all authority in heaven and on earth. Our sins grieve God, and he delights in our obe-dience, an obedience we owe him. But obedience is one ele-ment of the Christian life, not the whole. Indeed, the emphasis on obedience places the will ahead of the heart. It places our resolve (or self-discipline) ahead of our loves, even though the Bible places supreme emphasis on the heart and love—the heart is the "wellspring of life" (Prov. 4:23; see also Matt. 22:34–40). In short, obedience is neither the root nor the highest fruit of Christian living.

From beginning to end, God's love and grace go before his demands. We love because God first loved us (1 John 4:19). The love of Christ, who died for us, compels us to live not for ourselves but for God (2 Cor. 5:14-15). It is "the *grace* of God," not the *law* of God, that "teaches us to say 'No' to ungodliness and worldly passions" (Titus 2:11-12). Commands don't change people, love does. Unless God first loves a man and reconciles that man to himself, he cannot obey God's commands.

If we tell an atheist, "Store up for yourselves treasures in heaven," he cannot, for the command is nonsense to him. If he believes there is no god in heaven, why should he plan for it?

If we tell a teenager who despises her mother, "You must respect your mother," she cannot do so. She cannot *show* respect if she does not *have* respect. She may *obey* her mother, but she will do it grudgingly, with rolling eyes and slouching shoulders. She needs a changed relationship with her mother—a change of heart.

Similarly, while it makes sense to call a godless man to repent, it is a bit strange to tell him to stop sinning. We might as well command a drowning man to swim. It is true that the drowning man needs to swim, but the problem, precisely, is that he cannot. Likewise, a man who has enthroned his career or his appetites as his gods will not and *cannot* obey a command to put God first. As Paul says, "The sinful mind is hostile to God. It does not submit to God's law, nor can it do so" (Rom. 8:7).

The law has very important roles. It labels sin and shows people their sinfulness. It promotes civil order and reins in our wilder impulses. It states what we owe to others. Because every law reflects God's character, it shows us how to grow in conformity to him. But law, by itself, cannot change the heart.

The Root of a Godly Life

I recently spoke to a Christian businessman with a passion for discipleship. Frustrated by the slow progress of certain men, he asked me, "Dan, tell me, how do you get people to *change*? Where do they get *ability* to change? How can I get them"—he was punctuating every word—"to do ... what's ... RIGHT?" Because my friend had broken with Nike Christianity, he was ready for my reply: "Commands can change the behavior of children or employees, if you have the ability to punish disobedience. But law, by itself, never renews the heart. The love and grace of God change us. The truth changes people if the Spirit has renewed them and given them 'ears to hear.' But teachers don't have the power to change hearts. *We* cannot 'make' people do what is right."

Who can? Jeremiah said Israel would change when God gave his people a soft heart to replace their heart of stone (Jer. 31). Paul said the preaching of the gospel of Christ is foolishness—unless God's Spirit grants the ability to understand truths that are spiritually discerned (1 Cor. 1:21–2:14). In short, the *root* of obedience is God's prior grace and the *fruit* of obedience is conformity to his person and his plans. Jerry Bridges says:

> We do have a duty and obligation to God. He is the Sovereign Ruler of this world, and in that capacity, He has "laid down precepts that are to be fully obeyed" (Psalm 119:4). But He motivates us to obedience, not on the basis of His sovereign rule, but on the basis of His mercy to us in Jesus Christ. . . . I am committed to seek to act in love toward everyone. But I am committed in these areas out of a grateful response to God's grace, not to try to earn God's blessings.[2]

That is the gospel principle. We don't produce good works in order to *acquire* God's love but because we have his love. Everything hangs on the conjunctions. We obey, not *in order to* obtain God's salvation, but *because* God has saved us. Scripture motivates obedience by describing God's prior love. At Sinai, before declaring the law, God reminded Israel of his covenant-making love:

> You yourselves have seen what I did to Egypt, and how I carried you on eagles' wings and brought you to myself. Now if you obey me fully and keep my covenant, then out of all nations you will be my treasured possession . . . a kingdom of priests and a holy nation. (Ex. 19:4–6)

2. Jerry Bridges, *Transforming Grace* (Colorado Springs: NavPress, 1991), 78, 75.

I am the LORD your God, who brought you out of Egypt, out of the land of slavery.

You shall have no other gods before me. (Ex. 20:2–3)

So God's grace enables and impels us to live for him. Yet there are ways to think about obedience that partially detach it from the principles of covenant and grace. Like so many others, I experienced this very detachment for years.

The Motives for a Godly Life

When I was a new Christian, my teachers clearly taught that I owed the Lord my obedience in all of life. Yet I was a bit muddled as to why I obeyed. If asked to explain, I answered three ways, which we can call the way of wisdom, the way of trust, and the way of gratitude.

The way of wisdom says, "It is only reasonable to obey God's law. After all, he created all things, so he knows how they work. Therefore, we expect his commands to be effective, to bring us good." As Moses said, God gave Israel his commands "for your own good" (Deut. 10:13).

The way of trust says, "God loves us and would never mislead us." We should behave as he directs and trust him to make it work. If we do what is right for him, he will do right for us.

The way of gratitude judges that it is fitting for us to obey God without reserve because God first gave himself without reserve to us when he redeemed us. Because he has done so much for us, we should be willing to do much for him.

These perspectives contain profound truth. They are certainly superior to the *way of merit*, where people obey God to earn or retain his favor. And they surpass the *way of fear*, where people obey God to avert punishment. It is always good to obey God's law, yet he cannot be pleased with anyone who obeys him strictly to merit rewards or avoid penalties. Such obedience is selfish, even manipulative.

Yet, if we pause, we see that the ways of wisdom, trust, and gratitude *partially* obey for God's sake and partially for selfish reasons. There is trust and gratitude toward the Lord, but there is also a desire to gain benefits and to relieve debts. Thus they fall short of the noblest motive for obedience, the desire to obey God for his sake, out of love for him.

Bernard of Clairvaux, perhaps the greatest theologian of the twelfth century, said we cajole the *unwilling* with promises and rewards, not the willing. Who offers men rewards for doing what they want to do? Do we pay hungry men to eat? Do we pay thirsty men to drink? So, Bernard says, if we demand a reward to obey God, we love the reward rather than God.[3] In his words, "The soul that loves God seeks no other reward than that God whom it loves. Were the soul to demand anything else, then it would certainly love that other thing and not God."[4]

Suppose that three men go running five days each week. Suppose, further, that we ask each one why he dedicates himself to running.

- The first answers, "I run because my father died of a heart attack at fifty-four and I want to live long enough to retire and to see my grandchildren grow up."
- The second replies, "I run because I can eat anything I want when I run and I still don't gain weight. Running also makes me nice and tired, so I sleep soundly at night."
- The third says, "When I run, my legs soar over the ground; the wind brushes my face; my heart beats like slow, heavy thunder in my chest; and I feel *alive*."

The first man runs out of fear; he is worried about the consequences if he stops. The second runs for its benefits; he eats and sleeps better when he runs. But for the third man, running is its own reward. The first and second men love health, food,

3. Bernard of Clairvaux, *On Loving God* (Kalamazoo, MI: Cistercian Brothers, 1973, 1995), 7.17.
4. Ibid.

and sleep. Running is an *instrument* they use to gain what they desire. Only the third man loves running as an end in itself. The obedience of many Christians resembles the first two runners. We obey to avoid what we fear or to get what we want. How many serve God and seek no reward other than God himself? Ideally, the man after God's heart loves the Lord for *his* sake. Yet we love God as he reveals himself in history and in the Bible. We love God for his grace and his gospel. The idea of loving God for his own sake is daunting. But he does not leave us to "work up" love for him. Rather, he draws us to himself.

Knowing Grace

Sadly, it is harder to appreciate God's grace today than it was a few decades ago, because no seems to be guilty of anything anymore. People have guilt feelings, but no guilt. Everyone is a victim, but no one seems to be a victimizer. Rarely does anyone do anything that they admit to be *wrong*.

As a student radical, Katherine Powers committed several crimes in 1969 in an attempt to start a revolution. She helped rob a bank in which one of her confederates killed a policeman who had nine children. Investigators found a large store of weapons and ammunition in her apartment, but Powers eluded the FBI for years. She moved to Oregon, changed names, and created a new life. Then, in 1992, she became depressed and decided she had to reclaim her identity and become Katherine Powers again. To do that she had to turn herself in to the authorities. When she surrendered, she said, "I never intended to hurt anybody." And she explained that she turned herself in "to live with full authenticity in the present." Her husband added, "She did not return out of guilt. . . . She wanted her life back. She wanted her truth back. She wanted to be whole." So Powers returned to society for therapeutic reasons. In this atmosphere pastors sometimes feel like buggy whip salesmen, offering a product nobody wants.

Many believe that the concept of real guilt—as opposed to guilt feelings—needs to be abolished. Guilt-deniers reject the idea that they do anything wrong. Or if they did, it was long ago and unintentional, when they were a different person. Paul saw himself differently. Thirty years after his conversion, after decades of ceaseless labor and suffering for Christ, Paul still said, "Christ Jesus came into the world to save sinners, of whom I am chief" (1 Tim. 1:15 NKJV). He did not say, "I *was* chief," but "I *am* chief." He neither distanced himself from nor denied his past, when he blasphemed Christ and persecuted the church. He admitted his sin and advertised it as proof that no one is beyond the pale of God's grace (1 Tim. 1:15–16).

David's worst hour proves that this grace even covers sins committed after we come to faith. David, the man after God's own heart (1 Sam. 13:14). He became Israel's great shepherd and king, strong yet merciful (2 Sam. 9). His zeal for God proved itself when he faced Goliath in single combat. His heart for God showed again, when, in his first act after he took the crown, he brought the ark of God to Jerusalem (2 Sam. 6). Yet, in one outburst of sin, with Bathsheba, Israel's best king broke all ten commands (2 Sam. 11). We can work backward through the Decalogue:

- #10: His sin began when he coveted Bathsheba, another man's wife.
- #9: He deceived that man, Uriah, in his attempt to cover up her pregnancy.
- #7, 8: He stole Uriah's wife and committed adultery with her.
- #6: When his cover-up failed, he ordered Uriah's death by exposing him and his men to murderous enemy fire in battle.
- #5: Surely David's sin dishonored his parents.
- #4: David even desecrated the Sabbath, by remaining impenitent for a year. His worship was hypocrisy, as he hid his sin and refused God's remedy.
- #1–3: In all this, David followed another god, making his desires into his idol and serving them, so that the name of the Lord was put to shame.

All this David did deliberately, callously, from a public position. By the law, David deserved to die for his sins. Yet God showed mercy. He sent Nathan to rebuke through an irresistible parable (2 Sam. 12:1–6), ending with the accusation to David, "You are the man!" (v. 7).

When charged, David responded simply, "I have sinned against the LORD" (v. 13). He offered no extenuating circumstances ("You can't imagine how my wives had been acting"), no excuses ("All the other kings do it"), no blame shifting ("She was bathing in plain sight"). He does not say, "I have sinned, *but* . . ." He simply admitted his sin, with a mere three words in the original. He didn't even beg for mercy. He simply admitted his guilt: "I have sinned against the LORD."[5]

Nathan's reply was just as terse, "The LORD has taken away your sin" (v. 13). David would bear consequences for his sin (his son will die), but God's mercy carries no contingencies. Nathan did not say, "You will be forgiven if you prove you are sorry" or "You will have to do something to make up for this." David's sins deserved death, but he repented and God forgave. No sin stands outside the perimeter of grace. David says, "The sacrifices of God are a broken spirit; a broken and contrite heart, O God, you will not despise" (Ps. 51:17). In Romans, David is the paradigm of the long reach of God's grace: "Blessed are they whose transgressions are forgiven, whose sins are covered. Blessed is the man whose sin the Lord will never count against him" (Rom. 4:7–8).

The man after God's heart is a sinner, and he dwells in societies of sinners. At work, he puts down his rivals and shades the truth to gain a slight advantage. At home, he rebukes his children a little too harshly, for sins *he* modeled for his children. With a friend, he puts up an argument, even when he knows he is wrong, because he would rather *be* wrong than *appear* to be

---

5. The encounter is all brevity and simplicity. "You are the man!" translates two Hebrew words. David's reply, "I have sinned against the LORD," translates three, and Nathan uses just three more.

wrong. In athletic contests and in checkout lines, he chooses not to correct errors made in his favor. He would weep over it all, if he were not so cold.

"I know it, at least I know it," we think. We cling to the gospel, but even our clinging is tainted, because we are too much glad that our sin is covered, and not enough sorry that we did it. We even need to repent of our repentance. Even our faith is faulty, mixed with doubt and selfish hopes of God's blessing. Yet there is hope, because salvation rests not on the *quality* of our faith but on the *object* of the faith—Jesus. So God saves us even from the defects in our faith. Because we know this we return again and again to the gospel.

Loving the Gospel

It is so easy to forget the gospel. Even ministers of the gospel can do it; even the apostles did it, as Peter showed. In Acts 10, God welcomed a Roman centurion named Cornelius into the family of faith, without works, without giving up his Gentile heritage. God chose Peter to preach the gospel to Cornelius, a God-fearing Gentile, but Peter had a hard time accepting the charge.[6] God gave him a vision of a sheet lowered from heaven, holding all kinds of clean and unclean animals. Three times God said, "Get up, Peter. Kill and eat." Three times Peter refused to eat the unclean food. Three times a voice from heaven said, "Do not call anything impure [or unclean] that God has made clean" (vv. 11–16). While Peter wondered what this meant, Cornelius's servants arrived at his house. Peter had no idea who they were, but the Spirit told Peter, "Go with them" (vv. 17–22). Surely Peter was stunned to learn that the men were Gentiles, but he obeyed and went. When Peter arrived at Cornelius's house, a crowd of Gentiles awaited him. Peter greeted them, then asked, "May I ask why you sent for me?" (vv. 24–29).

6. *God-fearing* denotes Gentiles who believe in God and accept the Decalogue but not laws of food, circumcision, and sacrifice. Laws prohibiting close contact with Gentiles would force a centurion to forfeit his post.

When I read this, I want to laugh: "Peter, you are an apostle and herald of the gospel! Surely you know why God sent you there!" But no one laughed. Instead Cornelius urged Peter to speak: "Now we are all here in the presence of God to listen to everything the Lord has commanded you to tell us" (v. 33).

Peter began, "I now realize how true it is that God does not show favoritism but accepts men from every nation who fear him and do what is right" (vv. 34–35). Again, I want to laugh at Peter: "How can you say, 'Now I realize'? Surely you know, Peter. You saw Jesus heal Gentiles, talk to Samaritans, and all the rest. How can you say, 'Now I realize God accepts people from every nation?' You already know that!"

We laugh, yet we are so much like Peter. We know the gospel, but we forget it. We need to grasp it more deeply, more truly. We all have moments when we say, "Now I realize; now I understand the gospel."

My father belongs to the generation of stoics who became men in the Depression and World War II. My father loved me, but he never *said,* "I love you, son." He was proud of me, but he couldn't say so. Men raised by such fathers, often have two contrary traits. On one hand, we are confident and self-sufficient; we despise flattery. On the other hand, we yearn for praise from a father—or father figure. We want to be so good or do something so great that they will *have* to say, "I love you. I am so proud of you." But our fathers may be unable to say that. Our fathers may be dead. Then what happens to the desperate longing for the words, "I am proud of you"?

Our cure is in the gospel, for the gospel proclaims a Father who loved us when we ignored him, cursed him, and ran from him. He loves all his children, all whose parents never said, "I love you." His love is free, unconditional. There is nothing we can do to make him love us more than he does. When we alienated ourselves from him, he loved us, pursued us, and reconciled us to himself. He adopted us as his children, welcomed us into his family, where Jesus is our older brother (Heb. 2:11–13).

Sadly, Christians get tired of the gospel, especially if we care-lessly repeat its briefest form—"Jesus died for our sins." But, if we breathe in the gospel, we realize that it meets our deepest needs. So for everyone who seeks a father's praise, the gospel says, "Stop striving. God loves you without a performance, without conditions." The gospel liberates us in more ways:

- Justification cures the problem of guilt and condemna-tion. God, the judge, has justified us by faith, so we lose our right to condemn ourselves.
- Reconciliation removes alienation and loneliness. We need not wonder if we belong, or if anyone loves us.
- Redemption liberates us from the power of sin. Jesus delivered us from captivity to sin, death, and the devil. However we may feel, we are no longer trapped by sin.
- Jesus' propitiation put aside God's just wrath toward our sins. His love for us and our love for him casts out fear.[7]
- Jesus' bodily resurrection gives us reason to affirm this life, and his victory over death gives us reason to hope for life eternal.

At each point, the gospel meets heartfelt needs. At each point, people should say with Peter, "Now I realize! Now I understand the gospel!"

Living as a Man After God's Heart

The Christian subculture is full of "how-to" books. They stress rules, techniques, and methods to success, and they forget the gospel. They roll out lists of things men should do to please their wives, control their tempers, nurture their children, and find inner peace, all guaranteed by successful Christian leaders and athletes. If Jesus appears, he probably functions as an example, not as the Savior. Too often, the apostles are case studies more than fellow heirs of salvation.

7. A proper fear of God remains, due to his grandeur and holiness.

To live as men after God's heart, we need more than good advice. We need deliverance and a changed character. We don't need skiing tips, we need the ability to ski. Spiritually, this happens when God remakes us in his image. We are sinners created in his image and recreated in the image of Christ. Because Christian living begins and ends with God, techniques and advice can never by primary. Because we are sinners, Christ's redemption goes first. Because our goal is conformity to the image of Christ (Rom. 8:29), it also goes last. That is the focus of this book. But first, we need to understand our culture's images of masculinity, since they can blind us to the image of godly masculinity.

Discussion Questions

1. Why does legalism appeal to almost every Christian at some time? To what extent are you a "just do it" Christian? What is the cure for legalism?

2. How do people change? How have you answered that question in the past? How do you answer it now?

3. List all the motives people *can* have for obeying God. What are your main motives for living as a disciple? How might you move to the higher motives?

4. How do you handle your sin? Are you a guilt denier? Why is it hard to confess your sins? What makes it easier to confess them? Do you need to confess any sins to God or others?

5. Do you forget the gospel? Why? Do you believe the cure for many fundamental problems is found in the gospel? List some "heart problems" people have. How does the gospel cure them?

| 2 |

Images of Manhood

It is important, at this moment in Western culture, to know what it means to be a man and to act like one. On one hand, our culture affirms sexual experimentation of every kind. Some would redefine marriage, while others abandon it. Meanwhile, in heterosexual marriages, it is ever more likely that the wife's career and income will be primary. As warfare increasingly relies on electronics and weapons systems that strike at a distance, women now join combat teams, not just support teams.

The reaction is predictable. If we examine popular images of manhood, we see men bulging and rippling with muscle, festooned with facial hair, wielding guns and knives. At the movies, men are either buffoons or killers. In video games, the buffoons are gone. If we take these presentations of manhood seriously, they compound our culture's problems. What if a boy is neither athletic nor combative? Do we really want him to think that readers, chefs, and musicians are unmanly? That their slender build should lead them to doubt their masculinity?

Beyond doubt, Scripture instructs men to *act* like men, to act in ways that fit their gender. Acting like a man includes a willingness to go to war to defend one's people, as we see in the story and the psalms of David (e.g., 1 Sam. 17; 2 Sam. 23; Ps. 18). When David says he loves the Lord because "he trains my hands for battle," he means *literal* battle in which he crushed military enemies (Ps. 18:1, 29–50). Acting like a man also has a sexual component. The law of Moses uses the word *abomination* about a dozen times, to decry idolatry, fraud, and sexual sin such as

29

homosexual acts: "You shall not lie with a male as with a woman; it is an abomination" (Lev. 18:22 ESV; see also 20:13).[1]

To act like a man also includes dressing like one. Moses says, "A woman shall not wear a man's garment, nor shall a man put on a woman's cloak, for whoever does these things is an abomination to the LORD your God" (Deut. 22:5 ESV). Paul's somewhat perplexing teaching about hair length in 1 Corinthians 11 makes the same point. Nature itself, he declares, teaches that "if a man wears long hair it is a disgrace" (1 Cor. 11:4–15 ESV). As an educated and well-traveled man, Paul knew that men from certain cultures had long hair and that Jewish men grew long hair for Nazirite vows. He wasn't demanding short hair for all men everywhere. But in *his* Greco-Roman culture, men normally kept their hair short. In that cultural context, he says, nature teaches men to keep their hair short. That is, men should dress and act like men, and women should dress and act like women. In *his* culture, Paul wanted men to wear short hair, because long hair made them look like women. "The issue is not hair per se, but the natural desire to identify with one's own gender."[2]

How does one act like a man today? To stay with clothing, the West has so many subcultures that it's difficult to label the "right way" for a man to dress. Sexually, our culture seems to assume that no real man is monogamous. Just as important, we need to consider the work, emotional life, and personal goals of men. If we aim to avoid today's errors, we must be wary of retreating to older stereotypes that also owe more to old cultural norms than to Scripture. We must "test everything; hold fast what is good" (1 Thess. 5:21 ESV).

It is wise to "test everything" because boys get ideas about manhood in the oddest places. I discovered my first notion of masculinity in a doctor's office. As a little boy, I was active, but

---

1. In the law, an *abomination* typically refers to "acts that go against the moral fibre of God's created world." This includes acts of idolatry, theft, and sexual disorder. See Jay Sklar, *Leviticus* (Downers Grove, IL: InterVarsity Press, 2014), 238, 99.

2. The reader who wants to study this passage may consult Dan Doriani, *Women and Ministry* (Wheaton, IL: Crossway, 2003), 74–81, and the additional sources cited there.

short, slender, and often sick. Looking back, I now see that the members of my family, who valued toughness, wondered if little Danny would make the grade. The doctor set the defining moments in motion when he decided I should receive shots for the allergies that weakened me, starting at the tender age of four. First came diagnostic "scratch tests" in which the doctor hooked a curved, antigen-tipped needle through the skin on my back, piercing it twice, then withdrawing it. Little as I was, I lay silent and motionless, for all ninety-six needles. Afterward, I received five to seven shots per week for several years.

For whatever reason, I was a "very good boy" through this torment. I never whimpered, never complained. The doctors and nurses quickly noticed this and decided it could be useful. When I was in the office and an older boy blubbered at the prospect of shots, the doctor would wave me in, calling out, "Nurse, bring in exhibit A. He knows how brave boys act." The nurses led me into the needle corral and drew serum into rapier-like syringes, while seven- and nine-year-olds endured the humiliation of watching a wraith-like four-year-old endure the pain with a cool that boasted, "Bring on your needles! Do your worst. I fear you not." My parents told this story for decades, for by it I had met some unspoken code of masculinity. Whatever my size or health, my bravery became, for my family, a badge of my toughness, my masculinity.

The ego would cling to this, but sometimes I wonder if I was truly brave, or if I just have poor nerve endings. More important, what exactly does the ability to endure physical pain have to do with true masculinity? Is tough-minded suffering a *biblical* measure of manliness? Or is it merely cultural?

We live in a day marked by competing concepts of true manhood. Are real men hard or soft? Are diapers and dishes beneath their dignity, or do real men plunge their hands into those waters? Do true men bear pain, physical and emotional, in impressive, impassive silence, or are they so self-assured that they shed tears openly and speak of it freely? Do real men provide for their families, keeping food on the table even if they have to manage two jobs? Are they supposed to earn heaps of money if they can? Or do they pursue a life where work and free time have found better balance, even if income vanishes? Do real men have the confidence to walk away from a high-paying but stifling job, knowing they can get another? Do they believe it better to have less, with integrity, than to have more, with compromise? Further back, does virtue have gender? Is the greatest man almost identical—in character, behavior, and roles—to the greatest woman? Or does the form of greatness shift when gender changes?

Everyone who is still reading this is old enough to have pulled a few models of masculinity off the rack. They may seem to fit at first, but later they pinch in one place and billow out in another. Once they show their poor design, we want to toss them out and try something new. But friends, families, and society still find them workable, so we should consider a few of them: the tough guy, the good provider, the softer man, and the self-actualized man.

The Tough Guy

The "tough guy" model of masculinity has nearly expired, but it was the first that I absorbed. Adults say, "Big boys don't cry," and I believed it. I proved my masculinity at the doctor's office. Other men get their reputations through fights in alleys or in business suites, through battles in military uniforms or athletic uniforms. Millions of men adopted the tough guy model of masculinity as they grew up. They became traditional men who ruled the military and the business world, at least until the 1980s. Traditional tough men get up early, work hard, admire discipline, provide for their families, sacrifice for others, and love their country. They know their responsibilities, but they may not know their heart, or the heart of their wives, children, or friends (if they have any). They cannot cry. They choke on phrases like, *I love you.* They are dutiful and strong, but their strength is one- or two-dimensional. Most are poor communicators and cool husbands or fathers. This leads us to ask: Is there anything biblical or godly in the tough guy code? Does God approve of quiet sacrifice and emotional self-control?

In fact, it is commendable to be tough enough to endure physical pain. Endurance is a biblical virtue, and the ability to persevere through suffering supports it. Men should remain faithful despite persecution, and that requires willingness to endure fear and pain. The New Testament compares Christian living to war, athletic struggles, races, and boxing (1 Cor. 9:24–27; 2 Tim. 2:5; Heb. 12:1–4). All of these demand endurance and suffering. Likewise, traditional male activities such as waging war and performing manual labor require men to ignore pain. Of course, the waging of war keeps getting cleaner (not to say easier) as we fire at targets many miles away. Work gets easier too, as more men work with computers than with hand tools. Still, men must protect their families and work hard despite pain. Scripture assumes that men will toil and defend their nation.

Above all, Jesus models noble toughness, in three ways: (1) he finished arduous tasks, (2) he waged war and prevailed, and (3) he defied pain for the sake of others. First then, Jesus finished the task of redemption by offering himself to atone for sin on the cross (Matt. 20:25–28; John 19:30). Second, he entered solo combat against his family's great foe and defeated him. He tied up the strong man because he was stronger (Matt. 12:29). He crushed the head of the ancient serpent (Gen. 3:15; Rev. 20:2–3). He defeated the agent of death (Heb. 2:14–15). He silenced the accuser (Rev. 12:9–10). Third, Jesus endured intense suffering, even death—death on a cross—but he scorned the pain and shame in order to achieve his goals (Phil. 2:5–8; Heb. 12:2–3). Scripture presents Jesus, in all this toughness and sacrifice for others, as an example to us. Notice the phrases that mark Jesus as our example:

> Whoever wants to become great among you must be your servant, and whoever wants to be first must be your slave—just

as the Son of Man did not come to be served, but to serve, and to give his life as a ransom for many. (Matt. 20:26–28)

Let us fix our eyes on Jesus, the author and perfecter of our faith, who for the joy set before him endured the cross, scorning its shame, and sat down at the right hand of the throne of God. Consider him who endured such opposition from sinful men, so that you will not grow weary and lose heart. (Heb. 12:2–3)

There is, therefore, more to the tough guy model of masculinity than we might first think. Yet the tough guy persona has unbiblical elements that hurt men in several ways. A hyper-traditional model says men are tough, independent, self-controlled, self-governing, self-contained. They say, "I'm tough and I don't need no help from nobody." The tough guy model may promote endurance, but it also promotes a kind of silence that suppresses honest self-disclosure. It encourages men to keep their troubles to themselves and solve them on their own or to suffer in silence, because that, they think, is what real men do. It fosters the evasive language many men use to talk about their troubles, so that we have to decode it.

- "Things have been a little rough at home" may mean, "My wife has hired a divorce lawyer."
- "I'm not the husband I should be" may mean, "I work eighty hours and throw raging fits almost every week."
- "I should give more attention to my children" may mean, "I'm not sure I remember how old they are."

Tough guy thinking denies fundamental Christian principles. The tough guy says, "I can solve all my problems," but the Bible says we cannot. The tough guy says, "I am self-sufficient," but God says we are not. The tough guy says, "I don't need no help from nobody," but the Bible says we will never, by ourselves, meet our greatest needs.

Tough guys will please God in some ways. Still, if a man tries to live by the tough guy model of masculinity alone, he will find it difficult to grow as a Christian. The tough guy is too self-contained, too pinched emotionally to build strong, open relationships with family or friends. And without solid relationships, he may be more susceptible to other faulty models of masculinity, beginning with the provider model.

The Good Provider

The good provider is a cousin of the tough guy. The good provider believes he is responsible to get married and to provide a comfortable life for his family. The good provider liberates his wife to be a homemaker, to cook and clean, to decorate and entertain, to volunteer in the community, to organize schedules and, generally, to make their home a haven in a heartless world. The good provider strides into the world, slaying dragons, cutting deals, and moving tons of rocks for the family's sake. He brings home the bacon, and his wife cooks it up. The reward is admiration, but the price is pressure to produce, even if it means endless labor and mindless conformity to the world of gray suits, blue collars, or business casual. The good provider works hard to provide financially, but he gets home so tired that he cannot provide emotionally. Again, is this notion of manhood biblical or cultural?

As with the tough guy, Scripture commends parts of the good provider model. First, Scripture always assumes and sometimes commands that men provide for their families. From the beginning, before the fall, Adam worked God's garden and kept it. The patriarchs all worked, tending flocks and herds. Many of Moses' laws protect the rights and lives of farmers. Jesus was a carpenter and could build with stone and metal as well. Paul was a tentmaker who was glad to work with his hands lest he be a burden to anyone. Further, he forbade idleness and ordered early Christians to work lest they prove to be a burden (1 Thess. 2:7–9;

2 Thess. 3:6–11). As he said, "If a man will not work, he shall not eat" (2 Thess. 3:10).

In addition to these examples and commands, God himself models the good provider role. God is the Father and, in a way, is like a husband of Israel, and he provides well for her. He bestowed wealth on the patriarchs, Abraham, Isaac, Jacob, and Joseph. After delivering Israel from Egypt, he fed her food called manna from heaven when she wandered in the wilderness. God also gave wealth to David and Solomon and other good kings (1 Chron. 28–29; 1 Kings 10) and even to the common folk of Israel (Ps. 128). As provider, David also compared God to a good shepherd, who leads the flock to green pastures and quiet waters (Ps. 23). Indeed, Psalm 104 shows that God provides for the earth and all its birds and beasts. Even Jesus is a good provider, not so much materially as by delivering and protecting his people.

So the good provider model has biblical roots. A good man *does* provide for his family. Yet we can distort "the good provider" model in ways that make it more cultural than biblical. For example, we often misquote Paul from 1 Timothy 5:8, making him say, "If a *man* does not provide for his family, he is worse than an unbeliever." But he actually says, "If *anyone* does not provide for his *relatives*, and especially for his immediate family, he has denied the faith and is worse than an unbeliever." In its original context, Paul sought to ensure that men care for widows and other poor relatives, not just their wives and children. Second, the word translated *provide* does not mean to "earn" or "acquire" but to "plan" or "look out" for something. That is, Paul does not require men to *earn* all the money. Rather men must ensure that the family has the resources it needs.[3] It is fine, therefore, for a woman to help secure the family's resources. After all, the noble woman of Proverbs 31 sells garments and real estate.

American women now earn more college degrees and master's degrees than men. As the knowledge economy grows in

---

3. The subject of the sentence is masculine, but the conventions of Greek grammar, where masculine is the default gender, allow it to include both men and women.

prominence, wives frequently earn more than their husbands. Although that can cause discomfort, there is no law against it. A man fulfills his obligations if he plans for his wife to earn most of their income, whether for a few years or more permanently. If her skills bring her a better income, what is the harm, if both husband and wife work faithfully in an honest calling? By implication, a godly man can take the majority of the child care. In biblical times, coparenting was the norm, since work ordinarily occurred at home. That is why the Bible addresses both fathers and mothers, but fathers somewhat more.

The good provider image does pose dangers, however. First, it promotes the idea that a man is what he earns. It pushes us to conform to our acquisitive culture, which judges gaining and spending to be the essence of the good life. Second, the accent on earning pushes men to work long hours and to shove relations with family and friends aside. Third, the good provider syndrome can contribute to the dark side of mobility and rootlessness. To pursue higher income, men may move to get higher salaries. As we haul anchor and sail away from family and friends, we lose people who know the best and worst of who we are. Severing the cords of history and tradition, we lose the friends who share stories about sweet babies, terrible storms, and great contests. I will not even mention the consequences for our wives and children.

Good providers are by no means a rare breed, but, like tough guys, they are a more traditional kind of man. But other models of masculinity are also emerging.

The Softer Man

The softer man is a thoughtful, gentle breed.[4] He is sweet nurturer more than fierce protector. He takes pride in changing diapers and doing dishes alongside his wife. There are no guns in his house. The softer man may be fit, but he will not play contact sports. He is empathetic more than flinty. He can

4. For a pagan analysis of this man, see Robert Bly, *Iron John* (Westminster, MD: Vintage, 1990), 2–4, passim.

examine his emotions and feel your pain, but he may not know how to remove it. He says, "I feel so sorry for you," not "Buck up; it's time to get back to work." When he meets resistance, he becomes understanding rather than resolute. He will drink beer, but it will be something European or microbrewed, not a brand advertised on TV. He will drink beer, but in the kind of bar his mother might approve. He likes the great outdoors, but hesitates to enter a national park lest he contribute to erosion. He knows the eco-saying, "If you really love Yosemite, don't visit," and thinks it may be correct.

The softer man is not quite at home with his masculinity. He has heard the feminist critique of traditional, patriarchal men and thinks more than a few charges are true. He hesitates to exercise authority. He would never say, "I am the head of this home." He participates in a consensual decision-making process in a house where the question "Who is in charge here?" gets a complicated answer. The softer man certainly is not a tough guy, but he may not be soft. Rather, he sees the flaws in the tough guy and good provider persona and gropes his way toward something better. When an earnest woman tells him, "John, you need to learn how to cry," he wonders if he should gag or take her advice. He is less predictable, but has a harder time making decisions.

Like it or not, no man born after 1950 can be entirely free of softer man sensibilities. We have breathed the air of feminism, anti-authoritarianism, eco-awareness, and emotional expressivism. Society has questioned every traditional concept of masculinity, and we cannot help but investigate.

As much as the traditional man him might resist, the softer man has his points. First, concerning diapers, the Bible assumes fathers will be coparents, because work and family time were so intertwined until a couple centuries ago. For farmers, herders, and artisans, children worked alongside their fathers in their home or on their land. The industrial revolution and job specialization separated what had been joined.

Second, as for expressing emotion and feeling pain, a survey of the biblical data yields clear results. There are nearly two hundred instances of people weeping and shedding tears in the Bible, and the great majority of the criers were men. Sometimes the tears were shallow, as people pitied the losses they suffered for sin or folly. Women like Ruth and Hannah also wept with emotion. But most often men wept, and for good reasons. Jacob wept over Joseph's reported death (Gen. 37). Later, Joseph wept for joy when reunited with his family (Gen. 42–43, 45). David and Jonathan wept when they parted (2 Sam. 20), as did the Ephesian elders when they said good-bye to Paul (Acts 20). David wept again at the death of Saul and Jonathan (1 Sam. 30; 2 Sam. 1) and at the death of two sons (2 Sam. 12, 18–19). Godly Josiah wept when he read the Law and saw the extent of Israel's sin (2 Kings 22). He wept again when Assyrian invaders blasphemed God and threatened to capture Jerusalem (Isa. 38). Though they both lived in king's palaces, Ezra and Nehemiah prayed and wept over the misery of God's people after their captivity in Babylon (Ezra 3, 10; Neh. 1).

In the Gospels, Peter wept in repentance after betraying Jesus (Mark 14; Luke 22). Above all, Jesus wept. He wept in sorrow for his beloved friend Lazarus (John 11). He also wept for the city of Jerusalem that had rejected him and his way of peace and would reap the consequences (Luke 19). Jesus told men, "Blessed are those who mourn" (Matt. 5:4). Surely it is better to weep over sin and evildoing than it is to be indifferent. The godly know how to weep over wickedness (Ps. 119:136; James 4:9). Some men can go a decade without crying. Does that earn us a badge for manliness? Or does it show how much we let culture, rather than Scripture, define masculinity?

The softer man's ecological sensitivity is also good. After all, God appointed mankind to care for his earth (Gen. 2–3). The laws of Moses take interest in proper treatment of animals and in the preservation of trees, and so should we (Ex. 20:10; Deut. 20:19–20).

Finally, we must say that men ought to listen to the feminist critique of hyper-traditional concepts of male leadership. Men have often used their physical strength and social position to oppress and humiliate women. Men have silenced the voices and repressed the gifts of strong women. Men ought to listen to the charge that they have abused their leadership position by their selfishness.

Thus, as with the tough guy and the good provider, we can commend as well as critique the softer man. Nonetheless, the softer man seems uncertain about the roles of a man. He is alienated from his maleness, apologetic for his gender. He is so sensitive to criticism of the errors of traditional males, that his capacities to lead, to decide, to exercise strength for others, are nearly lost.

The Self-Actualized Man

The self-actualized man may be the dominant model of masculinity today. In *Habits of the Heart*, Robert Bellah interviewed a number of Americans and found that they live for their pursuit of happiness and purpose in life. They agree that people should pursue whatever they find rewarding, as long as they do not interfere with others' pursuit of their purposes. Some individuals find their purpose in self-reliance and hard work, others find it in relationships, but the freedom to change and grow is essential. Self-actualized men value the freedom to do as they choose, to do their best, and to fashion a life where they have power over their destiny.[5] They want to construct a noble identity.

With their talk of freedom and autonomy, self-actualized men disclose their individualism. They believe in a kind of democracy, but one where individual good trumps the common good. They live in "lifestyle enclaves" where people share patterns of behavior, appearance, and leisure, rather than true community. They also believe in meritocracy. As David Brooks has shown, meritocrats

5. Robert N. Bellah, Richard Madsen, William M. Sullivan, Ann Swidler, and Steven M. Tipton, *Habits of the Heart* (New York: Harper & Row, 1985), 3–26, 55ff.

locate their self-constructed identity in their accomplishments, not their lineage; in their college town, not their hometown.[6] Their merit should bring them a measure of material comfort, and the successful, at least, do not go through life hungering for money. Rather, they get a good education and work hard, and money finds them. Their individualism makes them question authority, but their skill puts them in authority. They attain worldly success but seek inner virtue. Therefore, they will forego earnings (as long as they are comfortable) to live a richer life. Self-actualized man defines himself by his post, but the post should leave time for travel and leisure.

As before, the self-actualized model of masculinity has positive elements. First, self-actualizers see that there is more to life than material success. Second, if self-actualization means developing our gifts and fulfilling our God-given potential, who can object? It is good to work hard and achieve proper goals. We are all made in the image of a God who has goals for all creation and particular goals for his people. God ordained Moses, and no other, to lead Israel out of Egypt. He commissioned Joshua to lead the conquest of Canaan. He called Solomon, not David, to build his temple. In the early church, God sent Peter to the Jews, and Paul to the Gentiles (Gal. 2:7–9). Later, Paul told Timothy to learn from "my teaching, my way of life, my *purpose*" (2 Tim. 3:10). The idea of spiritual gifts shows that God has specific tasks for people to this day. Further, the notion that God created, structured, and now governs all things gives "a degree of confidence in the reliability and predictability of life in this world" that encourages the pursuit of goals.[7] Indeed, though God exists outside history, his acts in human history are goal-driven. The goal of redemption drives his relations to mankind, from the fall of Adam to the death and resurrection

6. David Brooks, *Bobos in Paradise: The New Upper Class and How They Got There* (New York: Simon & Schuster, 2000), 25–53.

7. Christopher J. H. Wright, *Walking in the Ways of the Lord* (Downers Grove, IL: InterVarsity Press, 1995), 120–22.

of Christ. Since God is purposeful and since he created us in his image, we rightly pursue goals.

The problem, therefore, is not goals and achievement per se, but the tendency to choose goals and self-actualizing activities without a moral compass. Self-actualization can lead to lawlessness. Some men want to shuck off any burden that impedes their development and happiness. They feel free to violate promises and cast off duties they no longer accept. There is no ethical basis, no criteria, to judge one goal or way of life superior to another. If personal growth or satisfaction is the highest good, then men will pursue whatever promises that result. Personal gain replaces duty and "self-expression unseats authority."[8]

At worst, the search for freedom and self-actualization leads to irresponsibility and immaturity. As Rosaria Butterfield says, "Sin infantilizes."[9] In the name of finding and expressing oneself, men and women drift in and out of relationships and career paths, delaying marriage, parenthood, and true maturity. Women forget biological facts, and men bump around aimlessly, doing whatever they please. Some shout, "No one can tell me what to do." Others say, "I need to be true to myself and follow my heart wherever it leads." In the end, self-actualization becomes self-indulgence.

A Godly Man

We can recognize our culture's defective ideas about masculinity, yet we cannot easily escape them. Or if we do detect a mistake, we often react and commit the opposite error. For example, feminists reacted to those who accent male/female differences by ascribing all variation, except biology, to cultural influences. They discounted native differences between men and women. They tried to feminize men and to masculinize women. Men, naturally, react to the threat to their identity by lurching toward hypermasculine activities.

8. Bellah et al, *Habits of the Heart*, 77.
9. Rosaria Butterfield, *The Secret Thoughts of an Unlikely Convert* (Pittsburgh: Crown & Covenant, 2012), 39.

We have examined four models of masculinity: the tough guy, the good provider, the softer man, and the self-actualized man. We should identify the strengths and weaknesses of each, without reacting to them. As we know, when a reaction leads us to swing to the opposite extreme, we simply move from one error to another.

Instead, we seek a model that gives us the best chance to start afresh. We neither baptize our culture by sprinkling a few Bible verses on an essentially secular model, nor reject everything from it. After all, no culture can thrive if it discards all of God's ways. I propose God himself as the model for godly masculinity. Perhaps you noticed steps we already took in this direction:

- In the cross, Jesus exemplified toughness and self-denial for the sake of others.
- In creating the world and redeeming his people, God is the supreme provider.
- Like the softer man, Jesus knew how to cry.
- Like the self-actualized man, Jesus knew what he wanted to do with his life.

That approach will guide us throughout the book. God's saving grace is the foundation for godly manhood. As the man after God's heart seeks a pattern for life, we turn our attention to God himself. God's person and work will be our model in marriage, fatherhood, work, leadership, and friendship. For example, Christian studies of friendship typically begin with David and Jonathan, and Ruth and Naomi, before moving on to friendship in Proverbs. But we observe that God's friendships are marked by self-disclosure and helpful presence. As for work, the godly man knows and follows God's pattern of work and rest. The chapter on fatherhood does not list techniques for discipleship and discipline, it searches for the essential traits of our fatherly God—justice, love, and faithfulness—and applies them to fathers today. So the man after God's heart lives by grace, not laws; by character, not techniques; in short, by the pattern of the living God.

Discussion Questions

1. Among contemporary images of manhood, which comes closest to your tradition: the tough guy, the good provider, the softer man, or the self-actualizer?
2. If you asked those who know you best, which view would they say you live by? Which one seems most attractive to you? To most men in your community? Why?
3. Why do so many men sport the tough guy persona? Are tears a sign of strength or weakness? Who cries more—the immature man or the mature man? Explain your answer.
4. How does the biblical image of manhood correct your view and prevailing views today?

A Man and His Marriage: Companionship

From 1985 to 1991, a group of Americans became hostages in a civil war in Lebanon. The hostages fashioned a community in extreme adversity. They lived in airless, windowless cells, often scarcely bigger than a grave. Ceilings were so low they could not stand upright. They endured searing heat in the summer, bitter cold in the winter. They battled with mosquitoes and vermin. They wore the same clothes year after year. Filthy blindfolds infected their eyes. Shackled in steel chains nearly twenty-four hours a day, they had ten minutes a day to visit their "toilet," a fetid hole in the ground. They went months without a bath and spent long periods in shuttered rooms without light. Frequently isolated, they might also be forbidden to speak when together.

Despite the adversity, they forged a community. When permitted to speak, one man taught French and animal husbandry. Another made a chess set, a deck of cards, and crude versions of Scrabble and Monopoly from scraps of paper and tin foil. They played twenty questions and conducted verbal tours of the world's cities.

At their release, one reporter asked, "In your years of captivity, what was the worst day?" There were several candidates. Perhaps it was the days of mockery when guards blindfolded and chained them, then tossed off mock salutes, and shouted, "Heil Hitler!" Perhaps it was a day of degradation. One captive was prone to dizziness, so they spun him around, let him go, and howled in laughter as he flailed on the ground. Or perhaps the days when they prepared for their release, only to see their hopes dashed? Or the days when they were moved like corpses, wrapped in tape from head to foot and hidden in blazing hot compartments in trucks? No, they said, the worst day was Christmas day. On Christmas they felt their loneliness and separation from their families most acutely. And the worst Christmas day came when the guards denied them the right to say a word to any other captive. That was the worst, hardest hour because God designed mankind to flourish in relationships. Marriage and family are the primary avenues for companionship. But God made us to seek companions in dorm rooms, work teams, athletic teams, and civic clubs; at church, at home, even in prison.

We are social creatures, created in the image of a relational God. God is sociable and when he made us in his likeness, he created us with a yearning to connect with people. To be whole, we need companionship.

God designed marriage to be the prime source of companionship for adults. Jesus said that God himself joins men and women in marriage and what he joins no one should separate (Matt. 19:4–6). The companionship of marriage is exclusive and intimate, even passionate. But the passion of marriage leads to children, and they create a new kind of relationship. Marriage is a partnership between equals, but parenthood joins unequals. After marriage and parenting comes friendship and all the looser forms of companionship.

All relationships teach us about ourselves, and all hint at the character of God. In parenting, for example, we learn about God's sacrificial love and fatherly care. Children are a bundle of needs. Through them we learn the Godlike joy of giving, even giving to those who cannot reciprocate. In our sacrifices for them, we participate in God's mercy toward his children. We taste his compassion for us when we have compassion on children as they cry over silly things and serious things. But nothing matches that most intimate relationship, marriage, for what it can teach us about God and ourselves.

Marriage at Creation–Side by Side (Gen. 1)

From the beginning, God designed Adam and Eve, the first husband and wife, to relate in two ways: *face to face* and *side by side*. Face to face, each encounters the other in body and soul. Side by side, they encounter the world. Side by side—or perhaps we can call it "shoulder to shoulder"—they work to subdue the earth. They rule its animals, cultivate its plants, and develop its riches (Gen. 1:26–29; 2:8–12, 15). In Genesis 1, the emphasis falls on the side-by-side facet of Adam and Eve's relationship. God blesses the *work* of mankind, saying, "Rule over the fish of the sea and the birds of the air, over the livestock . . . and over all the creatures that move along the ground" (1:26). Adam and Eve reflect God's image by working. God, the king, rules all things, but mankind rules the world for God, as his vice-regents. Male and female serve together, side by side, partners in governing the good earth.

Genesis 2:20 calls Eve Adam's "suitable helper" for the task, and that has stirred quite a debate about the way men and women work together. *Chauvinists* claim, "See, this proves that women exist to help men!" *Feminists* reply, "No, it shows that men need help!"

But the point is simpler and happier than the debates of gender warriors would suggest. By calling woman a helper, God does not imply her inferiority. Remember, God often calls himself Israel's helper (e.g., Ex. 18:4; Deut. 33:29; Ps. 10:24; 118:7). Helping does not imply inferiority, for the stronger we are, the more we can help others. I can help my children with their math or science if I know more than they do. But when they know as much as I do, my capacity to help diminishes. If I know less than they do, I can hardly assist them. So, to correct chauvinists, we say, "God designed women to help, but *you have to be strong to help*." Then, to correct feminists, we say, "God designed women to help, so you should be *willing* to help."

The task of governing the earth for the Lord receives the accent in Genesis 1. Men and women form a team, offering each other strong and willing help in a grand task. This is the "side by side" of marriage. The "face to face" takes center stage in Genesis 2.

Marriage at Creation–Face to Face (Gen. 2)

Genesis 2 retells the story of creation from a new perspective, using a slightly different sequence. In Genesis 2, God formed Adam in verse 7, "The Lord God formed the man from the dust of the ground." But he made Eve some time later, as verses 21–22 say: "The Lord God made a woman from the rib . . ." Thus Adam and Eve were not a married couple from the outset. This gap between the creation of Adam and Eve reveals vital principles touching men, women, and marriage.

Adam's Bachelor Life

God gave Adam the bachelor a series of tasks. The Lord charged him to work the garden, to care for it, to guard it (2:15). The mention of gold, onyx, aromatic resin, and rivers in other parts of the world (2:10–14) hints that the task would eventually expand beyond the garden's borders. Yet, as splendid as the earth was, Moses implies that something was amiss in Genesis 2:18–21:

> The Lord God said, "It is not good for the man to be alone. I will make a helper suitable for him."
>
> Now the Lord God had formed out of the ground all the beasts of the field and all the birds of the air. He brought them to the man to see what he would name them; and whatever the man called each living creature, that was its name. So the man gave names to all the livestock, the birds of the air and all the beasts of the field.
>
> But for Adam no suitable helper was found. So the Lord God caused the man to fall into a deep sleep; and while he was sleeping, he took one of the man's ribs and closed up the place with flesh.

In Genesis 1, we recall, a refrain ended each day: "And God saw that it was good." That phrase *God saw that it was good* recurs six times (1:4, 10, 12, 18, 21, 31). But now we read, "It is *not good* for the man to be alone" (2:18). This jolts and puzzles us. God detects something wrong in paradise, even though sin has not entered it. God proposes a remedy for Adam's problem: "I will make a helper suitable for him"—then doesn't make that helper. Instead, God appears to ignore Adam's problem and sets him to the task of naming the animals. Now we are baffled and God is displeased, but there is no sense that Adam is troubled—not yet. But the naming will give us a link.

Naming is an aspect of Adam's *dominion* over creation. Just as discoverers name stars, comets, and diseases today, so rulers named things from of old (see Dan. 1:6–7). Certainly the naming required Adam to observe and ponder: "What is this beast? What is its essence? What is a telling name for it?" The verses describing the process are repetitive. God brought the animals to Adam "to see what he would *name* them; and whatever the man *called* [one], that was its *name*. So the man gave *names* . . ." The task, the repetition implies, took quite some time. Then suddenly, Adam's singleness, his lack of a helper, reappears. "But for Adam, no suitable helper was found." Why does Genesis return to the problem of loneliness now?

As Adam named the animals, he had to notice that all had companions, all had mates, all except him! All came in pairs, but where was his partner? He surely marveled at God's creatures, but he must also have noticed that none was a suitable companion for him. Dogs make the point. It's fun to romp with a dog, to play rough, to throw a Frisbee it catches mid-air. And it's relaxing to pat a contented dog that snoozes beside our reading chair. Dogs give almost unconditional love, and some even work hard. But dogs are limited creatures. If we want to frolic, fine, but if we want to discuss life's joys or sorrows, they fail us. We can relate to dogs at their level, but they cannot rise to ours. Only people can discuss matters of the heart.

I believe Adam saw this as he named the animals. God had Adam name all the animals *so he would see his aloneness as loneliness.* Work and animals would never fulfill Adam. He needed more and he knew it. Therefore, God returns to Adam's solitude in 2:20.

The Cure for Adam's Loneliness

However long it lasted, the parade of animals impressed Adam with both his superiority and his solitude. The more he watched the animals, the clearer it became that he had no companion among them. The original literally reads, "As for Adam, he did not find a helper suitable to him" (2:20). Adam was looking, but not finding. Now that Adam sees the situation God's way, God creates a woman for a man who is ready for her. Ray Ortlund paraphrases Genesis 2 perfectly:

> As the last of the beasts plods off with its new name, the man turns away with a trace of perplexity in his eyes. God says, "Son, I want you to lie down. Now close your eyes and sleep." The man falls into a deep slumber. The Creator goes to work, opening the man's side, removing a rib, closing the wound, and building the woman. There she stands, perfectly gorgeous and uniquely suited to the man's need. The Lord says to her, "Daughter, I want you to go stand over there. I'll come for you in a moment. . . ." Then God touches the man and says, "Wake up now, son. I have one last creature for you to name." And he leads Eve out to Adam.[1]

When Adam meets Eve, he utters humanity's first recorded words. He does not whistle, "Vive la difference." Nor does he moan, "Here comes the old ball and chain." He breaks into poetry. "Now, at last," he cries. At last, after his fruitless searching, "This is now bone of my bones and flesh of my flesh" (2:23). Here stood

---

1. Ray Ortlund, "Marriage," in *Recovering Biblical Manhood and Womanhood,* ed. John Piper and Wayne Grudem (Wheaton, IL: Crossway, 1993), 101.

the companion for whom he had learned to yearn. She shall be his partner. She is not a threat due to her equality or a menace due to her differentness. Rather he thrills at her capacity to fill his longing for companionship and communion. The woman, bride and wife, is a helper suitable for a man, because she is of his flesh, yet other than his flesh. For this reason, he rejoices at her sight and marries her. She completes him.

It is all too easy for married couples to lose sight of this "face to face" dimension of marriage. As the years roll by, as children and career and worthy causes press upon us, even good marriages can devolve into little more than co-laboring with nice people of the opposite sex who share our beds and kitchens. The relationship becomes ever more "side by side," and the "face to face" recedes.

Even people who teach about marriage can forget this. One year my wife suffered an intestinal infection by the Giardia microorganism. On February 1, she got what seemed like an ordinary but severe stomach virus. Strangely, she got better, then worse, then better, then worse again, for five or six days. Her doctor judged it inconsequential, then left town for several days. The symptoms persisted, and when he returned, we took her in again, but key test results were delayed. We were still awaiting the results on day twelve, but when my wife got up, threw up, and sunk back into bed, I decided to take her to the hospital at once, with or without the test results.

That process took all morning, and when I got back home, I tackled the dirty dishes and laundry that had been moldering for days. The illness fell during my second semester of seminary teaching. My reward for a successful first term was an academic overload in the second. Beyond the extra classes, I also had to deliver a special lecture that week. During the same days, our freezer broke, the children and I got colds, and electrical problems erupted throughout our house. As a result, I was unable to return that night or even the next day as I cared for children, house, and work. The next day, my wife, much improved, called and asked when I would be coming in. I was just beginning to get organized, and something in me wanted to stay at home and get more work done. But, if you are keeping track, this was the fourteenth day of an illness that began February 1 . . . Valentine's Day! I *had* to visit her in the hospital.

On the way to her room, I stopped by the hospital's flower shop. It was only 11:00, but all the classy arrangements were gone, so I went for *big* and grabbed the largest and most expensive bouquet in the refrigerator, something with an abundance of huge yellow blooms. I was just steps away from her door, when—feeling my presence?—she peeked around it. Our eyes met; we embraced in the doorway. She drank in the flowers and, moist-eyed, whispered, "These are the most beautiful flowers I have ever seen." That wasn't quite true, but I knew what she meant.

We had to cancel the grand date we had planned for that evening. (When children are small, the probability of fulfilling romantic plans for Valentine's Day is inversely proportional to the effort invested in those plans.) Yet we have never had a sweeter Valentine's date than we did that morning, sitting in the hospital hallway for two hours, sipping Sprites, holding hands, and watching the people go by. For my wife is bone of my bone and flesh of my flesh and, in the weeks of her illness and in the hectic weeks before it, I had lost sight of that.

The Ideal for Marriage (Gen. 2:24-25)

During the career-building, child-rearing years, men are prone to forget the face-to-face of marriage. It helps to return to Genesis 2 and see Adam and Eve thrill at their companionship, at the excellence each saw in the other. Let Adam's delight in discovering his wife be your standard. Yet marriage thrives on order as well as delight. The last lines of Genesis 2 state the elements essential to good order in marriage: "For this reason a man will leave his father and mother and be united to his wife, and they will become one flesh. The man and his wife were both naked, and they felt no shame." (vv. 24–25)

Genesis 2:24 lists three equally essential points that together make a strong foundation for marriage. If firm, they are as sturdy as a three-legged stool, but if one leg fails, it will surely collapse. We need all three elements of this trio to develop a healthy marriage.

Leave

"A man will leave his father and mother" shows that the bond between husband and wife trumps the bond between parent and child. It marks marriage as the foundational institution. Some may wonder why God led Moses to specify that the *husband* must leave his family, but says nothing about the wife. The answer is that in that culture everyone assumed that the wife left her family. No one had to say it. But Moses adds, "The husband must leave too. He must not take his wife into his father's house and place her under his authority. He must start a new family."

Wedding ceremonies wisely embody this in the moment we call the giving of the bride. The father takes his daughter's hand and gives it to the groom, not (originally) to create a photo opportunity, but to show that his daughter is leaving his household and entering another.

Be United

"A man will . . . be united to his wife" means husband and wife build intimacy into that new family. They "cleave," as the King James Version puts it, meaning they stick close together. They are "glued together," says Paul, quoting Genesis 2 in Ephesians 5. They become companions for life, growing in affection and fidelity. They work at their relationship, despite its trials and vicissitudes.

Once, after I had spoken on marriage, a youngish mother of three small children approached me. With her husband just a few feet away, she said, "You know, Bob and I are coming off a pretty bad year. His business was demanding, the kids were difficult, and we clashed frequently. Sometimes . . ." She paused.

"Sometimes, we didn't even *like* each other. But it's starting to get better."

This woman, this couple, was onto something. Their marriage was "unhappy," but they knew better than to give up. They were pursuing what the old wedding vows called "troth," as in "I pledge you my troth." Troth is cleaving. Troth is staying power. Troth is a pledge of lifelong fidelity.[2] It is reliability, stability, trust, loyalty, endurance, without preconditions. Prenuptial agreements that set the terms for the dissolution of a marriage before it starts are the antithesis of troth.

Troth is essential to marriage. Its pledge of lifelong fidelity logically precedes sexual intercourse, for it supplies the context for intimacy, for the vulnerability, self-disclosure, and abandonment of intercourse. Troth also permits men and women to bring children into the world without fear that their spouse will abandon them.

Our individualistic culture resists troth. For some, marriage is an arrangement that people enter to gain benefits such as affection, companionship, the kind of house two incomes can buy, and the designer life that allows model children. But, too often, divorce is thinkable whenever the costs of marriage outweigh its benefits for a prolonged period. Others repudiate the culture of divorce and broken commitments. But their "solution" is a decision to avoid all commitments. They shun marriage. They keep all options open.

The desire to keep options open destroys marital stability. People need a security that unlimited choosing annuls. We must do more than make loving *decisions*. We must make *commitments* and stick with them in ways that cut off other decisions.

Suppose you are in a business meeting when a colleague, David, informs your coworker, Joe, that an attractive young coworker named Jennifer is "interested" in him, even though he is married. Suppose further that David offers Joe his cabin

2. See James Olthius, *I Pledge You My Troth* (New York: Harper & Row, 1975).

for a tryst. Joe thinks a while, then declines the offer, saying, "Jennifer is attractive, and the offer of the cabin is generous, but I think it would be best for my career and my marriage if I avoided entanglements at work." Now think: would Joe's wife be pleased if she overheard this conversation?

Not at all. Joe's wife does not want him to *consider* the offer. Wives want the language of fidelity, not calculation. They do not want husbands to ponder the question and decide what is best. They want unshakable resolve, not deliberations. They want their husband to shout, "No way, I'm married."

Without the pledge of fidelity, marriage is merely a wager *for* the persistence of feelings and a wager *against* the ravages of time, illness, and unequal development or achievement. But the man after God's heart does not wager. He loves as God loves— graciously, permanently. If the thought creeps in that his marriage doesn't look like a good "deal" for him, he remembers that Jesus hardly got a good "deal" when he took the church as his bride. If he thinks he could do better on the open market, he remembers that God told Israel, "I gave you my solemn oath and entered into a covenant with you . . . and you became mine" (Ezek. 16:8). He kept that oath, though the contribution Israel made to their relationship hardly matched his!

God's covenant faithfulness is our measure, our norm. The faithful love of Christ models the Christian man's marriage covenant. Jesus does not love the church *because* it is pure and spotless, he purifies the church *in order to* make it spotless. Just so, godly husbands love their wives *despite* their blemishes, not *until they get* blemishes. Thus, we do not size up our wives each week to decide if we will love them a while longer. The idea of ever-fresh decisions, even decisions to stay faithful, is naive.

During a sabbatical at Yale, I attended a PhD seminar that took a personal turn one day. An ardent feminist student described the tension she felt between her Catholic faith and her feminism. She declared, "I believe the church is patriarchal and oppressive to women." Further, she repudiated parts of the

Bible that squelch women and contain "texts of terror" for them. Then she made a confession, "Every morning I get up and ask myself if I can be both a Christian and a woman." She hesitated and sighed, "And every day I decide I will remain a Christian . . . even though I know it is killing me as a woman."

We can respond to this in several ways. We can grieve the effects of feminism in this woman's life. We can admire the tenacity of her faith. But above all I think this student's position was unstable. Eventually, she must either renounce her brand of feminism or renounce the faith. There is something wrong with a faith that daily considers denying the faith. Of course, this applies to marriage too. *There is something wrong with a marital fidelity that is always open to the end of fidelity.* If we ponder the option of divorce every day, we will probably use it one day. To endure, we must stop asking, "Shall I endure?"

Both the woman from Yale and Joe who vetoed the affair exhibit "decisionism." Decisionism, so common in America, invites people to reevaluate everything annually if not daily. Decisionists keep their options open. They want to be free to reconsider almost any past commitment—marriage, career, beliefs, friends, even sexual orientation. Decisionism leads some into divorce, because it keeps that option open. It leads others to shun marriage. They hate divorce; they would never divorce, as their parents did. But they decide to drift from one semipermanent relationship to another.

Scripture calls marriage a *covenant* a man makes with the partner of his youth (Prov. 2:17). A man who divorces his wife breaks faith with her, for she is the wife of his marriage covenant (Mal. 2:14). One way to keep our covenant during the dry seasons is to think about our covenant of marriage the way God thinks of his covenant of redemption. God's love for us remains the same, however poor the love and obedience we offer him. God has maximum troth. The man of God will pledge himself to love as God loves, with permanent devotion to his wife.

That said, we need to remember that our sin and weakness deprive us of the strength we need to keep our vows. (I once vowed I would never get angry again. The idea was noble, but not very practical.) We want to follow God, but, too often, we cannot follow through. Thus we turn to the Lord daily for strength to fulfill our pledges and for mercy when we violate our pledges.

Despite our failures, a place for troth remains. We should still pledge to love our wives "till death do us part." Within the security of such a commitment, we discover what it means to "be united."

One Flesh

After "leave" and "be united," we come to the third leg of marriage, "one flesh." One flesh refers to the sexual aspect of marriage. The next line underscores this, "The man and his wife were both naked, and they felt no shame." The sexual aspect of marriage hearkens back to the idea that Adam and Eve must "be fruitful and multiply." Reproduction *is* central to our sexuality. Yet we notice that this statement about marriage does not mention children. Perhaps it was superfluous for Moses to mention children again in Genesis 2, since they are so prominent in Genesis 1. Still, the silence about children suggests that while they are the normal *result* of marriage, they are not *essential* to marriage. A couple is truly married even if they miss the blessing of children.

Further, if children are not essential to marriage, but sexual expression is, then God blesses sexuality even apart from procreation. God designed sex for procreation, but physical intimacy also expresses and deepens love, even if children are not in view.

Finally, while the nakedness of Adam and Eve refers to their physical intimacy, it also refers to their spiritual intimacy. In biblical language *nakedness* refers to both physical and spiritual exposure (see Isa. 47:3; 2 Cor. 5:3; Heb. 4:13). To be exposed without shame is to have nothing to hide (see Gen. 3:7–11). Because Adam and Eve knew neither sin nor guile, nothing shameful separated them. The idea of nakedness without shame suggests their perfect trust, ease, and openness.

Today, a proper sense of our sinfulness makes spiritual self-disclosure painful and complicated. We have far too much to hide simply to enjoy it. Yet in a marriage marked by love and troth, we can tell the truth about ourselves. We know our beloveds will not use the truth against us. We know we will love each other after the truth is revealed.

Conclusion

Our yearning for safe self-disclosure reminds us again that when God made us in his image, he made us for companionship, for intimacy. We should have friends, but marriage is the first and deepest source of companionship. To develop that companionship, we need to foster both the "face to face" and the "side by side" of marriage. We need to carve out time alone for walks, dinners, movies, sports, and vacations. Face to face we develop and maintain shared interests. But we also grow closer when we work together. As we govern the world for God, raise a family, and till our gardens, side-by-side affection and respect increase. If we quiet the critical tongue and foster mutual encouragement, unity develops whenever we labor together in kitchen or community. Shared labor promotes respect as we see each other's skills at work.

Still, our sinfulness complicates companionship both inside and outside of marriage. The captives in Lebanon irritated one another too—one snored, another was proud, a third was too assertive. Husbands and wives bother each other too. But the God who built us to yearn for companionship also will enable us to overcome both petty irritations and big problems. Living in God's strength and showing Godlike fidelity, we can overcome the sin that disrupts companionship and flourish in a shared life.

Discussion Questions

1. Is your marriage more face-to-face or side-by-side? Why? How can you make more face time?

2. If you could spend several days alone with your wife, what would it be like? What might you learn?
3. Of the elements (1) leaving, (2) being united, and (3) becoming one flesh, which have you done best in your marriage? Why? Worst? Why?
4. What happens in hard times if we think of marriage with a decisionist mentality? Why is it important to think of marriage as a covenant rather than a decision?

A Word on the Legal Status of Marriage in the West

At the moment that I write this short essay, socially aware Christians are justifiably concerned about the legal and institutional status of marriage in the West. The focus of attention today is on same-sex marriage. Throughout Western Europe and South America, several nations have decided to legalize same-sex marriage or to recognize civil relationships so that same-sex couples have the legal rights and privileges of marriage. In federalist nations, the same shift may occur on a state-by-state basis. Courts increasingly argue that interference with same-sex marriage is a prejudicial assault on human dignity and a deprivation of human rights. This positions conservative Christians as foes of human rights, which is hardly a welcome development. There are several results. First, wherever we live, same-sex marriage either has come or is coming soon. Second, it will not be easy for Christians to gain a hearing for their position. Third, we now know, if we ever doubted it, that there are no Christian nations. In pluralistic democracies, leaders are beholden to the will of the people, not the will of God.

Christians have a variety of opinions about these developments. Many are pleased by the way rights have been extended to an often-oppressed group. Whatever our views of marriage may be, we should know that the law of Moses often insists on equal legal protection for all (e.g., Ex. 23:8; Deut. 16:19; 21:15–17). On the other hand, Genesis states and Jesus reaffirms God's good plan for marriage: "From the beginning the Creator made them male and female. . . . 'For this reason a man will leave his father and mother and will be united with his wife, and the two will become one flesh'" (Matt. 19:4–5 NET).

As always, we need to put current events in context. Specifically, Western nations have been falling away from biblical norms for decades. Divorce has become easier and easier, accelerated most notably by no-fault divorce laws that allowed either party to a marriage to terminate it at will (that is, regardless of the wishes of their spouse). Decades ago, easy divorce codified disregard for Jesus' word, "What therefore God has joined together, let not man separate" (Matt. 19:6 ESV).

A few decades ago, cohabitation was rare, and widely considered shameful. The term for it, *shacking up*, suggested that it was a practice for the underclass. Today premarital cohabitation is typical. Studies have found that a period of cohabitation already preceded most first marriages by the mid-1990s. Today, that number is far higher. We now ignore another biblical norm. In the United States and Great Britain, the most recent studies report that over 40 percent of all children are born outside of wedlock. These numbers are rising steadily and in almost every demographic group. Yet deliberately childless marriages are more common. Finally, there are ever more marriages with no sexual intimacy. This means that Western cultures have disregarded the created order–marriage, then sexual intimacy, then children. Today there is no strong link between sex and marriage, sex and procreation, or procreation and marriage.

The confusion about the order of cohabitation, marriage, sexual intimacy, and procreation will create additional challenges in coming years. For example, everything is in place for polygamy to become the next challenge to God's design for marriage. Advocacy groups already make the case for polygamy, and unofficial polygamy is on the rise. It will be all too easy to make a legal and experiential argument for polygamy.

Legally, at the moment polygamy is illegal in all Western nations, but enforcement is lax as officials increasingly tolerate unofficial polygamy among Muslims in France and Mormons in America. Reports say that Canadians leave their polygamists alone. If an official hauled the members of a local polygamist community into court, how (unless the accused chose to incriminate themselves) could they prove that the group is practicing polygamy? If society sees no essential connection between sleeping in the same bed and marriage, what evidence could be presented? Besides, if "male and female" is irrelevant to marriage, how can the number of participants become its one immutable feature?[3] Can anyone argue that a marriage between two men promotes the social good more than a marriage between one man and two women? Moreover, the so-called right to privacy assumes that governments have no legitimate interest and no right to intervene in private acts between consenting adults.[4] As a thought experiment, try to construct a principled argument (as opposed to an emotional or historical argument) against polygamy that doesn't also condemn same-sex marriage. If we approve one, we must approve the other.

Experientially, people will say polygamy is loving and compassionate. "Yes," they may concede, "monogamy is ideal, but we hardly live in an ideal world. Many women long to marry but can't find a suitable mate because men have no money, no character, no interest in marriage, or no interest in women. If a man can support several wives, financially and emotionally, how can anyone deny an interested woman the right to love, companionship, and children? Even if it isn't ideal, we constantly accept things—like divorce—that are less than ideal. Besides, several of the world's religions have accepted polygamy."

So then, how do cohabitation, common divorce, same-sex marriage, births outside wedlock, and (one day) polygamy affect the cause of Christ and the gospel? In a vital way, nothing changes. Jesus is still Lord and Savior. As Christian ethicist Russell Moore said, the gospel doesn't need family values to flourish: "In fact, [the gospel] often thrives when it is in sharp contrast to the cultures around

---

3. Mark Steyn, "The Marrying Kind," *Atlantic Monthly* (May 2005): 142–43.
4. Unofficial polygamy means there is one legal wife. Additional wives are not reported at the courthouse or claimed on tax returns, but the additional parties still take marriage vows before witnesses.

it. That's why the gospel rocketed out of the first-century from places such as Ephesus . . . Corinth and Rome."[5] The Roman Empire lacked a moral system that promoted healthy marriages. In fact, the very contrast between Christian marriages and the wreckage of pagan marriages, which included slave concubines, easy divorce, and sexual chaos, *strengthened the appeal of Christianity.*

A nation's authorities may permit, tolerate, or even promote marriage-like arrangements that fall short of God's plan. But let us remember that those acts do not compromise our freedom to love our wives, husbands, and children. Courts permit many things that are contrary to biblical morality. Abortion is legal in most countries, but we can still have children. Legislatures promote gambling, since states expect to profit from it. But the state cannot drag us to casinos any more than Rome could force its people to attend gladiatorial shows.

For those who are prone to despair, consider the status of abortion today. Through the persistence and courage of life-affirming believers, abortion has declined in many areas. In the 1980s, my state of Missouri had an abortion rate that exceeded 20 percent. Today it is 8 percent, and the rate is lower in several nearby states. Since the abortion rate remains as high as ever in some states (near 40 percent in New York), it seems that gentle persuasion can create a moral consensus.[6] Not long ago, this sort of progress in the protection of the unborn seemed impossible.

More importantly, social trends in no way restrict our freedom to marry, have children, and love each other. If anything, they should prompt us to rededicate ourselves to Christlike love in marriage. The Christian marriage ideal attracted many pagans to the faith in

5. Russell Moore, "How Should Same-Sex Marriage Change the Church's Witness?," *Moore to the Point* (blog), June 26, 2013, http://www.russellmoore.com/2013/06/26/how-should-same -sex-marriage-change-the-churchs-witness/.

6. These statistics are the most recent numbers from U.S. government websites. We understand that trends may continue, accelerate, or reverse themselves and that abortifacient medications introduce uncertainty about the real abortion rate.

the apostolic age. When the Reformers restored the biblical teaching on marriage five hundred years ago, it enhanced the call to the gospel. When Reformers like Martin Luther married and became faithful husbands and fathers, their conduct beautified the gospel. May our marriages become a similar testimony to God's purposes.

Jesus said, "From the beginning the Creator made them male and female." We use this statement to promote God's ideal and rightly so, but let's remember that Jesus made that statement to correct an error of *his* age—arbitrary divorce. On that front, church conduct looks all too similar to the culture around us. How then shall we live?

First, we should tend our marriages and regard our spouses as God's great gift (Prov. 19:14). At its best, Paul says, the love of a Christian marriage reflects the love of Christ for the church (Eph. 5:25). Strong marriages adorn the gospel (Titus 2:10). Waves of good marriages will make the case for God's plan more effectively than any state or federal law.

This year I officiated at a wedding on the campus of a major American university that was founded on secular principles. At the reception, I sat next to a professor who did his doctoral work at that school and now teaches at another secular university in the same state. He said that the great majority of his fellow professors are secular. Nonetheless, he said they love their Christian students. On the whole, they are far more likely to come to class faithfully and well prepared. They are willing to argue their convictions, they are active in campus life, they volunteer for worthwhile projects, and they keep their commitments.

The Christian faith has lost the home-field advantage in Western cultures. We have to accept reality as it is, not as we wish it to be. That means we will need to acknowledge legal marriages as the state does. As always, we are free to distinguish between a legal marriage and an ideal marriage, between marriage as humanity sees it and marriage as God intended it. (Long ago, pastors distinguished between the *being* and the *well-being* of marriage.) That leaves us free to articulate, and, more importantly, to live out our concept of marriage. May we seek lives that are beautiful, and words that are coherent and peaceful. That is the surest way to promote God's good plan for salvation and a good life, one that includes God's plan for marriage and family.

| 4 |

A Man and His Marriage: The Three Faces of Love

From the field of evolutionary psychology, we have good news and bad news. The good news is that men and women are designed to fall in love. The bad news, they say, is that we are not designed to stay there. Indeed, the tendency to fall out of love is so strong, psychologists say, that we should view a golden anniversary the same way we view a dog walking on two legs. We should not judge whether it is done well, but marvel that it is done at all.

From the field of statistics we also have good and bad news. The good news is that the number of divorces in America has leveled off and may even be falling. The bad news is that divorces are down largely because so many people refuse marriage altogether. They simply live together awhile, then split up. Meanwhile, the divorce rate for those who do marry is still well above 40 percent.[1]

The root of the decline of marriage is the loss of a Christian concept of love. People get married for selfish reasons. Whether they want children or someone to care for them, whether they seek a regular sexual partner or a cure for lone-

---

1. Most statistical studies conclude that nearly 45 percent of all marriages will eventually end in divorce. Additional marriages end with an unresolved separation. Divorce statistics vary according to educational level, income, age at first marriage, among other factors. But some sophisticated studies continue to publish alarming findings. A 2002 study found 23 percent of all marriages in the United States ended in divorce or separation within the first five years. The same study found that 54 percent of nonreligious Americans and 39 percent of religious Americans saw their marriage end in separation or divorce within fifteen years. See Andrew Cherlin, *The Marriage-Go-Round* (New York: Alfred Knopf, 2009), 203–12.

liness, egocentricity drives too much courtship and marriage. Whether it shows itself as lustful *eros* or a desire for the benefits of a traditional marriage, self-interest rules and self-love cannot long sustain a marriage.

Marriages often start as a hot romance and end as a cool arrangement. In idealized romance, the fuse may be long or short, but once it begins to burn, the rest is supposed to be history. In romance we find the most attractive person in the world—or at least the most attractive person available in our pool of potential partners—the most attractive person "in our league." For a man, attraction may begin with a woman's physical appearance. A woman may take more interest in a man's ability to provide, if he has or can be expected to find a professional position. Kindness, sensitivity, and a willingness to commit count, too, because most people hope to marry for life.

Men and women both like to spend time with lively, pleasant people who pay attention to them. ("Can you believe it? She thinks I'm fascinating!") The blend of attraction and attention fill us with warmth and excitement when our beloveds are near. We foresee a good life together.

But after a while, the fires of romance—or perhaps infatuation—burn low. The virtues of the beloved become familiar and the vices become grating. Even the best music becomes wearisome if we listen to it every day. Similarly, it seems, even a good spouse becomes predictable, even stale. The strengths are so familiar, the weaknesses so noticeable. As the years pass, we all grow wrinkled, colorless, and saggy. Then what? If we marry for romantic feelings, and the feelings fade, the marriage faces a crisis. Some think of leaving. Or the romance can degenerate into an arrangement.

In an arrangement, the two parties are two individuals joined in a mutually agreeable and advantageous relationship. Husband and wife are two equal, autonomous, self-actualizing individuals. They negotiate their relationship. Each gives what they wish and gets what they can. No roles are set in advance, so everything is negotiated. Husband and wife both bring something to the table and expect to get something back. If each contributes to the other's happiness, through income, nurture, domestic skills, or amiability, then each can expect a return.

An arrangement can seem agreeable, but when a marriage deteriorates into an arrangement, infidelity and divorce become ever-present possibilities. Why remain faithful if a spouse fails to stay as attractive or interesting as he or she once was? Why stay married when the arrangement, the deal, becomes unsatisfactory? Whenever husband or wife thinks the cost of marriage outweighs the benefits for an extended period, whenever one party determines it feasible to obtain a higher-caliber spouse, divorce becomes an option. Some businessmen trade up for a younger wife every decade or so. As J. Paul Getty, the oft-divorced oil billionaire, said, "A lasting relationship with a woman is only possible if you are a business failure."

The Root of Our Distress

Again, the root of these troubles is the loss of a Christian concept of love. Both the romantic and the arranged marriage can be selfish forms of love. One seeks erotic pleasure, the other the subtler pleasures of security or ease. But in each the husband and wife seek what they hope another will do for them. That is, the quest for a romantic marriage and the quest for a good "arrangement" can both be driven by self-love, and self-love will not sustain a marriage.

In fact a healthy marriage will manifest three faces of love, labeled by the Greek words *agape*, *philia*, and *eros*. *Agape* is the selfless, sacrificial, Christlike love that touches stranger, neighbor, enemy, friend, child, and spouse alike. *Philia* is attraction for a special friend whom we admire due to shared interests or skills, due to their humor, intellect, or personality. *Eros* is romantic, sensual love, when fingertips and lips pulse at the thought of contact. *Marriage thrives when three forms of love join together.*

The First Face of Love: Romantic Love

Romantic love is a passion, a yearning, for another person who is desirable in a powerful and mysterious way. Eros makes us want to reach the depths of another person and bring them into the world of our deepest selves. When physical yearning and spiritual or psychological fascination join, there is romantic love. Scripture does not *command* eros—there is no need. Romantic love is natural; it comes over us. Yet God invites husbands and wives to it and Scripture commends it.[2]

Eros is born of *need* for another person who promises to complete us. The Song of Songs describes it this way: "O daughters of Jerusalem, I charge you—if you find my lover, what will you tell him? Tell him I am faint with love" (5:8; see also 2:5). Eros loves one particular person, not all people in general. It chooses *one* who is uniquely appealing and promising. Eros finds that, in all the world, there is just one person whom it desires. Both the lover and the beloved say, "I am my lover's and my lover is mine" (6:3; see also 2:16; 7:10; 8:6).

The Song of Songs describes the admiration that betrothed and newly married people feel. Solomon describes the delight of romantic love this way (4:1–7):

> How beautiful you are, my darling!
>> Oh, how beautiful!
>> Your eyes behind your veil are doves.
> Your hair is like a flock of goats [she is blond].
> . . . .
> Your teeth are like a flock of sheep just shorn,
>> coming up from the washing [they are white].
> Each has its twin;
>> not one of them is alone [when she smiles, there are no gaps].

2. I propose that even romantic love is grounded in God's love. There is no erotic component in God's love for his people, but the Lord's love is intense and personal. He is a jealous God. He desires our faithful love, and we are his treasured possession (Ex. 19:5). He says, "I have called you by name, you are mine" (Isa. 43:1 ESV). So focused love rests in God's nature. On God's blessing of romantic love, see Lewis Smedes, *Sex for Christians* (Grand Rapids: Eerdmans, 1976), 92–93.

Your lips are like a scarlet ribbon [they are thin and red];
   your mouth is lovely.
. . . .
Your neck is like the tower of David,
   built with elegance;
on it hang a thousand shields,
   all of them shields of warriors.
Your two breasts are like two fawns,
   like twin fawns of a gazelle
     that browse among the lilies [how breasts resemble fawns
       browsing among lilies is a mystery, but the main idea
       is clear].
. . . .
All beautiful you are, my darling;
   there is no flaw in you.

Parts of this poem sound strange to us, but we cannot mistake its sentiment. A man in love declares, "In all the world there is one person whom I desire, only one who completes me."

Solomon also praises romantic love in Proverbs 5. But first, he warns his son of the seductive adulteress. Her lips drip honey, but her steps lead to ruin and death (vv. 3–14). Promiscuity will devour both strength and riches. But Solomon objects to immorality, not *eros*. His remedy for sexual temptation is not abstinence, but the intimacy of marriage, as we see in Proverbs 5:15–19:

Drink water from your own cistern,
   running water from your own well.
Should your springs overflow in the streets,
   your streams of water in the public squares?
Let them be yours alone,
   never to be shared with strangers.
May your fountain be blessed,
   and may you rejoice in the wife of your youth.
A loving doe, a graceful deer—
   may her breasts satisfy you always,
   may you ever be captivated by her love.

"Drink from your own cistern" means quench your appetites with your wife. Keep your sexual powers in the home. Do not waste them, but treasure them, like the water that was so scarce in Israel. Sexual potency is a resource we must guard and channel, never pouring it into public places, never sharing it with strangers (vv. 16–17). Then our fountain—that is, our capacity and desire for children—will be blessed. Love will grow and endure. Like gazelles, we will mate for life (vv. 18–19). By keeping sex in marriage we avoid the trap of adultery. We also bring children into a secure environment.

But sex is more than a means for procreation and a control for unbridled sensuality. Solomon says there is a morally permissible love-ecstasy. He tells his son, "May your wife's breasts satisfy you. May you be *captivated* with her love." The term translated *captivated* (*shagah*) commonly means *drunk* in Hebrew (Prov. 20:1; Isa. 28:7). Solomon does not advocate literal drunkenness. Rather he means that a man may fall "under the influence" of erotic love for his wife. A husband may forget himself, losing some of his self-control.

God made us with a capacity to forget ourselves and the world when caught up in certain activities. We immerse ourselves in noble tasks that demand our highest skills. We get "in the zone" in athletic contests. We "lose ourselves" in absorbing books. When that happens, awareness of time, of surroundings, even of self diminishes. We have to rouse ourselves to reenter the real world.

Proverbs permits husbands and wives to lose themselves in love in just this way. We can get carried away in romantic love. We can enjoy each other in ways that break the boundaries of ordinary life.

Christians don't always know how to take Solomon's delight in married sexuality. Thomas Aquinas, a medieval theologian, said sexuality is "always evil" because it produces an "excess of pleasure" that keeps the soul from its highest good, which is the contemplation of God.[3] Now Aquinas was a monk, so we may

3. See my article, "The Puritans, Sex, and Pleasure," in *Christian Perspectives on Sexuality and Gender*, ed. Elizabeth Stuart and Adrian Thatcher (Grand Rapids: Eerd-

wonder how he knew that sex and theological contemplation don't lend themselves to multitasking, but he probably was right. Many people can do two things at once, but conjugal relations and theological meditations make a poor pair.[4]

The seventeenth-century Puritans had a higher view. They said sexual union can knit husband and wife together emotionally and strengthen their love for each other. But they struggled to break free of the medieval Christian's fear of passion. Citing Paul's admonition to consecrate everything by the word of God and prayer (1 Tim. 4:4–5), they urged couples to pray for several days after their wedding before coming together. They warned against overheated eros, even in marriage, and taught men to pray before every physical act, lest God curse their unborn offspring.[5]

If Christians past suffered from undue modesty and reserve about their sexuality, contemporary Christians often go to the opposite extreme. They accept our society's celebration, even obsession, with physical love. A couple of surveys have found that married evangelical women have more frequent sex, on average, than "swinging" singles. But the way we celebrate sexuality today, I half-expected some church to advertise, "Become a Christian and enjoy sex like never before." The Puritans probably did have a prudish streak, but we should hear their warnings against using sex for nothing but selfish indulgence. It is possible, even in marriage, to use our spouses for our own pleasure, as objects, rather than loving them as people. Marriage joins two people, not just two bodies.

We have trouble finding the golden mean that rejoices in the gift of sexuality but remembers the sin of sensuality. But Proverbs got it right. It celebrates ecstasy, but warns against reckless loss of self-discipline.

---

mans, 1996), 33–52.

4. In Aquinas's system, the idea that sex is evil does not necessarily mean it is sinful. If a husband and wife have relations for the sake of procreation, the act is considered evil but permissible.

5. Doriani, *Puritans, Sex, and Pleasure*.

In most Western marriages, the problem is not the getting of eros but the keeping. The feeling of love fades. Like funerals, weddings have the power of prompting reflection in the attendees. Sitting through the ceremony, we do not wonder, "Will these people *find* love?" but "Will they *keep* it?" Slouching in the pew, the divorced ponder their marriages, and many who are still married wonder if they can rekindle romantic fires that have burned to ash. To prevent the fading of love, we should learn from the second face of love, *agape*.

The Second Face of Love: Selfless Love

The biblical word for selfless, Godlike love is *agape*. Agape is the love that causes God to redeem deformed, rebellious sinners. We see agape in the Good Samaritan, who stopped to save a (presumably) Jewish man who, by the customs of the day, might spit in his face if he knew who was touching him. We see agape when Jesus washes his disciples' feet—even the feet of Judas—getting nothing in return but wet, dirty hands.

Agape seems like the opposite of eros. Agape flows not from need but from fullness or sufficiency. Agape "does not yearn to get what it needs, but empties itself to give what the other needs. . . . Agape is neighbor love: it goes out to all people just because they are there."[6] Agape is indiscriminate. It goes out to all, regardless of their worth. Agape reaches the good and the bad, the beautiful and the ugly, alike. It loves them because they are there. This is agape: "God so loved the *world* that he gave his one and only Son" (John 3:16). Again, God "causes his sun to rise on the evil and the good" (Matt. 5:43–48). And again, "God demonstrates his own love for us in this: While we were still sinners, Christ died for us" (Rom. 5:6–8). Agape is divine, supernatural love. We can admire it, but it is against our nature to practice it.

Agape so contradicts our egocentric inclinations that we must ask where we can find the motivation, the strength, for

6. Smedes, *Sex for Christians*, 93–94. The next several paragraphs are indebted to Smedes, 93–98.

such love. Surely it is not adequate to admire Jesus as he washes feet. We must do the same. But no one can generate this love by himself. Rather, "We love because he first loved us" (1 John 4:19).

Agape and eros seem almost antithetical. Eros is passionate, agape is dispassionate. Eros seeks to fulfill its desires, agape fulfills a neighbor's desires. Eros begins with self-interest, agape begins and ends with the interests of others. Nonetheless, a strong marriage needs both agape *and* eros, both Christian and romantic love.

Keeping Love Strong: Agape and Eros Together

Marriages need eros. Christian love alone cannot support a fulfilling marriage. Suppose that a woman asks her husband, "Do you love me?" Imagine that he answers like this: "Of course I love you. The Bible says, 'Love your neighbor as yourself,' and since we eat and sleep together, I would have to say we are neighbors. So, yes, I love you." No self-respecting spouse could tolerate being loved with nothing but neighbor love. Worse still would be a profession of love that said, "We have been having some rough times lately. I also realize that you are dull and untalented, but God commands me even to love my enemies and, as unattractive as you are, I certainly don't regard you as my enemy, so, yes, I love you." Within marriage, no one wants to hear, "I love you because God commands it."

A marriage cannot thrive on sacrifice alone; it needs romance. In marriage, we need to feel special, desirable. We need to feel that we are the apples of our lovers' eyes, the one in all the world for them. In marriage, we need to feel that we are loved *because* of who we are, not in spite of who we are. A woman needs to feel beautiful, treasured. A man needs to feel respected, even admired (Eph. 5:33). He longs to hear, "My hero." She longs to hear, "My darling."

Yet eros by itself can never sustain a marriage. Romantic love fades. It also becomes selfish. It needs the tenacity and discipline of selfless, Christlike love. So agape and eros must join for marriage to endure and deepen. Christian love and romantic love blend when the person we love needs us and we need them, when they fulfill us and we fulfill them. Agape and eros blend when a woman loves her husband *because* he is tall, dark, and handsome, *even though* he chews his fingers, picks his nose, and supports five other disgusting habits. Agape strengthens eros several ways:

- *Agape enriches eros* with its realism. It sees the flaws in the beloved and loves anyway. It reminds us that our beloveds cannot satisfy all our dreams. It helps eros love the whole person.
- *Agape stabilizes eros.* Romance is a flower that blooms and falls. It is a ride in the amusement park, thrilling but unsustainable. Marriage has its delights, but we spend more time with our heads in the washing machine than with our feet in the Jacuzzi.
- *Agape gives endurance* to marriage when romance cools. Agape revives love when it flags, because small acts of sacrificial kindness make us feel more loved, make us seem more lovable, and make us want to love in return.
- *Agape corrects eros* when it might be distorted by selfishness or sensuality. Self-sacrifice keeps us from using our spouses or keeping them for ourselves.

On the other hand, *eros empowers agape*. Eros keeps agape from becoming cold and dutiful. It keeps marriage from descending into routine, a mere partnership in life's struggles. Romance gives us secret joy in serving the one we love. We take pleasure in serving the one we admire. We *like* to give happiness to the one we *love*. Such sacrifices seem light, not burdensome.

Romance also keeps the mystery in everyday life. The wink, the hug, the squeeze of the hand, the unexpected kiss lighten the tasks of cleaning up, doing dishes, tending yards, or watching finances. Clouds hover overhead when a tortured commute home punctuates a miserable day at work, but small acts of loving affection part those clouds.

The Third Face of Love in Marriage: Philia

The third, oft-neglected, face of love is philia, the love of friendship and affection. Philia can help bridge the gap between eros and agape. Philia is the fondness we feel for a friend. It is the delight we feel in spending time with someone who is lively, interesting, and warm. Obviously, philia stands somewhere between eros and agape.

- The mark of *eros* is the need for one other person, and the mark of *agape* is the absence of need for another, but the mark of *philia* is the desire, but not the *need*, for the company of another.
- *Eros* loves one, and *agape* loves all, but *philia* loves a handful of friends.
- God never commands *eros*, and always commands *agape*, but he commands *philia* occasionally (e.g., Rom. 12:10).

To evaluate the status of philia in your marriage, consider: If you were not married to your wife, would she still be your friend? Would you find her interesting? Good company? In the love of friendship we treasure the pleasant traits of our spouses.

My wife is my friend, and I admire many of her traits. We were friends for nearly a year before we began dating. The first time I went to church with her, I startled at the soprano voice rising so pure, so sweet, so strong, beside me. I marveled at the strength and range of the voice pouring from her. Later, I came to admire her touch as a piano accompanist. Whether playing piano, typing, or playing table tennis, she has hand-eye coordination I can only envy. She also graces our home with skill in the domestic arts. Though our society holds them in low esteem, she carefully inculcates them in our children. Her smile is quick and warm, and her ready laugh shakes her whole body. She learns the name and offers her warmth to everyone she meets. She makes people feel welcome, even if it means offering meals and beds to near strangers. I could continue, but you get the point. If I were not married to her, I would want her to be my friend.

It is important for men (and women) to treasure and even list the excellencies of our wives (and husbands), because the longer we live together, the better we know each other's faults. A man I know commemorated his thousandth day of marriage by presenting his wife a list of one thousand reasons why he loved her. He told his coworkers the next day. A candid fellow exclaimed, "A thousand reasons to love my wife! It would be easier to think of a thousand reasons for hating her."

As the years of marriage pass, it sometimes seems that our *marriage IQ*—our irritation quotient—gets higher and higher. We crack our knuckles or forget to put snack food away. It took me fifteen years to learn to hang up my towel properly, but it took my wife twenty years to remember to slide the driver's seat back when she uses my car. I banged my knee against the dash enough times that I have a permanent limp. Joking aside, we all offend our spouses too carelessly and take offense too easily.

Few people are genuinely easy to live with. When we first contemplate marriage, we hardly conceive the daily irritations that can bloom into daily tensions. Many were hidden—not maliciously—as we tried to make the best impression on a person who was also making their best impression on us. Just as important, the virtues that attracted us to our spouses often have a converse vice. A sloppy man admired the neatness and organization of his intended, but now her concern for order feels like ceaseless nagging. A financially careless woman admired her fiancé's financial self-discipline, but now he seems impossibly stingy.

A wise man might list the dark side of his virtues—not his wife's. For example, as a man with a PhD, I know that my tribe is not necessarily the most intelligent, but we are analytical and tenacious enough to become an expert (usually) on a topic so narrow that very few would ever want to read about it. Sometimes my wife admires these analytical skills. Unfortunately, I analyze *everything*. When driving, I analyze traffic patterns. When watching a movie, I analyze character and plot development. I cannot help but predict who will die in the action movies and who will marry in the romantic comedy. Sometimes my family drives me out of the room so they can watch in peace. In short, I can be annoying. Constant analysis is a vicious virtue. Wise men will recall their own vicious virtues and stop pouncing on their wives for theirs.

Irritations, petty and otherwise, do eros in. Disappointment that our spouses are not quite the women of our dreams can spawn complaints and criticisms that escalate into quarrels. Sadly, some of us have minds that excel in finding flaws; eyes that notice the one white thread on the black suit, the tiny smudge on the white paper. As the cycle of error and criticism continues, hard words can fly. We feel the pangs of shattered expectations. The fear that we have chosen poorly begins to gnaw at us. Here loyalty, faithfulness, agape, and a firm grip on God's grace must rescue us.

Love Restored

The family is a society of sinners. A Christian marriage is the union of two redeemed sinners, not two angels. I like to ask my students, "What are the two biggest sources of problems in a marriage?" They shoot back their proposals: Communication. Money. In-laws. Sex. Children. Time pressures. No, the two biggest sources of trouble in a marriage are *the husband* and *the wife*. They bring enough sin, enough annoyances, to undercut all three facets of marriage.

- *Eros* fades as we get gray, pudgy, and creaky. But apart from the passing of the years, we let ourselves get stale. We try to be interesting in public, but at home we become dullards.
- Men strain *agape* when they presume on their wives. We abuse love when we let ourselves get lazy and boring,

thinking, "She has to love me no matter what." Agape knows how to love neighbors, but why test your wife by acting like a mere neighbor?

- *Philia* is love of an admired friend, but there is so much to criticize. We subvert philia when we carelessly irritate our spouses, but note every irritation they inflict on us.

Given our propensity to the sins and follies that weaken love, what can we do? Obviously, wise couples try to nurture eros, agape, and philia. But we can't keep love strong in marriage by deciding to do so, any more than we can fix a chaotic schedule by declaring, "From now on, I'm getting up at 6:00 a.m." We can't simply *resolve* to stop sinning.

One way to retain love is to understand our failures better. Consider the irritations that plague so many marriages. Suppose a man frequently desecrates his wife's beautiful kitchen, tracking mud in from the yard and leaving food and dishes strewn about. He judges it a harmless token of his masculinity, but she views it as a sign of his insensitivity. In return, she criticizes him for negligence and constantly nags him to put things away. He replies by condemning her ingratitude and chastising her for forgetting how hard he works.

Cycles of petty offenses, criticisms, and countercriticisms can suck the life from a marriage. We know better. As Proverbs says, "A fool gives full vent to his anger" (29:11) and "A fool shows his annoyance at once, but a prudent man overlooks an insult" (12:16). But how can a couple break a chain of negligence and quibbling?

First, *listen to your spouse.* Men, if your wife says your mud and dishes are driving her to distraction, then they are driving her to distraction, even if you think they should not. Wives, if your husband says your nagging criticisms are driving him to distraction, then they are driving him to distraction, even if you think they should not. When we listen, we forego the right to explain ourselves first, to assert our claims last, and to give top priority to our account of things. Courageous listening observes the marriage without blinking, so we know it as it is, not as we prefer to imagine it. Merciful listening hears troubles in order to render aid, not criticize.[7]

Second, *remember grace*. A Christian marriage is more than two people trying to carve out a decent life by following a moral code. A third party is involved. If we pray, and even if we do not, the Father pours his love into our hearts to replenish fading affection and troth. Jesus shows us how to love. He modeled agape, loving us when we were weak, unattractive, even hateful toward him. He entreats us to show the same love if our spouses become unhelpful, unattractive, even spiteful. Agape loves despite unloveliness and covers a multitude of sins.

God's love rebukes men who think their wives are not quite good enough for them. It corrects women who think they cannot endure their husband's poor conduct another day. God calls us his beloved bride after all our infidelities. How then can men after God's heart spurn their wives when they fail to measure up to our standards, in ways great or small?

It should be easiest to forgive our wives' sins. After all, we love them, we want peace, and we know they are weak, not malicious. Sadly, it can be hardest to forgive those closest to us. Their sins hurt us more. They are often repeated, and they occur despite promises to change. Occasionally, a woman does something that so enrages her husband that he resolves to stay angry. He replays and exaggerates the offense to keep his wrath simmering. But then a thought surfaces, "Is this sin really so great it cannot be pardoned? Greater than my sins against God?" Of course, no one can mistreat us more than we have mistreated God. No wife can dishonor us more than we dishonor God. Therefore, if God forgives us, we must forgive

---

7. Even on earth, Jesus was the supreme listener, his selflessness giving a singular focus on others so as to hear them. Yes, Jesus' divine prerogatives enabled him to read people's thoughts (Matt. 9:4; 12:25; Luke 6:8; 7:39–40; 9:47; John 2:25), but he did not always use the prerogatives of deity (Matt. 24:36).

and seek reconciliation, instead of poking our wounds and licking our bitterness.

Christ's Love the Standard

The notion of forgiving our wives because God forgives us brings us to a core value. Remember, we do not live by five-step action plans. We follow the character of our Lord, as he remakes us in his image. Therefore, godly husbands see Christ's love as their pattern. As Paul said, "Husbands, love your wives, as Christ loved the church and gave himself up for her" (Eph. 5:25). I urge you to ponder Christ's loving ways with you and to consider how you could practice them in your marriage. Let me mention three points.

Humility. Christ is the head of the church, but he does not exercise his headship for personal benefit. Rather, he humbled himself in service, even to the point of death on the cross. So too husbands should see their authority as opportunity to serve, not to be served. Humble husbands do not dominate. They lead by consent, not decree. They lead, but also empower wives to lead with them.

Service. When Jesus gathered the disciples for the Last Supper, no servant stood by to wash their feet. So Jesus knelt down, like a house slave, to do it (John 13). If our leader washes feet like a menial servant, then we should serve too, in tasks as concrete as scrubbing a kitchen floor. Indeed, washing can be a vital expression of love. Even if wives work exclusively in the home, men should be helpful.

Patience. One can hardly read the Gospels without noticing how many times Jesus predicted his death on the cross and how many times his disciples failed to "get it" (e.g., Luke 9:22; 17:25; 18:32). Once Jesus said, "Let these words sink into your ears: The Son of Man is going to be betrayed into human hands" (Luke 9:44 NRSV). Luke immediately adds, "They did not understand what this meant. It was hidden from them, so that they did not grasp it, and they were afraid to ask him about it" (v. 45). Four times over, Luke accents their dullness. Yet Jesus, the model for husbands, patiently explained it again. Even when he arose, they could hardly believe it—and he patiently explained the resurrection to them two more times (Luke 24:26, 46). Let us learn from the Savior.

Conclusion

Marriages fall apart because people seek romance and romance fades. They fall apart because people craft *quid pro quo* arrangements, and the *quid* outweighs the *pro quo*. Vices loom larger, virtues seem to shrivel, and discontent sets in. When eros erodes and philia falters, a marriage that exists to meet the egocentric desires is imperiled.

Marriages endure when they join all three faces of love. Wise husbands and wives make time for their face-to-face relationship, to keep romance warm. They treasure their spouse's strengths, to bolster philia. They remember agape, love for the unlovely, for so God loves us. Eros and philia develop almost spontaneously, but agape is more deliberate. Its realism—"my wife is not very lovable today, but I love her still"—promotes troth. Philia and eros supply the pleasures of marriage, but marriages cannot endure without agape, the most Godlike face of marriage. For all three, we need God's grace to cover our failings and God's power to pour his love into our hearts. Then we can enjoy the stability of agape, the warmth of philia, and the heat of eros.

Discussion Questions

1. Which facet of love is strongest in your marriage: agape, philia, or eros?
2. Are you and your wife friends? How do you deal with the problem of high irritability quotients?
3. List at least twenty things you like about your wife (or husband). Was this exercise easy or hard for you? What did you learn from it? Share the list with your spouse and watch the results.

4. Read Proverbs 5 and Song of Songs with your wife. Discuss the concept of intoxication with love ("morally permissible love ecstasy"). When was the last time you prayed about your physical relationship, in thanksgiving or in petition?

5. Are agape, eros, and philia joining together to strengthen your marriage?

A Word on Pornography

Jesus never directly addressed the problem of pornography, but his statement from the Sermon on the Mount tells us all we need to know: "If your right eye causes you to sin, gouge it out and throw it away. It is better for you to lose one part of your body than for your whole body to be thrown into hell" (Matt. 5:29). Businessmen have said that a little greed is a good thing. Pornographers seem to believe that a lot of lust is a good thing. Jesus tells his disciples how damaging lust is when he offers eye gouging as a solution. Yes, Jesus speaks in hyperbole. He doesn't actually envision battalions of one-eyed disciples. (Besides, a one-eyed man can still look upon evil, and a blind man can still remember it.) He means it is better to suffer bodily pain in the present than to suffer spiritual pain for eternity. Jesus used the repugnant image of maiming and blindness to show that he hates lust. Yet the very purpose of pornography is to excite illicit desire, which should seem as horrible to us as the gouging of an eye. To say it another way, if our eyes tempt us to sin, we should strive to act as if we have no eyes. We should refuse to look at anything that excites lust.

Pornography may seem victimless, but it is not. It degrades women and pays them to degrade themselves. It incites adulterous thoughts. It is unfair to spouses, present or future, who cannot compete with models who polish their bodies for a living while photographers delete all defects. Surveys have shown that after men view pornography they register less satisfaction with their wives.

Still, most men feel the lure of pornography. Boys are curious and men get overheated. We are visual creatures, drawn to beauty, and the industry recruits beautiful people. Pornography also has addictive properties. The addiction is not physical, but the brain builds roads to pleasure that lead to habit formation, so that pornography can gain a strange grip on a man.

The way to break with it is well known. First, keep yourself out of the way of temptation. Be careful where you set your eyes. Avoid the books, movies, Internet sites, and magazines that lead to it. Paul said, "Flee from sexual immorality" (1 Cor. 6:18). He told Timothy to "flee the evil desires of youth" and to "pursue righteousness" (2 Tim. 2:22; 1 Tim. 6:11).

Second, if self-discipline doesn't work, carefully seek a friend who has the right to hold you accountable. We can entrust our stories to the right people. We shouldn't harbor secret addictions. If necessary, seek professional Christian counsel. Don't despair. Bad habits create harmful pathways, but if we neglect them long enough, they disintegrate. People can and do defeat addictive behavior.

The Lord gives us good reason to flee sin. We belong to Jesus. Paul says Jesus "obtained" (or "acquired") us with his lifeblood (Acts 20:28 ESV; see also 1 Cor. 6:20). We are free and we ought to live it: "You were bought at a price; do not become slaves of men" (1 Cor. 7:23). A disciple should shun sins that have the capacity to enslave or addict, whether drugs, alcohol, nicotine, or pornography. Of course, that is easier said than done. For that very reason we should be watchful, and seek aid when we feel trapped.

James 4:7 says, "Resist the devil, and he will flee from you." It doesn't always feel that way. Sometimes, the longer we resist the more intense a desire becomes. But temptations do fade eventually. Suppose a physician determines that chocolate is damaging his patient's health. To eat chocolate would constitute sinful self-abuse. But the desire for chocolate is strong. The patient may have to resist the temptation over and over before the desire begins to subside. So the devil flees, but not at once. On the other hand, if we succumb, Satan doesn't flee; he plops down on the couch with us. And since habits become ingrained, failure to resist on one occasion makes it harder to resist the next time. When we resist Satan, he must seek another time (Luke 4:13), but when we give in, we give

him more time. Suppose a man is traveling on business. When the
day ends, his friends may invite him to join them at a certain sort
of nightclub. Or he may return to a room where sensual movies
are available. If a man is fighting old habits, resistance may feel
difficult. But it isn't futile. A friend can promise to check in with
us, and we can promise to answer truthfully. Every time we resist,
it gets easier.

Still, we want to press beyond duties and methods. Shortly
after Jesus made his statement about our right eyes, he went on
to say, "No one can serve two masters. Either he will hate the one
and love the other, or he will be devoted to the one and despise the
other" (Matt. 6:24). We can have many affections but only one love
supreme. That is why Solomon says, "Guard your heart, for it is the
wellspring of life" (Prov. 4:23). The heart is the core of our being,
the seat of our affections, and our affections lead our faculties and
govern our actions. We either love God or the world (1 John 2:15).
Our will and reason follow the heart's deepest affections. We do
what we love.

I recently took our dog to the vet. Years ago, we set a financial
limit on how much we would spend to save our dog's life. Now the
vet was saying our dog needed a procedure that cost about $150
more than the limit we had set. Did we therefore let our dog die?
No, our reason follows our heart, so we *changed our reasoning*,
increased the limit, and spared our family pet. Our affections led
our thoughts and deeds. (If you don't want to overspend on a dog,
don't get one. Your heart will lead your reason to protect the furry
little beast.)

You see the application to our topic. Our loves drive our decisions. The mind is not an independent agent, it is the heart's loyal
soldier. If therefore you are given to pornography, consider your
heart. It's good to remind yourself that a devotion to pornography
will hurt you, hurt your marriage (present or future), and hurt
people who work in the industry. It's wise to remember that you

could get caught. As Numbers 32:23 says, "Be sure that your sin will find you out." You should know that it violates Jesus' teaching. But beyond all that, you need a greater love. We repent when we love something or someone more than we love our sin. We follow Jesus when we love and trust him. Humans are lovers. The wrong love scrambles and misdirects us. The love of God sets us on the right path.

| 5 |

A Man and His Children

The Need for Character

In time, every man faces his limitations as a father. We may see a father act with cruelty or foolish leniency, and begin to condemn, only to realize that we have done the same thing. We may catch ourselves imitating the worst of our own fathers, doing the very thing we swore we never would. Or we suddenly find that a cooperative child has become a turbulent teenager. None of the familiar ways of fathering work, and we have no idea what to do next.

Perhaps we do nothing wrong. We simply grasp the magnitude of the parental task and shudder. For some reason, when I first held my third child, a thought seized me, "She is in my hands, but not in my control. She is out of the womb, never to return. Now what? We just got our first two children under control, and now we're outnumbered." We have children on loan for twenty years, and we wonder, "Do I have what it takes to be a good father?"

Self-doubt is hardly the first thought we have about parenting. As young adults, most of us read a few articles or heard a few talks on parenting and decided we knew everything necessary to solve most parenting problems. We saw a child wailing on the floor of a store and thought, "If only those parents had read the article I saw in *Better Homes and Babies* last week, this would not happen." We witness a baby loudly refusing to eat his supper, and wish, "If I had a copy of last week's sermon, I'd give it to these pitiful people."

But after we become fathers, nothing looks so simple. As one man said, "When I was young, I had no children and six theories about the proper rearing of children. Now I am older; I have six children . . . and no theories."

No book of theories or rules is thick enough to cover every riddle parents face. Let no one deceive you. Seven-step plans never took anyone through all the challenges of parenthood. People think about parenting most when they face a problem and want a remedy. Naturally, friends and teachers want to help, so they make suggestions, complete with action plans. But if we view fatherhood as a series of problems and solutions, we miss the first principle. "Successful" parenthood depends on who you are, more than the techniques you know.

But what should a father be? Some teachers list series of virtues that godly parents exercise—patience, fairness, mercy, self-sacrifice, and tenderness. Parents should certainly be patient, fair, and merciful, but virtue lists can be as daunting as overstuffed rule books, since they imply that we should go *acquire* all these traits. We don't have to learn an eight-step plan, we just need to become a new person! How does that happen? By willpower? By an act of resolve? To say, "Be sacrificial, be tender," is a kind of law, too. Yet we must say something about character, for a man can master every method, but without love, he will fail as a father. Conversely, if a father loves his children, he can commit many minor managerial mistakes and succeed at parenting.

Fortunately, God does not simply say, "Be loving." God is love. Because he created mankind in his image, we have the capacity to love (Gen. 1:26–27). Further, God is remaking his children in his image. By his power, we share his moral character (2 Peter 1:3–8). We grow in Christlikeness, until we are conformed to his image (Rom. 8:29). Jesus says, "Be perfect, therefore, as your heavenly Father is perfect" (Matt. 5:48). The command is both daunting and hopeful. It is daunting because God is in heaven, far above us, and no disciple can attain his perfect virtue. Yet it is hopeful because he is "our Father." "Heaven" reminds us of his distance, but "Father" suggests his nearness. Perfection is impossible, but sons do resemble their fathers, so progress is feasible.

The Character of God and the Character of Fathers

God is the source and model for every family, every form of "fatherhood" (Eph. 3:14–15).[1] His fatherly care is the archetype for human fathers. Conversely, good fathers teach us something about God, as their goodness reflects God's. For example, David says, "As a father has compassion on his children, so the LORD has compassion on those who fear him, for . . . he remembers that we are dust" (Ps. 103:13–14). Hebrews compares human and divine discipline: "'The Lord disciplines those he loves, and he punishes everyone he accepts as a son.' . . . God is treating you as sons. For what son is not disciplined by his father?" (Heb. 12:5–10).

If good fathers share the traits of God the Father, we need to know God's character. Sometimes people explore God's moral qualities one by one, like a string of isolated attributes.[2] But there is a wholeness, a unity, to God's character. God is a person. Each facet of his goodness holds together in his character. In Exodus 34:6–7 God describes that character to Moses:[3]

> The LORD, the LORD, the compassionate and gracious God, slow to anger, abounding in love and faithfulness, maintaining love to thousands, and forgiving wickedness, rebellion and sin. Yet he does not leave the guilty unpunished.

We need to explore this foundational statement. Notice first the prominence of love and justice. *Love* appears twice. Further, compassion and grace are forms of love. "Does not leave the guilty

1. The Bible often compares God to a father: Isa. 9:6; 63:16; 64:8; Jer. 3:19; 31:9; Hos. 11:1; Mal. 1:6; John 1:12; Rom. 8:14–17; Gal. 3:26.
2. On God's justice and mercy, see Millard Erickson, *Christian Theology* (Grand Rapids: Baker, 1983–1985), 265–67, 297–98; Charles Hodge, *Systematic Theology* (Eerdmans, 1975), 1:367–74.
3. Scripture repeats it often, underscoring its centrality (Num. 14:18; Neh. 9:17; Ps. 86:15; 103:7–13; Joel 2:13–14; Jonah 4:2).

unpunished" signifies God's justice. Moreover, love and justice meet in God's patience: he is *slow* to anger. They also meet in his mercy: he notices, but forgives, wickedness.

Theologians debate which is most central in God's relations with his rebellious-but-treasured creation: his love, justice, or holiness. When children misbehave, parents ask a similar question: Should we stress the rule they broke (holiness)? The consequences of their actions (justice)? Or should we forgive and teach them to do better (love)? Exodus 34 gives primacy to God's love, so godly fathers should too. Exodus 34 lists several facets of love, leading us past vague "love talk." As God describes his character in Exodus 34, every word describes the facets of parental love.

Compassion is the feeling of love. When life goes against our little ones, compassion makes us feel sorrow and sympathy for them. We mourn when they mourn and rejoice when they rejoice, so they know they are not alone in the world. When a child falls hard or cries at the doctor's office, when they moan that they have no friends, compassion makes us tender. We don't berate them for acting like babies. Of course we instill toughness, but we give them permission to feel pain, and we feel it with them.

Grace is love's delight in bestowing favors on children. Grace assures our children that we delight in them purely, uncondi-tionally. Grace means we care for our children whether they deserve it or not. Grace takes pleasure in showing a child snow or a Christmas tree for the first time. Gracious parents give their children ice cream even if they have been naughty that day. Grace remembers God's undeserved favors and grants additional undeserved favors.

Patience is love's capacity to wait. Patience withholds chas-tisement or correction from wayward and immature children. It checks the temptation to demand too much too soon, to rebuke too freely. My children first tried to set the table when they were four or five. They realized everyone deserved one copy of each utensil, but sometimes they put the knife on the left and the fork and spoon upside down on the right. Patience said, "Good job, honey. You gave everyone a knife, a fork, and a spoon." A few years later, they folded laundry. One child insisted that it was impossible to match our avalanche of white socks correctly. Patience worked beside her, reducing the pile, so the differences between the remaining socks became clear. Later, the time comes for driving lessons. Teenagers can persuade cars to do things we never thought possible. (How can a car with 65 horsepower lay rubber?) Patience remembers that driving is a complicated skill and says, "Let's try again."

Every aspect of God's character teaches fathers how to live, but some are weightier than others.[4] Love is certainly paramount (Matt. 22:40). Jesus also mentioned what he calls the "weightier matters of the law: justice and mercy and faithfulness" (Matt. 23:23 ESV). Micah cites the same trio: "He has showed you, O man, what is good. . . . To act justly and to love mercy and to walk humbly with your God" (Mic. 6:8).[5] Alongside love, justice, mercy, and faithfulness form the core of godly parenthood.

Some view love and justice as opposites, but justice is a form of love. *Justice is love's concern to give each child what is due.* Parents "do justice" when they perform the duties they owe their children. Justice means parents provide food, clothing, and shelter for their children (1 Tim. 5:8; 6:8). Provision includes an education or apprenticeship that prepares each child for a suitable vocation. In the spiritual realm, parents fulfill their duty by instructing their children in Christian faith and living. Just parents establish household rules that promote a wise lifestyle. Our house has several, including (1) always tell the truth, (2) treat one another with respect, and (3) don't hit your siblings unless

---

4. Even God's omnipotence and omniscience are germane. Pondering God's omnipotence, we recognize the limits of our power. His omniscience reminds us how hard it is to know our children or ourselves.

5. Micah literally reads, "They have told you, O man . . ." "They" means the Law and the Prophets, who agree that these points summarize God's will.

they *really* deserve it. Just parents seal their rules with encouragement and discipline. They distinguish between childish errors and rebellion. They try to discover what really happens, so they can acquit the innocent and address the guilty. *Mercy* is the willingness to overlook and forgive sins. Mercy manifests both love and justice. Merciful parents recognize a child's errors, thereby exercising justice. They also forgive them, exercising love. Merciful fathers see their child's sins, grieve over them, and correct them as tenderly as possible (see below). Merciful parents treat children better than they deserve, especially by forgiving their crimes and misdemeanors. But there is more. The Hebrew term for *mercy* in Micah 6:8 is *hesed*. *Hesed* is covenant loyalty and solidarity. Since covenants are usually between a stronger and a weaker party, *hesed* requires the strong to help the weak. Micah does not simply urge us to *be* merciful, he says, "love mercy"; that is, delight in it.

In the film *Schindler's List*, the commander of a Nazi labor camp personified evil by executing prisoners for both discipline and sport.[6] Schindler, who saved Jews from the camp and worked them in his factories, spoke to the commander one day (paraphrasing slightly), "You think the ability to kill is power. But real power is when we have every justification to kill and we don't." When can we take a life, but then forgive, "*that* is power," says Schindler. This intrigues the commander. In the next scenes he forgives a stable boy for mishandling his saddle and forgives a worker for smoking. Next, a servant fails to remove a stain from his tub. The prisoner cowers, but the Nazi says simply, "Go on. I pardon you." In the next scene, he practices saying, "I pardon you," in front of a mirror. Then suddenly, as the boy runs off, he reconsiders, grabs a gun, and shoots him. The commander found mercy intriguing, but did not love it. But that is not enough; we must *love* mercy.

6. *Schindler's List*, directed by Steven Spielberg (1993; Universal City: Universal Studios Home Video, 2004), DVD.

Mercy and justice appear to stand in tension. When parents deal with sins and follies, justice urges punishment, whereas mercy urges forgiveness. But justice and mercy are complementary. Children are sinful, weak, and ignorant enough to do many things that *could* merit discipline. Justice needs mercy, for justice without mercy descends into severity. Yet mercy needs justice, for mercy without justice declines into indulgence and sentimentality. Justice and mercy must cooperate.

Faithfulness is staying power. Faithfulness means children need not fear abandonment. They can count on living at home for two decades, with two parents. Faithfulness is the reliability and loyalty that spell security for a child. Faithfulness relieves fathers of the need to decide if they will remain as husbands, fathers, and heads of homes. Faithful fathers commit themselves to persevere precisely when perseverance seems most burdensome.[7]

Jesus calls faithfulness a weightier matter. Micah agrees when he summons Israel to "walk humbly with your God." "Walking" is consistency. "Walking humbly" means knowing our inability. "Walking humbly with your God" signifies more than a self-discipline program. Faithfulness means that children can expect their parents to be *almost* the same, yesterday, today, and for a long time. Spasms of goodness and flirtations with virtue are vain. Faithful fathers *dependably* manifest God's love, compassion, mercy, and justice. As we saw, we can simplify these traits to two, love and justice.

Love, Justice, and Parenting Styles

The best fathers faithfully demonstrate both love and justice with their children. Indeed, we can describe types of father, by asking if they practice love and justice together. Try to locate yourself on this diagram:[8]

7. See also chapter 3 and Olthius, *Pledge*, 20–23.
8. See Gary Smalley, *The Key to Your Child's Heart* (Nashville: Word, 1992), 49–58.

Love			
		-	+
Justice	-	Neither love nor justice: *neglectful*	Love without justice: *indulgent*
	+	Justice without love: *dominant*	Love and justice: *godly*

Most homes have at least one dominant parent. *Dominant parents* are high on justice and low on love. They have lofty standards and expectations, but offer their children less support as they try to reach them. Dominant parents act as if rules matter more than children. When dominant parents lead a home, law rules. These laws may be rigidly enforced and little explained. Dominant parents say things like, "The rules are the rules. You broke it, now you must face the punishment," or "I don't need to explain myself to you. I'm you're father [or mother] and you'll do as I say."

Dominant parents forget that God never intended the law to be an impersonal force. His law expresses his character. Because God is truthful, we tell the truth. Because God is love, we love. Dominant fathers forget that God told his people that he gives his laws "for your own good" (Deut. 10:13). Jesus declared, "The Sabbath was made *for man*, not man for the Sabbath" (Mark 2:27). That is, we do not simply keep Sabbath laws for the law's sake. The law blesses us.

Dominant parents think, "Conform to the rules—my rules—and you will accepted and trouble-free. Break the rules and you will not be accepted—and I hope you can bear your punishment." They mete out punishments for all violations of family rules and find it hard to suspend them, even if there are excellent reasons to do so.

Children suffer when love and justice fail to connect. Children born to dominant parents often "clam up" or rebel as teens. They have a poor self-concept, due to a lack of unconditional love. They reject their parents' values because they could never truly embrace them.

Neglectful parents are less common in Christian homes. Neglectful parents provide neither just rules nor loving support. They view children as a burden, an interference. Neglectful parents ignore their children. They use child care freely and make television and video games into surrogate babysitters when they are home. They listen poorly, touch rarely, and hardly look their children in the eye, except to correct them. They hate to drop their pursuits for the sake of their children.

Divorce, long hours at work, generations of poor parenting practices, and ordinary selfishness all contribute to negligent parenting. Whatever the roots, such parents devalue children. Seeing that they are not worth their parents' time, children of neglectful parents think they have little value. They lack motivation and self-discipline. In time, they will find people who care for them, but what kind of caring will that be?

Permissive parents show love without justice, direction, or discipline. This parent is warm and supportive, but fails to establish and enforce rules in the home. Permissive parents are lenient, perhaps from fear that discipline will lead children to rebel or to dislike them. They want to play the role of older friend more than parent. Permissive fathers are sacrificial, supportive, encouraging, understanding—and indulgent.

Permissive parents raise children who know they are loved, but the children tend to think everyone loves them in the indulgent way their parents do. They disregard social rules, indulge themselves, leave messes for others to clean up, and manipulate people. They typically lack self-discipline. They are the type that parks their car in the handicapped space and races into the store thinking, "That law doesn't apply to *me.*"

Godly parents are loving and just, and faithfully so. Godly fathers have the virtues of the dominant and permissive parents, without their vices. They have defined rules and standards, but they also explain them carefully so children can see their value and accept them as their own. Godly parents punish disobedience, but they take special circumstances into account, give clear warnings before discipline, and offer clear explanations afterward.

Godly parents supply the warm support, the touching, the eye contact, and attention that mark loving parents. They distinguish between real needs (food and clothing) and felt needs (the latest *something*), but they sometimes indulge innocuous desires. For example, at a certain age, children think their parents need to watch everything they do, as in, "Watch, Daddy, I'm kicking the ball," or "Watch, Mommy, I'm going off the diving board." Some say that if a tree falls in the woods and no one hears it, there is no sound. Maybe. But children certainly think that if they do something and no parent sees it, it did not happen. It's silly but innocuous, so godly parents play along. They save their protests for bigger issues.

The spirit of a parent is revealed by their response to certain test cases. Imagine two with me.

Case 1: Dinner is ending one of the last beautiful days of the fall. The rules say, "We clean up the supper dishes before we play." But the girls plead, "It will be dark very soon. Can we all go outside and play soccer first, then do the dishes?"

Case 2: A frantic boy reports that he just remembered he has a report due tomorrow. He needs a ride to the library (seven miles away) to get a book immediately. But the night is already full. Consider how dominant and neglectful parents might respond to these situations:

Case	Dominant parent	Neglectful parent
#1 Dinner vs. play	Rules are rules. If you hurry, you will still have ten minutes of light to play.	I don't care when you do the dishes, but I can't play tonight. I'm too busy to play games.
#2 Library trip	You knew you had this assignment. You need to be more responsible. You'll have to suffer the consequences.	Your assignment is *your* problem. I've got my own problems. You have to work this out yourself.

Case	Indulgent parent	Godly parent
#1 Dinner vs. play	Of course you can play. I'll take care of the dishes for you. You just have fun.	Yes, let's play outside together. But when it gets dark, we'll do the dishes together.
#2 Library trip	You're tired and under lots of pressure lately. Stay here. Tell me what you want me to get for you.	This isn't the first time you forgot an assignment lately. I'll take you, but you'll have to make up for my lost time.

Discipline also draws out the contrasts between the four types of parents.

- *Dominant parents are inflexible.* They think, "You broke the rules, now pay the price."
- *Neglectful parents are undiscerning.* They discipline based on trouble caused, not evils done.
- Indulgent parents are weak. They beg their children to be good, to stop making scenes, to stop embarrassing them. Their authority dissolved long ago. The kids rule, and they know it.
- *Godly parents are strong but discerning and flexible.* They understand exceptions but look for patterns of trouble or neglect. They hate to discipline, but even more they hate to see evil in their children and will act to remove it. Therefore, regarding the library trip, after investigating, they may let a child get a low grade to impress the need for greater responsibility.

Children need clear, rational, and enforced rules—rules that work. They also need unconditional love, shown by time and affection. Godly parents provide both, and researchers verify the results. Compared to others, the children of loving and just parents are secure and self-controlled, interested in their parent's faith and values, and capable of heeding authorities.

I suppose it is safe to assume that everyone who reads this book wants to be a godly father (or mother). But how? Three issues remain:

- Godly fathers establish good rules for their families.
- Godly fathers have a plan for dealing with the inevitable violations of the rules.
- Godly fathers strive to inculcate a heart for God.

Godly Rules

One way to establish good rules is to adapt the Ten Commandments to family life. The first three commands teach us to worship, pray, read the Bible, and honor God at home. We hallow every joy with praise and sanctify every sorrow with prayer (James 5:13). The fourth command requires that we build worship, rest, and reflection into our harried lives, that we control our schedules instead of letting them control us.

The fifth command, "Honor your father and your mother," is central. We expand it this way in our home—honor means a child will:

- Follow the general rules of family life. For example, clear your dishes after meals.
- Obey one-time commands and requests. For example, run upstairs and close the windows.
- Perform daily tasks without fail. For example, make the bed, do homework.
- Obey without complaint. Yet if a child thinks his parents erred, and they say so respectfully, wise parents will discuss it.

Commands six to ten apply readily. "Do not murder" means we treat one another with respect. We don't hit, torment, or insult our siblings. The seventh command reminds parents that strong homes rest on strong marriages. "Do not bear false witness" means we never lie. We tell the truth unless it causes needless pain. In that case we simply remain silent. "Do not steal" means children respect each other's possessions. We don't borrow things without asking. "Do not covet" forbids children to envy the possessions, achievements, or attention their siblings get. For their part, parents make it easier for children to rejoice in others' success if they distribute praise evenly.

Parents may need a few more principles for siblings. For example, older children may not use their physical strength or their mental ability to defraud younger children. But younger children may not use their social skills and apparent innocence to provoke older siblings or get them into trouble.

Establishing good rules is important, but parents fret more over enforcement. How can parents do justice when a child violates the principles of justice? How do parents *discipline*?

The Discipline of Children

Discipline ranks among the most difficult parental tasks; a proper discussion might take another book. The difficulty lies with the parent as much as the child. We misinterpret our children's motives. We have baggage from our childhood experiences of excessive lenience or harshness. We get angry about petty offenses one day because we are tired and grumpy, and ignore major sins the next because we feel mellow. We get upset about things that cause us trouble, even if they aren't immoral, and let immoral acts go if they cause no harm. For example, which child is more likely to get a rebuke: a boy who trips and tears a new garment, or a boy who breaks rules by running across a carpeted floor with grape juice in his hand but spills nothing?

To remind parents of their flaws, let's define discipline this way: *Discipline is the process in which bigger sinners attempt to convince littler sinners to mend their wicked ways.*

That is not a true definition, since discipline is positive as well as negative. It involves both nurture and admonition, both education and punishment (Eph. 6:4). But the main point stands:

parents cannot consider themselves models of humanity and treat their children as miscreants. We suffer too much from bad patterns and bondage to custom, as well as ordinary sinfulness, to tout ourselves as exemplars of virtue.

Bad Patterns

Most of us have two recordings going in our heads. One is "My mother said this, my mother did that." The other is "My father said this, my father did that." We tend to accept and imitate the recordings we like, almost blindly, and to react, just as blindly, against others.

For example, I had one called "What to do when something spills at the dinner table." To understand it you must know that my father's family escaped from communist Russia in 1935. Growing up in Stalinist Russia, where millions died of starvation, he came to the United States at the height of the Depression. So my father had zero tolerance for spilled milk or juice when my brothers and I grew up. Contrary to the second law of physics, our action led to an opposite but *unequal* reaction. When we spilled things, he exploded with rage. At an early age, I vowed, "When I have children, I will never yell at them for spilling anything."

I kept my vow. I lost my self-control more than once, but never for spilling. My children, dimly aware of this, came eventually to knock cups over almost every day. Maybe it looked like a game to them: topple a cup and watch Mom and Dad jump up and scramble around to sop it up. One day, as another cascade of milk or orange juice drenched table and floor, my wife fixed her eyes on me and said, "I'm thankful that you are true to your vow not to yell, but we're losing about a gallon of milk a week by now. We have to do something."

She was right, and we did do something (see below). But mark this: Mindless *imitation* of our parents lets them establish the agenda for our parenting, but so does mindless *rejection*. When we react to our parents by reversing whatever they did, they are still setting the agenda. Godly parents liberate themselves from the pattern of imitation and rejection and find their own wisdom.

Bondage to Custom

To find our wisdom, we must also evaluate our culture's customary wisdom. It also dominates us more than we might think. It is customary today for parents to use three forms of discipline: spanking, loss of privileges, and banishment from civilized society (aka grounding). All of these have a place. On *spanking*, Proverbs commends the use of the rod. Spankings should sting, but never hurt a child physically. Therefore half-ounce wooden "spanking spoons" are preferable to the hand, which can be too heavy. "All discipline seems painful," says Hebrews 12:11 (ESV), making it fair to say that if there is no pain of any kind, sinful behavior has not been disciplined. The pain of a spanking teaches a child that sin leads to pain.

Deprivation of privileges sometimes works too. If a young boy and his friend tear up the basement, perhaps that friend should not visit for a season. If an older girl violates a curfew, she may justly lose one night out the next weekend. But other deprivations hardly stand to reason. For example, some parents deprive children of audio or video privileges for almost every offense. If their room is a mess, no music. If they fail to do homework, no video. The punishment is arbitrary and wrongly accentuates one privilege.

Banishment from civilized society also works on occasion. If a boy eats like a caveman, perhaps he should eat alone in his room once. If two siblings bicker all morning, parents may forbid them to occupy the same room for a while. But sending children to their room for every offense makes no sense.

Liberation from Custom

Unfortunately this trio does not give parents enough room to educate. And sometimes none of them seems to work. My wife once put it this way as she struggled with a child who was going through a period of mild rebellion: "I don't know what to do with her. She's too old to spank; she hardly notices the television or radio. Take away her privileges? All she does is piano and soccer, and they are both so worthwhile. I certainly don't want to ground her—I'll punish myself as much as I punish her." I said, "Good point. I'll get back to you on that."

Six weeks later (theologians answer questions slowly sometimes), I was reading Exodus 21:22–25 and realized that it addressed my wife's question:

> If men who are fighting hit a pregnant woman and she gives birth prematurely but there is no serious injury, the offender must be fined whatever the woman's husband demands. . . . But if there is serious injury, you are to take life for life, eye for eye, tooth for tooth, hand for hand, foot for foot, burn for burn, wound for wound, bruise for bruise.

Lest you worry, I had not suddenly developed a vindictive streak. Though it sounds harsh, the purpose of this law is actually to restrain vengefulness. It forbids excess, as in, "If you knock out my tooth, my friends and I will knock out all of yours." The law forbids spirals of violence, declaring, "*One* tooth for *one* tooth, nothing more."

This "principle of proportional punishment" is foundational for the Bible's penal code. It governs property violations (Ex. 22:4–6), personal injury (Lev. 24:19–20), and manslaughter (Lev. 24:17, 21). It is perhaps clearest in the case of perjury, where the convicted perjurer must suffer precisely the punishment that his lie would have inflicted on his victim (Deut. 19:16–21).

In the home, the goal is reform—discipline not punishment. Therefore we can call it the "principle of proportional discipline." Proportional discipline is neither too harsh nor too lenient. It is relevant to the misdeed and is measured to suit it. If tooth crimes merit tooth punishment, then "food crimes" deserve "food punishment," and clothing crimes merit "clothing discipline."

For example, if grade school children spill juice day after day, proportional parents will warn them, then take juice off their menu for a day or two. When we instituted it in our house, the spills promptly stopped.

Or consider that chronic cause of parental distress—a child's habit of dropping book bags and coats on the floor the instant he or she enters the house. With a shrug of the shoulders, coats and bags slide to the floor smoothly and effortlessly. Too often, mothers shout and threaten—and pick it all up. This teaches children that they have a noisy maid. If they ignore her for a moment, nothing happens. Instead, try a book bag punishment for a book bag crime:

"Honey, I see that you don't care very much about your book bag, since you drop it in the middle of the floor so much. So, unless you stop, we will put it away for a couple of days."

"But how will I get my books and lunch to school?"

"Well, I guess you can take them to school in a grocery bag."

"A *grocery* bag!? Are you kidding! Everyone would laugh at me!"

"All right, you have one more chance to hang up your bag, but if you drop it on the floor again tomorrow, that will be three days in a row, and it will go on the shelf for three days." (My oldest and youngest children each endured this exactly once. Our middle child resolved, "That will never happen to me"—and it didn't.)

This works for all sorts of crimes and misdemeanors. Abuse your new coat, lose your new coat (and get an old ugly one from the old clothes box). Abuse the television and lose the television. Fail to do chores on time, get double chores the next day. If two children bicker for a solid hour while playing, they lose the right to play together for an hour.

Occasionally, someone tells me this is cruel. Let me be clear. Children may go to school without *their* coat, but we never send them, in winter, without *any* coat. Again, children may briefly go without juice, but we never malnourish them. No child contracts scurvy by going two days without vitamin C.

More importantly, I believe it is far crueler to yell at children and threaten them while never doing anything to root out their sin and error. It is far crueler to teach, by our inaction, that sins have no consequences.

This leads to the essence of discipline. All parents discipline their children. But if we lose sight of justice, we discipline for the wrong reasons. We discipline them for acts that are troublesome or embarrassing to us, even if they are accidents. But we overlook sin and rebellion if they cause us no trouble. But if parents discipline their children for selfish reasons, they destroy its essence. God disciplines us, individually, that we might live well and enjoy his righteousness and peace (Heb. 12:9–11). He disciplines us corporately to purge evil from the land (Deut. 13:5; 17:7). Similarly, parents should seek to free their children from evil. This is our thought as we discipline: *"I love you too much to let you think that what you did has no consequences."* Discipline is like a vaccine. It inflicts lesser pain now to avoid greater pain later. One question remains. Can godly fathers change a child's heart?

A Heart for God

We have discussed the character, the rules, and the discipline of a godly father. But how shall we convey it all to our children? We cannot simply command children to develop character. Fathers cannot control a child's character the way they can control behavior. The heart of a child is partially hidden. It belongs to him and to God, not to us. The heart of a king and the heart of a child are in God's hands. Only God can quicken a heart, and only the child can respond.

Still parents can help inculcate character. By sharing our heart for God we can mediate God's presence. Proverbs 13:20 observes, "He who walks with the wise grows wise, but a companion of fools suffers harm." As Moses says in Deuteronomy 6:4–8:

> Hear, O Israel: The LORD our God, the LORD is one. Love the
> LORD your God with all your heart and with all your soul and

with all your strength. These commandments that I give you today are to be upon your hearts. Impress them on your children. Talk about them when you sit at home and when you walk along the road, when you lie down and when you get up. Tie them as symbols on your hands and bind them on your foreheads.

Notice the sequence. First, parents know, love, and obey God. *Then* they can impress things on their children. To develop the spiritual life of their children, parents must first develop their own. Many parents prematurely ask about techniques for spiritual nurture. They want to know how to have good family devotions or when to talk to their children about the faith. Good questions! But *who we are* matters more than the techniques we master.

Living faith expresses itself naturally, whenever we are with our children. So, when do we talk about our faith? Breakfast is a good time, for then we can gain a spiritual perspective on the day. Lunch works, because we can evaluate the morning and make midday corrections. Supper is fitting, because we can review the day and prepare for the evening. Bedtime is sensible, because tired children tend to be spiritually receptive.

Just as every time offers opportunities, so does every place. At the store, we discuss money and the difference between needs and desires. After an athletic contest, we consider exercise and competition, the importance of doing our best and trusting the results to God. Reviewing a television program or video, we ask what kinds of humor enrich and what kinds humiliate. After church, we recount what we learned in worship or Sunday school.

As we share our hearts and minds with our children, they acquire our understanding of God. This has an enormous impact on children. When our children were young, we didn't watch much TV, but we tended to watch together. We had one television and discussed what we saw, including commercials. Likewise, when we listened to popular music, we analyzed the lyrics. This paid off one day when two children, ten and eight, started playing an old Billy Joel song they had found in a closet. I tuned it out until I heard the upbeat nihilism of the song, "Only the Good Die Young." Hearing my children bouncing to the music downstairs, I knew we had to talk about the lyrics. Descending the steps, I heard one child shout over the music, "That's not true at all!" The other replied, "Yeah, remember Great-Grandma? She was really good and she lived to be ninety-eight." Mission accomplished. Indeed, "He who walks with the wise grows wise."

Christian parents nurture their children as they walk and talk together, discussing friendships, school, sports, and social pressures. Some men delude themselves with notions of "quality time" as in, "I don't have much time with my children, but at least it's quality time." But we can't treat children like business appointments. We can't appear at their bedroom door on Saturday and say, "It's 9:00 a.m. Are you ready for our quality time?"

It is nearly impossible to schedule quality time. *Quality time comes through quantity time.* Noble plans for "quality time" often sour. Routine time together supplies the hours we need so golden minutes will emerge. Children need us to be home several nights a week and through weekends. Most children need their father's presence more than they need a little more money from his extra work. Working together, fathers teach children how to work. Traveling with Dad in the car, they start to learn to drive. Invite a young child to join you on an errand and he will jump in. Use it.

Conclusion

I once went to a baseball game with my middle daughter. We happened to have seats that put us in good position for a foul ball. I mused, "I've been to lots of ball games, but never caught a foul ball. It's a shame we didn't bring a glove, because if a ball comes our way, it will have too much speed and spin to catch with our bare hands. Still, we might get one if a ball bounces off someone's hands a row or two ahead of us." Sure enough, seconds later, the batter sent a hard foul straight toward us. One row ahead, a man rose for the ball. I prepared for the bounce, but at the last instant, he ducked. I threw my hands in front of my face, and, just as I had predicted, the ball spun off my palm and bounced to another fan a few feet away. A tragedy? Not at all. My daughter and I had a great conversation about hopes and disappointments. Quantity time led to quality time.

Fatherhood is glorious but daunting. To show love, justice, and faithfulness is a noble but elusive aspiration. Every father is a sinner. Our supreme hope lies in the grace of Christ, not parenting techniques. We want to enact wise laws and to practice firm but gentle discipline, but whence comes our strength? Again, "He who walks with the wise grows wise." If we walk with our wise Father God, he will impart wisdom to us, to share with our children.

Discussion Questions

1. As a parent, are you oriented more to justice or to mercy? Which of the four parenting types best describes you?

2. If God is truly remaking you in the image of his love, compassion, grace, patience, faithfulness, and justice, as described in Exodus 34, what does that mean for the way you treat your family?

3. Describe your current patterns for disciplining your children. Restate the principle of proportional discipline in your own words. Where might you practice it in your home or in other relationships?

4. Do you spend enough time walking and talking with your children? How can you find more time with them?

5. How do the "recordings" of what your father and mother said and did influence you today?

A Word on Becoming a Father

The Current Situation

In most Western nations, rates of reproduction have fallen well below the replacement rate of 2.1 children per woman. At 2.0, depopulation begins. At 1.5, population is crashing, causing social upheaval through an aging population. Recent census reports from the World Bank, the United Nations, and CIA World Factbook, all readily available online, have very similar assessments of birth rates. For example, they estimate the European Union's birth rate at 1.6 (a small rise in recent years). Financial crises in nations like Greece, Spain, and Italy are primarily population crises. There aren't enough young adults working to support an ever-higher proportion of retirees.

The census studies report that almost all of Africa has a birth rate of 3 to 7, while South America trends around 2.5. The USA, France, New Zealand, Ireland, the United Kingdom, Brazil, and Turkey are the only leading industrialized nations that are near the replacement rate of 1.9–2.2 children per woman. China, Russia, Canada, the Netherlands, Portugal, and Switzerland are all around 1.5. Germany, Greece, Spain, and Italy, as well as most formerly communist lands–Austria, Hungary, Romania, and Poland are lower, at 1.3–1.4. Without immigration, that leads to a 30 percent population loss per generation. South Korea, Taiwan, Japan, and Ukraine are still lower, so that population collapse and economic ruin threaten.

Rates do shift, and several Western nations have ticked upward recently, but the trend is clear. Industrialization, prosperity, and higher education levels, especially for women, all align with population decline. So does secularization and atheism. Formerly communist or socialist nations have very low birth rates.

Who refuses to have children? The pessimists who don't want to bring children into the world. The selfish, who shun the cost and bother of children. Have you heard the anti-child jokes? "The main purpose of holding children's parties is to remind yourself that there are children more awful than your own." Or "Be nice to your children; they are going to choose your nursing home some day."

We can see the change without the benefit of statistics. Watch people react when a couple announces, "We are pregnant again." If they herald a second child, faces beam approval. The display shows that we no longer take the multiple-child family for granted. A second child creates another ideal family: mother, father, and two children. The body language changes for subsequent pregnancies. It suggests that three children are a sign of faith; four a sign of bravura; five, extravagance; and six, lunacy. Many Christians uncritically accept prevailing views. What does Scripture say about children, birth control, and family size?

The biblical faith is pro-child. The prophets railed against child sacrifice. Early Christians rescued pagan infants whose parents had left them on rubbish heaps to die or be claimed as slaves. The church has always been the child's advocate and the foe of abortion, infanticide, and child abuse. Still, the church has had its struggles. The ancient and medieval church preferred celibacy and so could not be robustly pro-child. Yet, since early theologians like Augustine, Jerome, and Aquinas believed marriage to be good primarily because of procreation, they indirectly promoted childbirth. When the Protestant Reformers affirmed the goodness of marriage, they elevated the value of sexual intimacy and its fruit, children. Luther championed childbearing, proclaiming that God created man and woman "to produce seed and multiply."[9]

The industrial and medical revolutions raised the issue of family planning in a new way. Once child mortality rates dropped and birth control became reliable, people had freedom to make plans about family size. Throughout human history, population loss had

---

9. Martin Luther, "On the Estate of Marriage," in *Luther's Works*, vol. 45, ed. Helmut T. Lehman (Philadelphia: Muhlenberg, 1962), 45–46. Luther wrote these lines in 1522, while still single.

been a constant danger. Suddenly, overpopulation became the perceived threat. Married couples now faced decisions. How many children should we have? Why should we have children? Is it wrong to avoid parenthood?

Above all, the *Bible is pro-child and consistent Christians must be pro-child.* Whenever anti-child mentalities spread, the faithful must speak and act on their convictions. When God created Adam and Eve, he called children a blessing. "God blessed them and said to them, 'Be fruitful and increase in number; fill the earth and subdue it'" (Gen. 1:28). Conversely, barrenness is a sorrow (Gen. 15:1–4; 25:21; 29:31–30:24). Paul says the children of believers are holy to God (1 Cor. 7:14). Scripture is not naive about children. Adam (literally) raised Cain, and David's favorite son stole his throne and his wives. Nor does God require people to have children. Jesus neither married nor had children, and Paul also approved celibacy for the sake of kingdom service (1 Cor. 7:7–9, 25–35). Further, many people either cannot find a mate or are unable to become parents. Indeed, it's possible to make child-bearing an idol, as we see in the life of Rachel, who declared, "Give me children or I will die!" When she showed that she would do *anything* to have children, she spoke and acted like an idolater. Children are a blessing, but not the ultimate blessing.

Children as a Blessing

Still, the Bible expects most adults to marry and have children, and calls them a blessing within marriage (Ps. 127). But *how* do they convey God's blessing? Why do men and women want to have children?

- Adults hope their children will carry on the family name, care for them in old age, or keep their marriage together.
- They want someone to love; they want someone to love them.

- Adults want someone to need them, admire them, make them feel young, obey them, and remember them when they are gone.
- Some seek social status by having a child who will do great things.

Some of these hopes may materialize, but a year or two of diapers and midnight moanings will dash selfish dreams. Besides, about the time children become useful, in today's economy, they leave home.

Jesus said, "It is more blessed to give than to receive" (Acts 20:35), and it seems that the chief blessings of parenthood lie in giving. If we give up the hope of gain, we can enjoy the blessings of parenthood. Parents *give*. They give the Lord the godly children he desires (Mal. 2:15). They give their children the gift of life. Once we give, the blessings can flow.

As a monk, Martin Luther never awoke with pigtails in his face and his blanket missing. After he got married, he saw that family life is a *school of character*. Parenting blesses us by teaching us to love sacrificially. Parents learn to give up their plans for happiness or fulfillment. They spend themselves for people who give little in return. Childless couples also sacrifice, but in marriage the husband and wife ordinarily contribute almost equally to the tasks of life. Children don't contribute the same way. They don't lighten the load, as a good spouse does; they increase the load in every way. Babies cry more than they smile. Little children are bundles of need. Teenagers bring more worries than celebrations. They teach us to expand the circle of concern. Herman Bavinck said:

> Children check selfishness in parents. . . . They uphold to their parents, as if in a mirror, their own virtues and defects, force them to reconsider their lives, soften their criticisms, and teach them how difficult it is to rule a human being. Out of the family life there

proceeds a reforming power toward the parents. . . . Family life
turns the selfish into servants, misers into heroes, coarse men
into considerate fathers, and tender maidens into courageous
mothers.[10]

The godly parent learns to sacrifice, to abandon the creeping
solipsism that dreams that our fellow humans somehow exist for us.
Infants have no capacity to meet our needs. As we watch children
grow to maturity, we see their *otherness* and independence. We
love them not as extensions of ourselves, but as people who are
one with us and alien from us.

Loving procreation is an important element of our creation
in the image of God. Genesis 1:27–28 connects parenthood and
the image: "So God created man in his own image. . . . God blessed
them and said to them, 'Be fruitful and increase in number; fill
the earth and subdue it.'" We don't fill the earth as animals do,
through blind drives.

When we become parents, our motives are like God's. Our life-
giving is rational, moral, loving, and creative. We imitate God's holy,
ordered fruitfulness. Parents love, instruct, guide, and discipline
their children as God the Father does. We give of ourselves, empty
ourselves, and watch children grow toward independence, much
as God does. When we become parents and raise children in the
faith, we demonstrate that God made us in his image.

There are few things we do that are more Godlike. When we
deliberately become parents, we give the gift of life, then love
and sacrifice for a profoundly valuable yet flawed person, just as
God does.

Then, once we relinquish the hope of gain or a "payoff," children enrich our lives. When little ones marvel at a Christmas tree,
when snowflakes first dance in their eyes, they restore our sense

10. Herman Bavinck, quoted in J. Norval Geldenhuys, *The Intimate Life* (London: James Clarke,
1952), 51–52.

of wonder. Their belly-laughs, stumbling acrobatics, and earnest lisping of family names are so life-giving.

When they are a little older, they restore play to life. We run, hide, honk noses, and play make-believe. Older still, they become our friends, even guides. In these ways, children are a blessing. How many blessings should we seek? The Bible doesn't say, therefore I cannot say. But if children are a blessing and God wants us to multiply, then at least know that godly couples will desire children and so seek the blessings he offers.

| 6 |

A Man and His Friends

Friendships abound during college, but during the years when men choose a marriage partner, establish a career, start a family, and order their finances, the pressures of life squeeze out the zeal men once had for their friendships. When men get older, especially if they are not married, they tend to go rogue, like the old, unruly bull elephants that banish themselves from the herd. Men need friendships, but for much of their adult life, they are so careless, they may not even know if they have true friends or not.

The Church—A Friend of Friendship?

Christians believe in relationships in general, yet the church is ambivalent about friendship. Churches gather for "fellowship" and "community" but do not promote gatherings for "friendship." Historically, the church has advocated spiritual direction where mentors lead novices toward discipleship. But the church hardly mentions the mutual direction that friends and peers offer each other. It is not hard to see why friendship has become a forgotten form of love.

First, if we compare the love of friendship (*philia*), to love of neighbor (*agape*) as Jesus describes it, we can understand the church's relative indifference.[1]

---

1. There are few sustained, theological treatments of friendship. Aelred of Rievaulx wrote *Spiritual Friendship* in the twelfth century, Jeremy Taylor wrote *Discourse of the Nature, Offices and Measures of Friendship* in the seventeenth, and Hugh Black wrote *The Art of Being a Good Friend* in 1998. Among secular authors, Joseph Epstein's *Friendship, an Expose* (Boston: Houghton Mifflin, 2006) is grounded in philosophers

- Agape is indiscriminate, extending itself to every neighbor or stranger; philia discriminates, extending itself to those whom it favors.
- Agape goes to all who cross its path; philia goes to a few who make sure their paths cross.
- Agape is inclusive, denying no one; philia is exclusive, denying many.
- God's love is the source and model of agape; human attraction is the source of philia.
- Agape is divine, unmerited love, given to the lovable and unlovable alike; philia is a human love based on affection for the desirable.

Some Christian literature about friendship illustrates the difficulty. Em Griffin explains that in the attraction between potential friends, "the thread of increased self-esteem is woven into each principle of attraction." A friend is someone who "makes me feel good about myself."[2] Griffin knows this may leave Christian readers uneasy, but he lists factors that foster that good feeling between friends: proximity, collaboration, physical attractiveness, competence (but not omnicompetence), affirmation ("we appreciate those who appreciate us"), the exchange of favors, and similarity of skill, background, and interests. The common thread, Griffin concludes, is "our overriding need for self esteem."

Most of us have some lingering doubts about our attitudes and lifestyle. Having people close who think and feel as we do can be very comforting. The law of selective exposure suggests that we avoid information that challenges our beliefs. Friendship is probably the purest form of selecting our own

---

since Plato and Aristotle. C. S. Lewis analyzed friendship in *The Four Loves* (New York: Harcourt, Brace, & World, 1960), 87–127. Plato's *Lysis* may be the first sustained discussion of friendship. See Benjamin Jowett translation, Electronic Classics Series, Penn State University, www2.hn.psu.edu/faculty/jmanis/plato/lysis.pdf.

2. Em Griffin, *Making Friends* (Downers Grove, IL: InterVarsity Press, 1987), 142–58, 206.

propaganda. Relationships with similar others make us feel good about who we are.[3]

Not only do friends make people feel good about themselves, they may also make others feel bad, for "to announce, 'You are my friend' to someone, is, by implication, to say to another, 'You are not.'"[4] This exclusivity, even selfishness, makes the church uneasy about friendship.

C. S. Lewis admires friendship, but he has caveats. Mutual affirmation and shared insights can, he notes, render friends indifferent to the opinions of others. A self-appointed group of friends easily acquires a superiority complex, becoming a coterie of snobs, proud that they rise so far above others in skill, virtue, or insight. Because shared convictions can galvanize people to take a stand, friendship can empower resistance to authority, for harm as well as good.[5]

Finally, friendship is more transitory than other kinds of love. Agape can appeal to duty and the love of Christ. With familial love, we have both social and physical motivations to show affection and fidelity. But fewer moral or spiritual resources sustain friendship. Friendship is amiable solidarity and, sweet as that is, it is not necessary for survival. For all these reasons, the church neglects friendship.

The Value of Friendship

Despite all this, the biblical teaching moves us to seek strong friendships. Ecclesiastes 4:9–12 describes the four advantages of friendship. First, friends work together effectively: "Two are better than one, because they have a good return for their work" (v. 9). Second, friends help one another in time of need: "If one falls down, his friend can help him up. But pity the man who

3. Ibid., 153.
4. Lewis, *The Four Loves*, 90.
5. Ibid., 112–25. It is said that some corporations transfer executives to prevent the development of friendships that could inhibit corporate loyalty.

falls and has no one to help him up!" So friends galvanize us for God-given tasks (v. 10). Third, friends offer comfort and companionship in life's cold nights: "If two lie down together, they will keep warm. But how can one keep warm alone?" (v. 11). Fourth, friends cushion the blows life deals us: "Though one may be overpowered, two can defend themselves. A cord of three strands is not quickly broken" (v. 12).

In short, friends *help* each other. Some of us like to give aid, but can hardly receive it. It embarrasses us to admit our need or ask for help. Or we can accept assistance, but only if we can reciprocate. If we cannot reciprocate, we would rather suffer in silence. But there is no accounting, no ledger, no sense of debt among true friends. There is no place for pride among friends. True friends see needs and meet them for each other. But perhaps the greatest gift is oneself, in companionship.

Sometimes a Man Needs Another Man

Marriage and family are the principal avenues for companionship. Yet marriage can never fully satisfy our longing for companionship. First, there are vast numbers of single adults, and ever more of them spend their entire lives single. Single people need companionship. Second, despite expectations, many marriages lack deep companionship. Third, even an ideal marriage cannot fulfill all of our needs for companionship. God did not intend one person to supply every social need. I have engaged in competitive sports for my entire life. When I return from a contest, my wife knows she is supposed to ask who won and how my team and I played. But the question is polite, not heartfelt. Even if we defeated a superior foe at the last instant, she cannot thrill at the tale; she doesn't care all that much. And that is fine! No one should expect a spouse to rejoice at each triumph, to weep at each setback, to converse helpfully upon each topic. It is an impossible demand, and one that treads near idolatry. Even married people need a circle of friends.

Besides, even the happiest married man wants to talk to another man about some things. Suppose a businessman suspects that he works long hours, in part, because he likes work more than family. At work, he is an important person. His words, his decisions, change things. People admire him; they laugh at his jokes and do him favors. At home, the children always seem to be squabbling, and his wife wears that familiar "Where have you been?" frown. A wise man will disclose his sentiments to his wife, but first he will talk to a man who faced the same problem.

Sometimes we need to talk to someone of our gender. Suppose a woman of unspecified age looks in the mirror and says, "I am getting wrinkled, gray, fat, and ugly." If she tells her husband, he may create a four-step analysis and action plan for her appearance. "You have very few wrinkles and gray hairs for your age, and besides you can dye your hair. And you're not fat, just a little overweight . . ." But a woman does not want an analysis of her physical condition, she wants love—and sympathy. She may get it from a woman who knows the melancholy sensation of watching her beauty fade. Similarly, a man may think, "I have no friends." If he tells his wife, she may take it personally: "I thought I was your friend!" Or she may commiserate when he wants someone to go and *do* something with—a guy. It may be best to call an old buddy.

Sometimes a Man Needs a Rebuke

Friendships can degenerate into mutual admiration societies. But friends also have the capacity to cause *creative discomfort*. Friends can make us feel good about ourselves, but true friends also inflict *constructive misery* on each other. Friends make us feel bad about ourselves if there is good reason for it. Certainly God, the model friend, stings in order to heal.

Friends correct each other, and they listen when the correction comes. Remarks that would seem judgmental from an acquaintance become loving counsel in the mouths of friends. "Iron sharpens iron" (Prov. 27:17), and sometimes the sparks fly. As

Proverbs says, "Better is open rebuke than hidden love. Wounds from a friend can be trusted" (27:5–6). Again, "The pleasantness of one's friend springs from his earnest counsel" (27:9).

Once, I saw a married friend developing a close relationship with an attractive single woman. A strong-willed man, he was also in a spiritual trough and in no mood to hear counsel. If I spoke, he might sever our relationship. But I spoke anyway, because I loved my friend more than I loved our friendship.

Friends challenge me too. Once my wife and I visited friends who had moved to another state. Carol had allergies like mine and was eager to share how she got relief by changing her diet. I was skeptical, so I tried to deflect her with a joke about oat chaff and rice husks. Her eyes flamed, her voice grew steel rods, and she interrupted me, "I see what you're doing, Dan. You don't believe a word of this, but you're too polite to say so, so you make it into a little joke. You don't have to do what I'm saying, but at least listen. It just might help you!" And I thought, "Wow, what a friend."

But we need to press past the values and dangers of friendship and consider how to preserve the best and avoid the worst of friendship. We need a model of an ideal friendship.

The God-Centered Model for Friendship

The Bible makes few statements about friendship. There is wisdom in Proverbs and Ecclesiastes, and we have illustrations from the lives of David and Jonathan, and Jesus and his disciples.[6] Sadly, many talks on friendship run through a string of verses from Proverbs to generate an atomistic list of human virtues titled "The Traits of a Friend." The format is legal: "A good friend

6. David and his mighty men (2 Sam. 23:15–17), Elijah and Elisha (2 Kings 2:1–12) and Elisha and the Shunammite (2 Kings 4:8–37) may be additional models. Paul may also hint at friendships when he greets nearly thirty Roman believers by name, singling out Epenetus, Ampliatus, Stachys, and Rufus's mother (Rom. 16:3–16; see also 1 Cor. 16:15–17; Col. 4:9, 15). More important, among all his disciples, Jesus chose twelve as his "friends" (John 15:13–15). Within the twelve, he favored three, who shared the glory of the transfiguration and the shame of Gethsemane.

is faithful, righteous, and loving, willing to sacrifice, and willing to rebuke. If you want to please God and your friends, seek these traits in your relationships."

That, of course, returns us to Nike Christianity. We forget the gospel when we quote strings of Proverbs and say, "Do this and this. Be that and that." Proverbs do show us the way of wisdom. Sadly, we cannot follow the proverbs in our own strength, as Proverbs itself knows (Prov. 3:7–12). We must ground friendship in something deeper than duty. That "something" is the nature of God, the archetypal friend. He shows us how to be a friend, but more, he remakes us in his image (Rom. 8:29; Eph. 4:22–24). As he does, he grants us ability to do what the Proverbs say. Then we can do for others as he has done for us.

Most important, the Bible calls God a friend of his people on five occasions. Believers know, intuitively, that God is their friend. Though the Bible only calls God a friend a few times, we readily see that the central traits of God as friend are *self-disclosure and helpful presence*. They manifest themselves first in God's dealings with Abraham, whom Scripture calls the "friend of God" (2 Chron. 20:7; James 2:23).

In Genesis 18, the angel of the Lord visited Abraham and Sarah when they were ninety-nine and eighty-nine years old. The angel came to announce that he would *help* them, that Sarah would bear the child God had promised them twenty-five years earlier. The angel shared a meal with them and confronted their doubts. Then, as he prepared to leave, he asked, "Shall I hide from Abraham what I am about to do?" No, God had chosen Abraham to be the father of Israel, so now he revealed his plans to judge Sodom and Gomorrah (vv. 17–21). Thus God *disclosed himself* to Abraham. He was just and could not tolerate the wickedness of those cities. Abraham found this troubling and, as the Lord turned toward Sodom, he asked God if he would destroy Sodom if there were fifty or even ten righteous people in it. While Abraham had concern for Sodom, he was also probing the character of God. "Will you sweep away the righteous with the wicked? . . .

Far be it from you to . . . [treat] the righteous and the wicked alike. . . . Will not the Judge of all the earth do right?" (vv. 23–25). Is God just? Is he merciful? Yes, for he would spare the whole city of Sodom for the sake of even ten righteous men (v. 32). So God revealed his justice and mercy to Abraham, his friend.

The Bible also calls Moses the friend of God, in Exodus 33:7–11. As a friend, God *helped* Moses lead Israel out of Egypt. Still, as in Genesis 18, the strongest element of Exodus 33 is God's *self-disclosure*. Shortly after Israel left Egypt, the Lord manifested his presence with Israel in a "tent of meeting" located outside her camp. Many visited the tent, but when Moses went, the glory cloud of God would descend on it, and the Lord "used to speak to Moses face to face, as a man speaks to his friend" (v. 11 ESV). Later, the Lord disclosed himself more fully, letting Moses see his glory as it passed by on a mountain (vv. 18–23). He declared his nature to Moses: "The LORD, the LORD, the compassionate and gracious God, slow to anger, abounding in love and faithfulness, maintaining love to thousands, and forgiving . . . sin. Yet he does not leave the guilty unpunished" (34:6–7).

Isaiah called God the friend of Israel and emphasized his helpful presence. Although Israel had no claim on his friendship, the Lord called Israel and became her friend. Isaiah says:

> But you, O Israel, my servant, Jacob, whom I have chosen, you descendants of Abraham my friend, I took you from the ends of the earth, from its farthest corners I called you. I said, 'You are my servant'; I have chosen you. . . . So do not fear, for I am with you; do not be dismayed, for I am your God. I will strengthen you and help you. (Isa. 41:8–10)

Jesus shows the same traits—self-disclosure and helpful presence—in his friendship with his disciples.[7] In John 15:13–15

---

7. Jesus' foes accuse him of making the wrong sort of friends: they call him "a friend of tax collectors and sinners!" (Matt. 11:19 ESV; Luke 7:34 ESV). But this is more a slur than a serious analysis of Jesus' ways.

he says, "Greater love has no one than this, that he lay down his life for his friends [help]. You are my friends if you do what I command. . . . I have called you friends, for everything that I learned from my Father I have made known to you" [self-disclosure].

Of course, God's friendship with Israel does not directly model a *typical* human friendship. Above all, no human friendship could be so one-sided. God knows us perfectly, so we need not disclose ourselves to him, whereas he chooses to reveal himself to us. Further, he helps us despite our disloyalty, and we can, ultimately, give nothing to him. So self-disclosure and helpful presence take a different form in human friendships.

Beyond help and disclosure, true friendship entails something more. Indeed, serious studies of friendship always seem to define it as "more than" other similar things. Aristotle said friendship is pleasant, but more than pleasure; it is useful, but more than mere utility. C. S. Lewis said it is more than companionship, affection, or cooperation. Friendship features some "third thing"—an insight, a cause, quest, or passion.[8] Two children may move toward friendship because both just moved to town or both are brainy nerds, or both are estranged from cruel fathers. But there must be more. Aristotle says true friendship requires good character, since a man has to be good to qualify as a true friend. Only then can a friend do that essential service of improving our character. But a weak person cannot help us; they cannot even help themselves.[9] C. S. Lewis, operating from a somewhat narrower definition of friendship, adds that friends need additional connections:

> Friendship arises out of mere Companionship when two or
> more of the companions discover that they have in common

8. Friendship is notoriously difficult to define. Plato's dialogue on friendship, *Lysis*, ends with a lament that it is indefinable. Though Socrates, Menexenus, and Lysis "should imagine ourselves to be friends . . . as yet we have not been able to discover what is a true friend." If Plato despairs, Freud destroys. For him, same-sex friendship is essentially homoerotic and male-female friendship is simply erotic.

9. Aristotle, "Nicomachean Ethics," in *The Basic Works of Aristotle*, ed. Richard KcKeon (New York: Random House, 1941), 1082, 88–90 (book 9; chapters 4, 9; sections 1166, 1169–70).

some insight or interest or even taste which the others do not share and which, till that moment, each believed to be his own unique treasure (or burden). The typical expression of opening Friendship would be something like, "What? You too? I thought I was the only one."[10]

Lewis, armed with a concept of sin, knows that this insight or taste can be evil as easily as good. Indeed, a secret passion can seem shameful until a peer—a friend—approves it.[11]

C. S. Lewis says genuine friends share a common insight, a common point of view, a sense of the way the world works, and a vision of how it might work.[12] Pat Conroy's novels often feature teenage boys who become friends through athletic skill, reckless courage, a hunger for adventure, and similar experiences: "There is no stronger brotherhood than between boys who discover that both were born to fathers who waged war on their sons."[13]

So friendship is more than a mutual aid society or exchange of favors. Friends help each other, but they also share a secret, an enthusiasm, a *cause*, not just affection or a task. They have a common insight about the way the world is and a common dream about what it ought to be. Yet their bond surpasses the unity of people who hope to reach a goal together. People can work hard for a common goal even if they distrust or detest each other. Friends agree both on the goal and the way to reach it, for they share a vision of the noble life. Here true friendship is open; it delights to welcome others, if they share the same ideals.

This means that at creation Adam and Eve were, or had the potential to become, God's friends. In a way, their sin was a refusal of his friendship, his vision of life. Redemption is, in part, our restoration to the circle of God's affection.

10. Lewis, *The Four Loves*, 96. The next paragraph is loosely indebted to Lewis, 90–105.

11. Ibid., 113–14.

12. Ibid., 103, 113–19.

13. Pat Conroy, *Beach Music* (New York: Bantam, 1996), 363.

Once we know this pattern for friendship, we can read Proverbs with less danger of falling into legalism. The Proverbs are no checklist of duties. They describe friendship in its focus on helpful presence. Like God, true human friends faithfully render aid in the hour of need.

- "A friend loves at all times, and a brother is born for adversity" (17:17).
- "A man of many companions may come to ruin, but there is a friend who sticks closer than a brother" (18:24).
- "Do not forsake your friend and the friend of your father, and do not go to your brother's house when disaster strikes you—better a neighbor nearby than a brother far away" (27:10).

Two chief points emerge. First, everyone needs companionship. Second, the friendship of God manifests helpful presence and self-disclosure. These are the core of friendship. But we must consider the forces that separate men from the friendships they need.

The Practice of Friendship

Unfortunately, our society does not view friendship as the Bible does. To apply scriptural principles, we need to understand our culture.

The Ways of Men and of Women

Men and women approach friendship differently. Women seem to be gifted for intimacy (a man might say "wired for bonding"). They seek friendships and work at them.[14] If you doubt this, tour a card shop until you find the section labeled "Friendship." A typical man doesn't know this section exists, because he sends cards when required, plucking something from his wife's card

14. See Dee Brestin, *The Friendships of Women* (Wheaton, IL: Victor, 1989).

drawer if possible. He has never sent a friendship card. Women send cards to each other when there is no birthday, anniversary, birth, or illness to demand it. Friendship cards say, "As I sipped my tea this morning [a tea bag might be stapled inside this card], I thought of you." There are no "Friendship" cards for men; marketing departments know better.

Little girls are like their mothers. They hold hands and talk on the phone about "us." They send notes that say, "You are my very best friend." Boys don't send such notes. They do not discuss the status of their relationship.

I don't believe women outdo men in every way. Every good gift can be abused, and women's friendships are no exception. If the male quest for strength decays into autonomy and autocracy, the female quest for socialization can decay into enmeshment and codependency. Women form cliques and become jealous and gossipy. If one becomes miserable, the other, *literally* commiserating, becomes miserable too. Yet, on the whole, women form more constructive friendships than men, for they care about them more.

Men, by comparison, are careless about friendships, forming them almost accidentally. When men work or play together, it hardly matters who their partners are, as long as they are decent fellows who contribute to the goal. For example, suppose a man we'll call John goes to a basketball court looking for a pickup game. John only hopes to get on a decent team, with players who know how to pass, play team defense, and work together. A few minutes into the game, John finds that he can already communicate with one teammate, Mike, with a glance, a nod of the head, or by single shouted words, "Middle!" or "Outlet!" The next week, John is pleased to be on Mike's team again. The third week, John *hopes* to get on Mike's team. The fourth week, Mike and John arrange to be on the same team as sides are chosen. After three months, John and Mike are talking after the game. After seven months, Mike has to move. The next week, John goes to play ball without Mike. Then it hits him, "I miss Mike. You know, he was my friend."[15]

So it goes with men. They work with someone for a while, then one day it dawns on them that they are friends. Sometimes they only recognize a friendship after it is over. So men fall into friendships almost by accident.

Since men enter into friendships through a shared task, their relationships are typically *one-dimensional*. At work, men work and talk about work. In the neighborhood, they work on yards and barbecues and talk about them. At sports, they play as a team and talk about the team. Rarely will men talk about marriage or career in these settings.

I do not disparage one-dimensional relationships. We know so many people that most relationships *must* be shallow. How much can we expect from mail carriers, salesmen, and hosts of others with whom we have regular but routine encounters? But something is wrong if a man has *nothing but* one-dimensional relationships, if he relates to others strictly according to their functions or roles in his life.

In his book *Desiring the Kingdom*, James K. A. Smith says something very important here. He says it isn't enough to analyze our culture and create a solid theology or worldview of whatever topic interests us. We need to do what we know, not sporadically, but steadily. Specifically, a good *study* of friendship must lead to *practices* that promote friendship. It is not enough to understand friendship, people who want deep friendships must structure their lives so that they can (fairly easily) meet with them.[16]

We can explore the problem of shallow relationships by describing four types of friendship between men, comparing them to the divine standard; that is, the twin traits of *self-disclosure and helpful presence*. Three are flawed, but one shares the marks of God's friendship.

---

15. Of course, women unwittingly fall into friendships too. Susan Philips calls them "kitchen friendships" in "The Practices of Friendship," *Radix* 23, no. 4 (1995): 5.
16. James K. A. Smith, *Desiring the Kingdom* (Grand Rapids: Baker, 2009).

A Typology of Men's Friendships[17]

Good old boys: Presence without self-disclosure. Good old boys drink beer and swap stories at the bar. They often grew up together and stuck together through thick and thin. Good old boys are always there when you need them. They gradually build up a reservoir of stories and inside jokes that get an easy laugh, but they never express affection or emotion, because, "If you have to say it, you don't have it."

One-point friends: Limited presence, limited disclosure. One-point friends cooperate to reach a goal. These men have one thing in common and little more. They work on that one thing, talk about that one thing, and rarely move beyond it. They may be very emotional and expressive when they reach their common goals. After winning a big contract or sharing a big adventure, they may think nothing of weeping, hugging, and swearing their love for one another. But otherwise they literally stay at arm's length.

Leader and follower: One discloses needs, the other gives help. If one man clearly exceeds the other in a skill or an experience they both treasure, that man assumes the role of leader. If the men are roughly the same age, the superior will be "the man," and the inferior, his sidekick. If their ages differ, they may adopt a mentor/disciple pattern. The older man plays the role of mentor, guide, sponsor, and role model for the younger man, who may one day rise to the mentor's level.

Genuine friends: Helpful presence and self-disclosure. Genuine friendship may begin as a one-dimensional relationship. But something happens and the next dimension opens. Perhaps their wives like each other. Or they share an aspiration, a vocation, or a struggle. They wonder, "Is there more here than I realized?" Men who care about friendship stay alert for signs of the phase when true friendship can sprout. We can become one-point friends and establish an enriching relationship in a day. But

17. This typology modifies one by Jack Balswick, *Men at the Crossroads* (InterVarsity Press, 1992), 177–84. His typology includes Good ol' boys, Locker-room boys, Sidekicks-topkicks, and Mentors-novices.

mutual, profound self-disclosure is rarely easy or rapid. It takes time and effort. If one confides while the other shares nothing, the relationship becomes awkward. Self-disclosure entails risk, but the investment is worthwhile. It takes time to pursue a potential friendship. Since time is precious and since men grow together by working together, try to take on a project together. Get on the same team. As you help each other, take small steps toward self-disclosure. As friendship begins, you will admire your comrade's strengths. But we seal a new friendship when we see a comrade's sins and character flaws and continue to pursue the relationship anyway.

Friendships between Men and Women

When we speaks of risks and friendship, people often ask if adult men and women can be friends. Some stress the dangers of temptation and misunderstanding. Yet if we refuse friendships with the opposite sex, we cut off the insights, skills, and excellence of half the human race. Remember, Jesus struck up conversations with women and let them anoint him, weep over him, support his ministry, and sit at his feet (Matt. 26:7; Luke 7:37–38; 8:1–3; 10:39; John 4:1–26). He shattered the standards of his day by treating at least two women, Mary and Martha, as friends.

The rabbis of Jesus' day ordered the separation of the sexes. They thought casual contact between men and women was perilous, because they viewed women as empty-headed temptresses, whose very presence caused temptation. But Jesus did not blame lust on the mere presence of a woman; it took an improper response to a woman. Therefore, Jesus spoke to women—even disreputable women. Let no one object, "That was safe for Jesus; he was sinless." Yes, Jesus is sinless, but he was also a real man, tempted in all things as we are. Further, he intended his life to be a pattern for ours. He knew that when he decided to associate with women, it signified that male-female friendships are worthwhile, obstacles notwithstanding.

Among singles, friendships between men and women risk that romantic feelings may stir in one person but not the other. Yet single men and women can carve out safe space for a relationship. The key is open communication and the avoidance of mixed messages. If someone *says* they want a strictly "brotherly" friendship, they should *act* like it. Casual friends do not share late candlelight dinners. They spend time together in groups and public places. A trip to the zoo, with hot dogs and a pretzel for lunch, implies one thing; dinner and a concert, another. If romantic feelings rise in only one heart, it will be painful. But if it blooms in both, fine! (There is wisdom in the custom of using intermediaries to communicate about levels of affection.) It is healthy for a romantic relationship to begin as a friendship. The relationship will probably start more realistically, with fewer delusions.

Married men and women can be friends too, within limits. It may start indirectly, through the friendship of the husbands or wives. Eventually the two couples get together and form a foursome. Your friend's wife becomes your friend too. My wife, Debbie, and I have gone to the house of Steve and Sue and found that, at times, Steve and Debbie, both musicians, ended up by the piano, while Sue and I, both educators, talked about school at the coffee table.

These relationships enrich us at several levels. They provide another perspective on life, another way of seeing things. I also understand my wife better because I have seen her through the eyes of her female friends. Above all, there is the simple pleasure of talking to an interesting person. Of course, it is wise to be cautious, for an element of attraction could enter and cause harm. So a married man should not spend time alone with a married woman (a limit on "presence" in their friendship). They should also avoid intimate topics (a limit on self-disclosure) and cultivate a solid friendship between all four parties.[18]

18. If one friend has an area of needed expertise, perhaps they could discuss personal subjects. Again, the friendship between the two men and the two women should

Can a friendship between a man and a woman lead to pain or sin? Yes, but *every* good thing can be abused, whether food, drink, sleep, work, sex, technology, or friendship. The potential for abuse does not rule out the proper use of friendship. We simply handle it with care.

Obstacles to Friendship

Men gain social approval in our culture for being good workers, providers, husbands, and fathers, but not for being good friends. Of course, to be successful at work, a man needs to be *friendly*. Cordial men will form one-dimensional friendships to ensure that phone calls get answered, that vital data and favors flow back and forth.

But in our culture, millions of men are friendly, yet have no friends. We have a thousand associates and fifty of them *could be* our friends, but somehow not one *is* a friend. These friendly associations are like post-it notes—joined by a mild adhesive, with a link easily broken. Our society undermines deeper relationships in many ways, including (1) misconceptions about masculinity, (2) excess mobility, (3) our acquisitive culture, and (4) the misuse of social media.

In chapter 2, we discussed two leading misconceptions of masculinity, the "tough guy" and "good provider" models. Because the tough guy endures pain alone and suffers in silence, he projects a self-sufficiency that bars self-disclosure. The good provider's accent on earning pushes men to work long hours, until time elapses for relationships. In some cases, the good provider's insistence on supplying all his family's needs can have the effect of sequestering women at home, limiting both his wife's relationships and the use of her gifts. The good provider model also promotes a willingness to go anywhere, any time, to find a better job. Thus, it fosters the dark side of mobility.

---

ordinarily be primary, though one can think of exceptions. I want to urge caution without specifying legalistic rules.

Mobility is part of the culture of freedom that Americans treasure, but it destroys friendships by severing the regular contact friends need. It ends the joyful retelling of shared triumphs and sorrows—the tales of the unbearable boss, the impossible task accomplished. Mobility separates friends, and men recover slowly because they hardly try to recover. Mobility encourages rootlessness. As we haul up the anchors of family, history, and tradition, we become vulnerable to the call to reinvent ourselves. Family and friends are not there to remind us of the best and worst of who we are.

Mobility is not intrinsically immoral, but wise men know how to resist the careerism and materialism that jump at every increase in rank or salary. They buck the egoism that believes the flatteries of strangers who swear, "You are just the man we need." They deflate the naiveté that imagines that the perfect job exists. They also remember how precious friends are, and how rarely friendship survives a passage across the continent unscathed.

It is easy to stay in touch with friends who live across the state or around the world. But until we can teleport, than is no substitute for looking a friend directly in the eye, and hearing through the medium of air rather than ether.

When I counsel with a man, I often ask if he has friends. Half the time, the man says something like, "Yes, but he lives in Montana. Does that count?" Yes and no. I give thanks for the media that *almost* cancel the miles between loved ones. I say "almost" because nothing takes the place of a hug, of the physical proximity that lets us see the twitch in the eye, the hesitation in the voice that reveals everything.

People once found a number of light friendships in their neighborhood. Today we find innumerable pseudo-friendships online. Once we bumped into neighbors as we walked tree-lined streets. Then we shopped with hordes of strangers at malls. Now we can buy, see, or hear almost anything without leaving our homes. We lose the physical contact that allows relationships to develop.

The Pursuit of Friendship

We can see why friendship has failed to thrive in Christian communities. Obstacles abound, from careerism to misconceptions about masculinity. Friendship suffers from comparisons to divine love. Yet God has ordained, blessed, and modeled friendship as part of a good life. Through friendship we learn to make commitments and stick to them. We learn to listen, to empathize, to expose our dreams and fears to loving scrutiny. Friendship cures the loneliness of the single and the "gender loneliness" of the married. David and Jonathan, Ruth and Naomi show how friends teach each other, how they spur each other on toward good deeds.

Certain spiritual lessons are best taught by friends. Friends warn of hidden weaknesses and encourage hidden strengths. Their confidence impels us to take risks for the kingdom, to uncover buried talents. Friendship provides another source of companionship, taking pressure off marriage. Friends help us walk with God through their wise counsel and godly example. Friendship brings comfort in affliction, partnership in adversity, and joy in companionship. They build good lives together. But if we believe this, we must pursue it.

Discussion Questions

1. How many genuine friends do you have with men who live in your area? What do you gain from the friendships you have? What more could you gain?
2. If you don't have good friendships, why not? What can you do to craft deeper friendships?
3. What can you learn from women about friendship? From other men you know?
4. How do you describe your friendship with God? What can you learn from his friendship with his people, as the Bible defines it?

| 7 |

A Man and His Work

The Challenges of Work

A certain man once served as a media corporation's chief financial officer. His company produced television programs, radio programs, and magazines. Most focused on the news. All were wholesome. One year, to his surprise, his corporation acquired one of the sleaziest programs on television. My friend had no contact with the program, but as a corporate leader, he couldn't entirely separate himself from it. The man is a believer; some of his friends thought he should quit his job to avoid the pollution of the tainted program. In fact, some wondered why a Christian would work for any public media company. But my friend stayed on, convinced he should stay with his calling. The problem resolved itself a few months later when his corporation sold the show. Still, did he compromise his integrity, or did he wisely retain his ability to lead from a strategic position?

We encounter a steady stream of questions at work. Leaders raise some of them: Can a believer market the products of a low-end brewery, knowing their business model forces them to rely on heavy drinkers? Can a software engineer write programs for the more efficient distribution of lottery tickets? Should a painter quit her secure day job and devote herself to her art?

Some of us hardly think about the connection between our work and our faith. Christians resolve to tell the truth, keep promises, and avoid work on Sundays. But their faith hardly touches their business decisions about the products they make, or the way they sell them. Thousands of Christians produce, market, and sell tobacco, alcohol, lottery tickets—even pornography— without asking themselves if it is a proper way to earn their bread and use their gifts.

Work also forces more fundamental questions: Does my work matter? Will I have a job and a life-sustaining income in five years? It would be easy to give all our attention to professionals, business leaders, and artists, but honesty demands that we label a hard reality: the ideology of self-actualization says we should find fulfillment and flourish as individuals through our work, *but our experience is different.* Christian teachers sometimes *endorse the concept of self-actualization* and add that disciples can use their gifts to bring God's blessing to the world as they transform the workplace. But for most of us rhetoric and reality stand far apart. In recent years, the most common occupations in the United States have been retail salesperson, cashier, and (basic) food preparer. These posts don't offer especially fulfilling work, and the people in these positions have few chances to transform the economy.

Imagine the work experience of a few people. Lisa is a cashier. She often feels like a machine with arms and legs. She suspects that a machine *will* replace her one day. How would she earn a living then? Ryan picks up and delivers portable bathrooms. He knows his work makes construction projects, parades, and concerts possible, but he doubts that his work is significant. He's glad to earn a fair dollar, but he lives for the weekend and wonders if that's right.

Lisa and Ryan both have honest jobs. They do good to the people around them, and that pleases the Lord, whatever their pay or public status. But the church often fails to discuss work in ways that help them.

Lisa and Ryan are single adults who became friends at church. Their pastor says their work matters to God, but his illustrations feature doctors, teachers, engineers, and farmers, not truck drivers and cashiers. They wonder why no one talks about their kind of work.

At church last Sunday, they watched a video about stewardship. The narrator named three ways to use their time and talent for the Lord: serve in the nursery, go on a hospital visit, and host a home Bible study. The suggestions bothered Ryan and Lisa. They both have tiny apartments, no children, and no experience in hospitals. Above all, they want to put their faith into practice at work, where they spend most of the day, not in volunteer activities that they add at the end.

Ryan and Lisa ate lunch together after church and listed what they knew. First, they should work hard. No problem there: Lisa finds it makes the day go faster, and Ryan has a strict schedule. Second, they should be honest. Again, no problem. A camera watches Lisa all day, so she couldn't steal anything if she wanted to (she doesn't), and there is no market for stolen porta potties. Third, they should be ready to share their faith. But Ryan works alone and Lisa's small team already knows about her faith.

They agreed that there must be more. They met Michael and Sarah, a married couple in their discipleship group. Sarah works in corporate communications, and she began the discussion.

"I have more questions than answers, but here are some basics. First, God ordained work from the beginning, before Adam and Eve rebelled. So work is essentially good, no matter how frustrating it feels. Second, God commanded Adam and Eve, 'Be fruitful and multiply and fill the earth and subdue it, and have dominion over [it].' That doesn't mean we have the right to exploit the earth—God put Adam 'in the garden . . . to work it and *keep* it' (Gen. 1:28; 2:15 ESV). So we should respect and preserve creation even as we develop its resources."

She sighed and continued, "That's great as rhetoric, but I'm not sure I'm caring for creation. My company does more good than harm, but it's a big corporation. People say our industrial division makes chemicals that are bad for the environment, and I've heard that our legal department tries to crush our competitors. My job requires me to manage our corporate image, and I feel conflicted because I'm not sure I believe everything I have to write."

Michael markets sports equipment. He doesn't struggle with ethical issues the way Sarah does, but he has concerns too: "Well, my work is so hectic, I hardly have time to think. I have to cover for other people because no one takes initiative. I can't tell if they're lazy or if they can't see what needs to be done. But I like our company's motto—'Helping people enjoy the great outdoors.' Our equipment is good, and I love the idea of helping people stay healthy and enjoy God's creation."

Before long the foursome realized they had more questions than answers, so they decided to visit an assistant pastor and his wife, John and Jessica. They listened, then Jessica told her story: "I landed a job with a big company right out of college, but I was frustrated. My boss was an egotist and I felt claustrophobic, cooped up in a tiny space, staring at a computer screen, crunching numbers all day to set price points for clothing to maximize sales and profits. Like you, I had doubts about my work, but then I had an interesting experience.

"We had a line of women's sweaters that I didn't like. They seemed frumpy, but they sold well. One day I visited one of our stores and heard two women looking at the sweaters I despised. The women didn't look cool or beautiful, but they loved our sweaters. They said things like, 'I could wear this to our party this weekend. . . . I'd buy three of these if I could afford it. . . . You can see that this is well-made.'

"As I listened, it hit me: these *are* quality sweaters at a decent price. It isn't my job to get women to buy what *I* would like. I might not buy those sweaters, but who am I to judge what styles should please other people? I realized that my work made life a little better for these women, because I helped them buy quality sweaters that *they* liked. I remembered what a teacher once said: 'Work is the chief place where we love our neighbors as ourselves.'"

John had worked in construction and management before seminary, so he had a range of experiences. He began, "I'm glad to hear that you know the basics:

- God ordained work from the beginning, so it's good.
- We should govern God's creation for him, both developing it and caring for it according to the abilities he's given and the training we've received.
- We should do honest work in an honest way and do our best at it. Paul says, 'Whatever you do, work at it with all your heart, as working for the Lord, not for men' (Col. 3:23)."

He continued, "We struggle because there is a canyon between our principles and rhetoric about work and the daily reality. We meet a lot of great people at work, but from the start, we labor beside people who are incompetent, careless, and mean. It's quite a shock, especially in the beginning, when we feel powerless. Everyone gets orders that feel destructive, humiliating, or both, and every coworker is a sinner.

"No workplace is wholly good—not even the church. Every organization makes mistakes. And *someone* will resist, even try to sabotage, the best decisions. They may be lazy. They may hate change. They may envy your talent. But the higher our ideals, the more these things disorient us. Still, we can't give up because we're dismayed. Fifty years ago, many Christians opposed devotion to work. They said this world would end soon, so working for social and economic change is like polishing the brass on the *Titanic*—an absurd waste of time. On the other hand, if we are too idealistic, we can fall into the opposite error and assume that *our* work is *God's* work." John paused, "But there is another issue, and it's almost as daunting as the problem of sin. It is impossible for us to see our work as God does." Here we can leave John behind and go to the words of Jesus.

The Lord Sees Our Work

Jesus' parable of the sheep and the goats, in Matthew 25, describes the blessing that awaits God's people—his sheep, in the language of the parable—when we stand before him on the last day. We will learn that Jesus sees the results of our work far better than we do. The middle of the parable reads this way:

> Then the King will say to those on his right, "Come, you who are blessed by my Father; take your inheritance, the kingdom prepared for you since the creation of the world. For I was hungry and you gave me something to eat, I was thirsty and you gave me something to drink, I was a stranger and you invited me in, I needed clothes and you clothed me, I was sick and you looked after me, I was in prison and you came to visit me."
>
> Then the righteous will answer him, "Lord, when did we see you hungry and feed you, or thirsty and give you something to drink? When did we see you a stranger and invite you in, or needing clothes and clothe you? When did we see you sick or in prison and go to visit you?"
>
> The King will reply, "I tell you the truth, whatever you did for one of the least of these brothers of mine, you did for me." (Matt. 25:35–41)

That is, Jesus tells truck drivers like Ryan, "Your work is *important*. Without portable bathrooms, construction projects, outdoor concerts, and art festivals seem impossible." Like many people, drivers minimize their contribution. They say, "The farmer grows the food, I just deliver it." But where would we be without food processors, distributors, and truck drivers? Will people drive to Kansas to buy a cow, to Idaho for potatoes, then Minnesota for wheat?

Everyone in the food chain contributes. The supplier sells seeds, fertilizer, and farm equipment. We need the food processors, truck drivers, stock boys, and cashiers. Take the cashier. How do we *buy* food? Someone has to *take the money.* And the cashier is vital to her company. She is the last person a shopper sees. She can make a tough shopping trip end well. She fosters customer loyalty by showing that the store cares about its clients. In that way she loves people at work.

It's hard to see these things. Consider schoolteachers. The math teacher doesn't know that her algebra student is now an engineer who builds excellent bridges. The art teacher can't see that his student became an architect with visual flair.

In grad school, I wrote a letter to my fourth grade teacher:

> You taught me in fourth grade and I know I caused you grief. I didn't listen to you because I was trying to get everyone to laugh at me. You moved me away from my friends after one week. Eventually, you put me in a corner and surrounded me with your best-behaved girls. You constantly scolded me for not reaching my potential and you punished me with Cs I didn't deserve. You made the naughty life miserable and I thank you for it. For some reason I paid attention in class and behaved well the next fall. The letter "A" dominated my report card, no one was scolding me for a change, and it was so pleasant, I kept it up ever since.

I heard back: "Your teacher died this year, but I'm sure she would have been glad to hear . . ." So *she never knew* the result of her work. Teachers think, "Is anyone listening?" Students wonder, "Will I get a job?" We ask, "Is my work meaningful? Appreciated? If I disappeared, would the machine grind along as well as ever? Is my work significant?"

Picture a woman who tends the drive-through window at a fast-food restaurant. She may ask, "Do these people know how much salt is in this meal? Would it be better if we closed?" But I have prayed to find fast food when desperately hungry and night was closing in. God answered through workers who had no idea how important they were to my family and me.

A loan officer can think, "I crunch numbers and move money to generate profits for my bank, but I don't *make* anything." But the loan officer's decision may finance a business venture that will eventually employ hundreds. Both the meal and the loan may be an answer to fervent prayers. Jesus tells truck drivers, cashiers, and fast-food workers who live by faith, "You did it for me."

We cannot see the results of our work, but God can and he gives us roles that let us serve our neighbors. We pray, "Give us this day our daily bread," and God calls farmers, food processors, truck drivers, and cashiers to work to answer that prayer. Again, Jesus will bless his sheep on judgment day: "I was hungry and you gave me something to eat. . . . I was sick and you looked after me." We will say, "When? When?"

We often feed the hungry or tend the sick in our volunteer activities, but it would be a mistake to think Jesus chiefly has volunteerism in mind.

At work we have the greatest capacity to care for the needy. At work we have the greatest skill and training, spend the most time, and can bring the greatest resources to bear. If, by faith, we consecrate our work to God and aim to love our neighbors—our coworkers and customers—then our work serves him. And he will remember it forever. In Matthew 25, Jesus teaches this:

- If your work has *any* role that helps brings food to the hungry, Jesus is pleased.
- If you are a link in the chain that brings water to the thirsty, he smiles.
- If you have a task in the process that brings clothing and shelter to humanity, Jesus will reward you.
- If your work has a place in the system that brings health or physical care to the sick, Jesus counts it as service to him.

When Jesus says, "I was in prison and you came to visit me," he blesses all who care for the needy. Everyone who works in education, finance, transportation, technical support, administration, and management has a place in the blessing.[1]

In his excellent little book, *Work: The Meaning of Your Life*, Lester DeKoster suggests how broadly we should conceive of our work. Our work welcomes the stranger "if it keeps people connected" so they never become strangers in the first place. Therefore, all who "work in communications of any kind" welcome the stranger by helping people "sustain relationships" and create "a sense of shared humanity and identity."[2]

As we know, communication separates people too, through misinformation, gossip, and fear-mongering. That is why believers should work faithfully in communication. Indeed, even the industries that provide food, clothing, and health care are susceptible to abuse. Someone once said, "The goodness of our work calls for hope, but its fallenness calls for perseverance." Much of our work is a battle against evil and the results of sin. That is why we should be active in all honest callings. Then we can work with all our hearts, offering our labor to our neighbors and to the Lord, even if we feel invisible to our customers, supervisors, or families.

Our perspective on work is also clouded when we take our paradigms for work from the culture rather than Scripture. One college professor said his students view work as "a realm for self-fulfillment" and "optimal self-actualization." They expect to develop their gifts, find a fulfilling career, and flourish as individuals if they work hard and heed their mentors.[3] He calls this a myth that applies, at best, to people who already have the advantages of native intelligence, a network of supportive adults, and access to an elite education. Even in the West, many

1. Lester DeKoster, *Work: The Meaning of Your Life; A Christian Perspective* (Grand Rapids: Christian Library Press, 1982).

2. Greg Forster, "Work and the Meaning of Life: Key Insights from Lester DeKoster," in Educational Pathways Project, Foundational Ideas Tool, Kern Pastor's Network, 5 (unpublished workbook).

3. Douglas Schuurman, *Vocation: Discerning Our Callings in Life* (Grand Rapids: Eerdmans, 2004), 117–21.

groups rarely have such opportunities; higher social strata find their ideals elusive too.

Self-actualization came into Western (and church) vocabulary through Abraham Maslow's paper, published in 1943, "A Theory of Human Motivation." Like most essentially secular ideas that the church adopts, there is something valid in the desire to realize our potential and to do so, in part, through work. Indeed, the Bible links work and joy or satisfaction on a few occasions (Deut. 16:15; Prov. 12:14; Eccl. 8:15; Heb. 13:17). And Jesus found satisfaction in accomplishing the work of redemption (Isa. 53:11; John 4:34). But the prophets and apostles approach work more as a matter of faithfulness in a calling than as a place where we choose what we want to do (e.g., Num. 12:7; Ezek. 48:11; Matt. 25:21; 1 Cor. 4:17; 7:17–24; 1 Tim. 1:12).

Faithfulness at Work

This chapter has emphasized less noble work—cashiers, drivers, loan officers—because most of us do work that *is* less noble or *feels* less noble. Men and women who have high status tend to minimize their significance. More than that, even in the great callings, leaders cannot do whatever they want.

As the king of Israel, David had a zeal for worship (e.g., 2 Sam. 6). After God gave David "rest from all his enemies," he wanted to build a temple for the Lord's worship (2 Sam. 7:1–2). David told Nathan the prophet, who approved at once. But God said no. The Lord called David to fight for Israel. He was a man of war and blood (1 Chron. 28:3). There is no evil in fighting defensive wars. But in the temple mankind finds peace with God, and God wanted Solomon, a man of peace, to build it. David accepted God's will, even though it dashed his hopes (1 Chron. 22:7). But David did better than step to the sidelines. He supported Solomon in every way. David blessed Solomon with prayers; he assured Solomon of God's presence; he donated vast amounts of gold, silver, timber, and stone to the project; and he commanded Israel's leaders to support Solomon and seek the Lord (vv. 11–19).

Clearly, even kings and presidents have limits and disappointments at work. No one can do *whatever he or she wants*. We should accept our God-given roles and support each other, even if they have the role we wanted.

At the other end of the spectrum, we affirm that all honest labor is valuable. Martin Luther said the farmer shoveling manure and the maid milking her cow please God as much as the minister preaching or praying, if they serve faithfully. Working in our place, Luther said, we become agents of God's loving, providential care.[4] Through our hands, God answers the prayers of his children. We pray for our daily bread at night, and bakers rise in the morning to bake it. We pray for safety in travel, and engineers design safe vehicles. When we work faithfully, the naked are clothed, the hungry fed, the sick healed, and the ignorant educated. Our work pleases God, and by our work we love our neighbors as ourselves.

All honest work is dignified if we love our neighbors and strive to serve God in it. (Some work is *not* honest, of course. No Christian should accept a calling that requires sin.)

Someone will object: are you claiming that all work is equal, so that it hardly matters what we do as long as we offer it to God? Yes and no. Janitors and dishwashers can please God as much as surgeons and chefs—maybe more, if their attitude is better.

Nonetheless, no matter how fast they wash floors or dishes, the surgeon ought to operate and the chef ought to prepare food. That is their call, their training, and their gift. We must use our rare and refined capacities. Jesus said, "From everyone who has been given much, much will be demanded" (Luke 12:48).

We need to avoid two mistakes. We must not think that "sacred" work—church work—pleases God more than "secular" work. Many Christians rate "secular work" a notch below

4. Lee Hardy, *The Fabric of This World* (Grand Rapids: Eerdmans, 1990), 45–51; Gustaf Wingren, *The Christian's Calling: Luther on Vocation* (Edinburgh: Oliver & Bond, 1958), 9; Martin Luther, *Luther's Works* (St. Louis: Concordia, 1962, 1966), 44:98–99, 45:330–33.

"full-time Christian service." But even pastors can feel second rate. They can feel inferior to missionaries, who sacrifice more, since they leave the comforts of home and have to speak another language. But even missionaries have ranks. Those who serve in Africa surpass missionaries to Europe. Evangelists outshine support personnel, and city evangelists bow to frontier evangelists. But no one supersedes pioneer translators. At the pinnacle of these stands the Bible translator who lives in the jungle, without electricity, in a snake-infested tree hut. When stated this way, we recognize the absurdity of it. The Lord is pleased with faithful work in every calling. Yet there is still something to the notion, the inkling, that certain work is (somehow) more important. Specifically, we sense that we ought to steward our most strategic gifts.

That is the place for godly ambition. We should be ready for strategic work that we are uniquely qualified to perform. Is there an important task? Are you one of the few that can do it? Then you should be open to it. Try to block the question of salary or title or status or fulfillment.

The more strategic task *may or may not* offer a higher salary. It may or may not demand more time or greater sacrifice. But it probably will require more training, more experience, or a rare talent. Godly leaders can change a city or a culture. Isaiah 32:1–2 (ESV), says:

> Behold, a king will reign in righteousness,
>   and princes will rule in justice.
> Each will be like a hiding place from the wind,
>   a shelter from the storm,
> like streams of water in a dry place.

When "princes" lead under the righteous king, there is justice and shelter for the people. These princes change people's perception. Closed eyes will open, ears will listen, and "the fool will no more be called noble." Finally, the fabric of society will improve. "He who is noble plans noble things, and on noble things he stands" (Isa. 32:3–5, 8 ESV). So while David teaches that no king can do whatever he wants, Isaiah says leaders can change perceptions, plan what is good, and accomplish at least part of it.

A leader in a strategic position can shelter the weary and bring justice and peace to the land. Therefore, if you are a prince in some area of life, it is good for you to step up and lead, whether the pay or recognition motivate you or not. You may prefer to have more leisure and a simpler life, but if God has given you the capacity and opportunity, then serve as a prince in this world.

If everyone can wash dishes and one person can create a superior system for washing dishes, he should work on the system. If ten Haitians can farm the land and one sees how to bring marginal land into effective cultivation, then the one should do that.

Work as Duty

Christians work. Paul said, "If a man will not work, he shall not eat" (2 Thess. 3:10), and "If anyone does not provide for his relatives . . . he . . . is worse than an unbeliever" (1 Tim. 5:8). Paul also says *how* to work: "Whatever you do, work at it with all your heart, as working for the Lord, not for men" (Col. 3:23). Solomon said, "Whatever your hand finds to do, do it with all your might" (Eccl. 9:10).

God also sets a pattern and limit for work: "Six days you shall labor and do all your work, but the seventh day is a Sabbath to the LORD your God. On it you shall not do any work" (Ex. 20:9–10). This law commands both labor and rest. It forbids both ceaseless toil and laziness. Proverbs describes the sluggard: "The sluggard craves and gets nothing, but the desires of the diligent are fully satisfied" (13:4). It also mocks the lazy: "How long will you lie there, you sluggard? . . . A little sleep, a little slumber, a little folding of the hands to rest—and poverty will come on you like a bandit and scarcity like an armed man" (Prov. 6:9–11).

Work as Divine Activity

Because the God of the Bible works, we know work is divine activity. He plans, creates, and fashions reality. He splashes birds and colors in the sky above, and places animals, plants, and minerals on the earth below. He called worlds into life, then formed and arranged them to declare his glory (Ps. 8:3; 19:1). When he finished, he rested, establishing the cycle of work and rest. He still tends and oversees his creation (Ps. 104:10–22). In Scripture, God compares himself to a gardener, a potter, a shepherd, a farmer, a builder, a garment maker, a tentmaker, and a king.

Jesus also works, with delight, saying, "My food is to do the will of him who sent me and to accomplish his work" (John 4:34 ESV). He works as long as there is light, since his work has an urgency to it (John 9:4). The Father delighted in the work of creation and judged it "very good." The Son also took satisfaction in redemption. When he completed it, he declared, "It is finished" (John 19:30).

Our work is, therefore, Godlike activity. Godly men share the Lord's positive attitude toward work. We are glad to share his work by taking his commission to govern creation for him. We are the king's vice-regents.

At its best, the boundary between work and play fades as pleasure in our work reflects God's pleasure in us. Vigorous work and vigorous play both demand singular concentration. When we do the right thing, the right way, at the right time, it nourishes us. When we finish what God designed us to do, it does not drain us, it strengthens us. When we concentrate on God-given tasks, using God-given abilities, the hours fly. Work becomes blessed collaboration with God. Nehemiah described this when he told how the Israelites rebuilt the wall around Jerusalem. First, he said the wall went up, "for the people worked with all their heart." Later he said the wall went up because the "work had been done with the help of our God" (Neh. 4.6, 6.9, 16). This sense of participation lets us pray, "Establish the work of our hands" (Ps. 90:16–17). Again, "Unless the LORD builds the house, its builders labor in vain" (Ps. 127:1).

Work as Cursed Activity

But work also brings frustration, drudgery, and boredom. Some repetitive tasks have been taken over by machines, but laborers still have to follow the pace of machines. Around 1970, one worker lamented his life tending a machine: "Put it on, take it off. Put it on, take it off. In between I don't even try to think."[5] But today, machines tend other machines and we worry about the disappearance of manufacturing jobs and manual labor.

Yet billions of laborers in undeveloped nations face a lifetime of tedious toil. In India, I saw workers excavate the dirt for a four-story building with little hand shovels and straw baskets. Of course, they could not afford earthmoving equipment, but why no wheelbarrows, I inquired. If they purchased *good* ones, my host replied, they would be stolen immediately, and poor ones are worthless. Besides, efficiency is not the Indian way, he said. It is better if everyone has a job.

In the beginning it was not so. Yet when sin entered the world, work became toil—sweat of the brow and the frustration of thorns and thistles. Now sin pervades our work. Cars built on Monday mornings may suffer from hangovers. Projects completed Friday afternoon suffer from haste. Sin means many people cut corners as they produce goods and deceive as they sell them. It means large companies seek to destroy small ones, perhaps *because* the small companies have better products. The combination of ignorance and malice brings many sorrows.

5. Studs Terkel, *Working* (New York, Avon, 1972), xxxiv, xxxii; Hardy, *Fabric*, 32–33, 38.

Everyone experiences the curse on work. In my youth, I dug potatoes by hand under a blazing summer sun and washed dishes in such heat and filth that I dreamed of being promoted to busboy. I painted houses, unloaded trucks, put on roofs, fed machines, and knocked holes in walls. The details change, but we all know work can be hot, dangerous, backbreaking, demeaning, and boring. White-collar work may be cleaner, but it can be just as frustrating. Sometimes most of our work aims to reverse effects of the fall. Fallenness is more than things going wrong. It includes confusion about the right goals for our work. We misjudge our gifts and calling. We become obsessed about finding the right job and using our gifts.[6] Yet we invest our energies foolishly.[7] Even when we do succeed, we can hardly handle it. We become proud of ourselves, envious of our rivals, and greedy for our gain. Solomon said:

He who loves money will not be satisfied with money; nor he who loves wealth, with gain: this also is vanity.

When goods increase, they increase who eat them; and what gain has their owner but to see them with his eyes?

Sweet is the sleep of a laborer, whether he eats little or much; but the surfeit of the rich will not let him sleep. (Eccl. 5:10–12 RSV)

The Grandeur and the Misery of Work

Because work is both noble and fallen, we need the right perspective on it. Because work is essential to life, it leads us to ultimate questions: Who am I? Why am I here? What is wrong

6. I hesitate to use the phrase "our gifts" since it can lead us to think of abilities as our possessions. In a way, our abilities do belong to us, but many of our capacities came as genetic gifts. And if we hone skills and practice them, it's probably because someone introduced us to those skills. Since the Lord gave us our basic abilities and sent us guides to spur their development, our abilities are loans from the Lord.

7. I knew a highly talented man who wrote a novel as a side project. It was rejected by every possible publisher, yet even as the final rejections rolled in, he continued to work avidly on the *sequel*.

with this world and how can it be fixed? Our view of God shapes our opinion of work, and our view of work affects our idea of God. Those who despise work are apt to imagine their god does too. But if the living God works and designed mankind to work, then we must work.

We honor God when we design, manufacture, distribute, and sell. John Calvin believed God is active and effective, not just a god dwelling in solitary self-sufficiency.[8] Therefore, he said, we honor him by our activity at work, by *making* things.

Calvin was himself an entrepreneur. He took an active role in Geneva's government. He offered tax and property benefits to lure cloth manufacturers to the city to alleviate the employment problems of the Protestant refugees who streamed into the city from France.[9] Both Calvin and Luther refused to split life into sacred and secular activities. Both stressed our ability to honor God in daily tasks. They insisted that we serve God even in routine activities. By working, we provide for our families and bless mankind.

Luther and most Puritans (rough contemporaries of Calvin) stressed that people should serve in their place, the place assigned to them by God and man. For them, social structures were almost immutable. If so, the disciple serves in the position ascribed to him. But Calvin understood that society itself can be reformed, so that it is easier for justice and virtue to flourish. That is why he tried to persuade the city council to close Geneva's bars (and, failing that, to shorten their hours). Calvin understood that social structures make it easier or harder to live faithfully. In the United States today, extreme inequality between school districts makes it hard for poor parents to educate their children properly.

Keeping a biblical perspective on work often requires us to affirm twin truths that seem to be in tension. Here we see that we should stay in our God-given calling *and* reform our work

8. John Calvin, *Institutes*, 1.16.3.
9. Ibid., 1.2.2, 1.14.4.

environment if we can. Paul said, "Were you a slave when you were called? Don't let it trouble you—although if you can gain your freedom, do so" (1 Cor. 7:21). We also need to affirm that work is grand *and* miserable.

Because God works and intended mankind to work, even before sin entered creation, we should have a guarded optimism toward labor. Jesus worked with his hands, with building materials. In this way, he dignified all manual labor.[10] The Gospels confirm Genesis; God created all humans in his image, so that men from every station in life have dignity. God chose lowly shepherds as the first witnesses of the incarnation. Jesus' friends include fishermen and tax collectors.

Still, labor can humble and afflict us. The misery of work explains why certain men start dreaming of retirement in their forties. Our duty to provide for our families can press us into difficult positions. To provide for his family, an aspiring songwriter may become a sound technician.

We get drafted into positions we would never choose, but the Lord uses them. Because God gave him the power to interpret dreams, Joseph became Pharaoh's second in command and saved many lives. We may also find ourselves in an unpopular profession. Every year pollsters list the most and least respected occupations. Medical professionals and teachers always lead the hero list; and lawyers, insurance agents, telemarketers, and used car dealers head the list of villains. But Christians need to serve in dishonored occupations. Surely society needs more honest lawyers, insurance agents, and used car dealers!

On another front, each economic system seems to foster certain problems. Slave economies debased both slaves and masters. Communism tolerated indigence. Patronage systems instill corruption. The free enterprise system can reduce workers to

10. Tradition says that Jesus made yokes and plows for farmers. But the Greek term translated *carpenter* in Mark 6:3 includes carpenters, stonemasons, and metalworkers. It is fair to call Jesus a craftsman, builder, or construction worker.

commodities, as they sell their time and skill to the highest bidder. Loyalty between employers and employees erodes.

But there is good news too. The Bible promotes a robust attitude toward work. God filled the world with resources and charged mankind to nurture and develop them. Because God plans, we can plan too. Further, the variety of human gifts teaches us to live in a society of mutual dependence and mutual service. Each man assists his neighbors according to his God-given talents.

Some important work garners no wages. A mother is not paid to care for her children at home, but she works. Because work is more than a livelihood, many continue to work after they retire. Work gives us direction and purpose. Through work, we gain the satisfaction of contributing to something larger than ourselves. The joy of producing and achieving explains why some retired men work as hard as ever.

Admittedly, many work to pay the bills or to conform to roles society imposes on them. Society rewards workers and punishes slackers. But we do more than gain wealth and social status through our labor. Work is tainted by the curse, but it still has intrinsic value because God summons us to be his fellow workers. Still, to gain the most from work, we must discover our gifts and calling.

Work in a Blessed Calling

Colorado has a camp that rests under Horn Peak, rising to 13,500 feet, five thousand feet above the main lodge and eight miles distant. A small group climbed last summer, and somehow I became a lead guide as we made an ascent that is more arduous than dangerous. Unfortunately, "leading" meant keeping up with four athletic teenagers, including my daughter Abby. We made it to the summit despite howling winds that buffeted us and threatened to toss us off the final ridge, far above the tree line. During our descent, a rock gave way under my daughter's foot. She sprained an ankle, and we had to carry her the last three miles to camp. Three men helped, but a father's sweat is less odious than a stranger's, so I did the lion's share of the work. At 120 pounds, she is big enough that I wanted to start a chorus, "She ain't heavy, she's my daughter." It was hot, exhausting work, but, honestly, I never had a more satisfying afternoon all summer, because I love hiking and love my child. Work is not burdensome when you do *what* you love, for *people* you love.

But how do we find the right work—our place in God's plan? How do we distinguish God's voice from our desires, whether for prestige or possessions? The historic Christian answer begins by distinguishing two kinds of calling, our "universal calling" and our "particular calling."

Our universal calling is God's summons to everyone to believe in him; to repent of sin; to know, trust, and follow him (Rom. 8:28–30; 1 Cor. 1:9; Gal. 1:6, 15). Paul says God has "called" us to conformity to the Son (Rom. 8:28–30), "called" us to peace (1 Cor. 7:15), "called" us to freedom (Gal. 5:13), "called" us to be holy (Rom. 1:7; 1 Cor. 1:2).

But God also prepares us for a *particular* calling. It begins with genetic gifts and predispositions. It continues with his providential care, as he shapes us through our parents, teachers, friends, and employers. God leads us to our occupations. The Bible describes this as a calling too: Paul says he is called to be an apostle. God called Jeremiah, Isaiah, and Ezekiel to be prophets. By listing apostles and prophets first, I do not imply God only "calls" men into his service." Not at all. In fact, 1 Corinthians 7:21–22 says believers can be "called" to slavery!

Dedicated Christians who labor in business or the trades need to digest this. Many of them suffer from a vague sense of guilt. They think their work stands one notch below pastors or missionaries who "serve the Lord every day." In fact, the noblest thing we can do is to serve the Lord faithfully in the place God assigns us. A "secular" calling can be full-time service too.

Most of us exalt some occupations over others. Christians typically honor pastors. Secular people may honor political service. A couple of years ago, the tax return of a wealthy politician disclosed that he had donated only $600 to charity in an entire year. When asked why he was so miserly, he replied, "I have given my life to public service." I wonder, does he think bakers, truckers, farmers, garbage collectors, and secretaries do *not* serve the public? Though we may not extol political service, many Christians share the belief in higher and lower callings. But before God, the highest position anyone can hold is the one to which God gifted and summoned him.

This does not mean we can pursue whatever we choose. Too many people want to be professional athletes, musicians, and artists. No matter how strong our desire may be, we are not called to a job if no one ever offers us that job. Further, God may summon us to difficult tasks that deprive us of the peaceful pursuit of our preferred activities. And a man must pursue a career that lets him provide for his family. A man who aspired to be a concert pianist may need to become a music teacher or a banker—and keep playing for the joy of it.

Finding God's Calling

How then do we find our vocations? How do we know when it is time to take a new post—whether to provide for our families, meet great needs, or use our gifts? The Bible doesn't address these questions directly, because people didn't have the options we enjoy today. Most people were farmers or herders. Most simply followed their parents. Still, we can list a few principles.

First, consider what people invite you to do. Wise friends often see our gifts better than we do. They ask us to do what they see us do well. Second, our callings are usually also something we desire. What do you love to do? When do you feel pleasure in your work? When do you feel *alive*? What work would you do for free, if you were wealthy? When do hours of work seem like minutes? Every job has its burdens, but we tolerate them if we spend most of our time using our chief gifts. Third, where do you do the most good for others? If invitations, joy, and fruit converge, your calling is probably there.

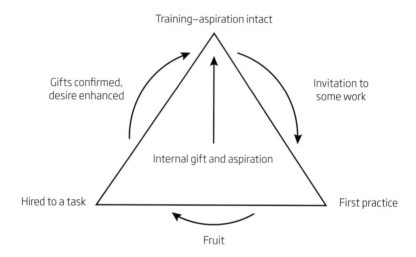

Ideally, a calling has at least these three elements:

- An internal aspiration, with the necessary training and preparation.
- An external verification: employers or customers will pay you a living wage for your services.
- An external result: the fruit or success that satisfies employers and customers.

In years past, sages counseled fathers to take children who planned to leave the family's work on a tour to visit workers in various trades: to the sea for sailing, to the garrison for soldiering, to the church for ministry. As they continued through markets, farms, and shops, parents watched for sparks of interest. The child picked something and tested the work. The work also tested the child. Thus good parents tried to assess and promote the child's inclinations. Today, friends can do something similar for each other.

Conclusion

Work is complicated. Its riddles seem all the more intense because work is so important to us. It is exalted divine activity and repetitive human duty. The frustrations of work make our fallenness clear, yet our achievements bring glory. May clear thought and faithful endurance enable us to settle into our work and see God's blessing there.

Discussion Questions

1. Do you ever have the experience of gaining strength from your work? How often does your work make you feel alive?
2. Do you agree that no job is entirely secular? How does that conviction affect your work? Do you work for God's honor and kingdom while you labor?
3. Do you have a lingering suspicion that "full-time Christian service" is slightly superior to all other callings? How would you answer your own doubts about the value of "secular" callings?
4. Do you believe your current *job* is God's calling to you? Review: What do people ask you to do? What do you love to do? Where do you bear fruit?
5. Is your view of work more like that of the Greeks, medieval theologians, or the Reformation? What are some consequences of failing to view work from the proper perspective? (See next section.)

A Word on Working Too Much and Too Little

Constant change is the mark of the global economy and most local economies. It seems harder than ever to find security or to settle into a satisfactory rhythm of work, rest, leisure, and family life. As a result, we work too much or too little, and rarely get the proportions right. We work too much because our pay is low or because an employer demands it. We work too little because we simply can't find a job, or because our work is dreadful and we can't wait to leave. Whatever our plight, we can't blame all our problems on outside forces. Mistaken mindsets or idolatries lead to problems just as often. If we love pleasure and leisure, we work less. If we love riches and fame, we work more.

Over the years, humans have adopted a number of perspectives on work, but I will mention three with lasting influence: (1) work is evil, (2) work is an instrumental good, and (3) work is intrinsically good.

The Greeks: Work Is Evil

Most Greek—and many Roman—philosophers judged that work was a curse, nothing more. It was, they thought, an unmitigated evil, to be avoided if possible. Greek philosophers said manual labor is undignified. Further, it robs men of time for friendship and citizenship. According to Hesiod, work originated with Eris, the goddess of strife, and labor came from Pandora's box as a punishment from Zeus. Cicero said work is unworthy and sordid. The Greeks considered work a burden fit for brutes and slaves. Like beasts, slaves enter the world, reproduce, toil, and die, leaving no mark. The Greeks valued freedom from bodily necessity. Our bodies require endless toil for food, clothing, and shelter. The fortunate have slaves to care for them. Their work gives freedom to greater men.[11]

11. This paragraph follows Hardy, *Fabric*, 6-16; and Leland Ryken, *Redeeming the Time: A Christian Approach to Work and Leisure* (Grand Rapids: Baker, 1995), 71-73. See also Plato, and Aristotle.

The gods of Greek myths both reflected and fostered disdain for work. They were idlers, not workers. They gave themselves to pleasures and the occasional foray into the affairs of mankind. Aristotle's god was the unmoved mover, thought thinking thought, but not acting. So the Greeks demeaned work. When the apostle Paul said it is good for disciples "to work with your hands" (1 Thess. 4:11), he cut against the grain of his culture (although the Stoics would have agreed).

Medieval Christianity: Work Is an Instrumental Good[12]

Ancient and medieval theologians believed work was an *instrumental* good. Work feeds and clothes the body. Its griefs crush pride and promote penance. Work prevents idleness, provides self-discipline, and lets workers give to the poor. These acts of charity please God and could help the benefactor obtain salvation. So leaders understood that work is an instrument that brought various benefits, but they thought work had no *intrinsic* value, no direct ability to edify.

Their disrespect for work had three sources. First, they generally followed the Greeks' disregard for bodily life. Second, they had confused ideas about salvation. They believed God is gracious, but they also thought they had to complete his grace by adding *their* works to it. Finally, since most theologians were priests or monks, they wanted to give their lives to study or contemplation. They had little interest in the active life, because it hindered contemplation.

Renaissance and Reformation: Work Is Intrinsically Good

Renaissance thinkers had a clearer view of God. A higher view of work followed. They called God a cosmic craftsman who displayed his wisdom and power by creating the universe. Renaissance thinkers called God the "Divine Artificer," the "Supreme Maker," the

12. See Hardy, *Fabric*, 16-26; and Ryken, *Redeeming the Time*, 73-75.

"Mightiest Architect." As a result, they honored craftsmanship, industry, and labor. Giordano Bruno said work was good because it made men develop their creative capacities, which would lead them to exercise control over the earth and fulfill the mandate God gave Adam at creation. Renaissance thinkers denied that work is bestial, since animals work without thought or variation, according to predetermined instincts. But men use their imagination to plan and execute. They innovate, fabricate, and amend the material of nature. Thus, while our work is simple in some ways, it is Godlike in others.[13]

Over and Under

We all know people who work too little. A capable and likable woman can't find anything but part-time work. A man has market-able skills, but refuses jobs that seem boring or beneath his dignity. Another likes work well enough, but is careful to avoid attention and big projects, because he wants to guard his time for backpacking and skiing. If we lay unemployment and underemployment aside, the prime cause of underwork may be the sense that our jobs don't deserve our best effort. If the pay is low and the esteem lower, why work hard?

But in my circles, overwork is far more common than lack of work. I have (unscientifically) polled a number of people, aged twenty-four to seventy-two. They had eight reasons for overwork. The first three are intrinsic to work itself; the last five extrinsic.

1. *Because of love of the work.* Engineers and inventors love to make things and scholars love their discipline, so they gladly devote extra hours to their work.
2. *Because of the nature of the work.* Certain professions and trades have a structure that demands long labor to complete

13. Hardy, *Fabric*, 27.

essential tasks. Farmers work long hours when plants are sown and harvested. Anyone who starts a business or leads a complex organization must do whatever it takes to keep the enterprise going. One man said, "There is a lot that has to be done, and I'm responsible for it."

3. *Because of essential skills.* Anyone who possesses rare, strategic skills has an obligation to use them faithfully. A trial lawyer must press on till a case is resolved. The son of a man in my poll was born with the great vessels of the heart reversed. The surgeon who performed that life-giving surgery is one of very few who can. For that reason, wherever he goes, a plane may come to pick him up to take him to the hospital where he can save a life.

4. *To survive.* A man or woman will hold two or more jobs because none pay enough to guarantee money for food, clothing, and shelter.

5. *To advance in a career.* Younger adults work hard to prove themselves to their superiors, whether to keep a job that someone else wants, or to position themselves as candidates for a higher post.

6. *To earn status.* Some work for titles, position, and power. Others hope for simpler privileges—a small raise, a decent work space, or the right to a vacation.

7. *To become wealthy.* People long for the capacity to buy whatever they want, whether for themselves or others.

8. *To prove worth or significance.* People work to keep score, to prove an enemy wrong, and to silence the voice of authority figures who told them they were nothing.

For most readers, overwork is the greater problem than laziness. I first sketched some of these comments years ago, during spare moments in a very busy week. It started on a Saturday, when I presented a seven-hour seminar. Sunday, I preached twice and taught Sunday school in a large church. Monday, I lectured for four hours in regular classes and led a devotional for a student group. Tuesday, I spoke at a community Bible study and lectured two hours for a colleague who had an emergency appendectomy. Wednesday, after a regular class, I preached in chapel, led a discussion on mentoring, and, covering for my pastor, spoke on parenting at seven. Ultimately, I delivered twenty-six talks in seven days. The week was both exhausting and exciting. It was exciting because the sessions went well. I enjoy the surge when a sermon or lecture goes as planned. And the rapport in a seminar with well-prepared students is exhilarating.

To be honest, the ego also found it satisfying to be in demand. I gave several talks as a last-minute substitute. It felt good to be trusted in time of need. Like many pastors and professors, I can quickly craft a tolerable talk. We plunder something from an old lecture or sermon; add one section; delete another; then sketch an introduction, illustration, and application; so that a useful (if not outstanding) talk emerges. I discovered this capacity one day, like a package at the door, when I was in grad school and my pastor fell ill moments before a worship service began. So I should take no pride in it (but maybe I do). In emergencies, the speaker writes some notes, prints others, then draws arrows so he knows what goes where. We dash out the door and find moments to secure the main points while sitting at red lights or ignoring announcements. An element or so will flop, but momentum gathers. Soon everyone is learning and laughing together.

My busy week was exhilarating but costly. Home life suffered. Duties piled up or got shoveled onto others. And after the rush of activity comes the crash. Public figures get addicted to adrenaline and need *something*–a crisis, a public presentation, or a jolt of caffeine–to restart the body's engines.

If I'm honest, I can detect the presence of false gods at play. I'm willing to complain about long hours. But just as no one reaches an eighty-hour work week without regularly loitering around seventy, so no one speaks twenty-six times in one week without choosing or allowing a baseline of fifteen or more.

There are good reasons to work long and hard. Sometimes hard work is the only thing that keeps us from unemployment. But many of us *prefer* to toil to the edge of exhaustion, knowing we might overshoot and collapse. Some love the work itself. They feel alive when they write music or serve clients to perfection. Others love a cause and will do anything for it. They guide rafters and jump into wildfire zones for minimum wage. They volunteer to stuff envelopes and make calls for their political candidates. Others want financial security and will do anything, however tedious or perilous, for the salary and benefits. A final group needs to prove something. Their gods whisper, "Prove yourself in your status and wealth."

If you are prone to needless overwork, you need to know why. My reasons were mixed. I love to teach and I believe in God's cause (good). But I also feel the lure of status (not good). Worse than that, my father's salvos of verbal abuse provided the catalyst for ambition formation. Most days, when I was twelve to fifteen, he told me that I was lazy, good for nothing, useless, worthless, and always would be. I resolved, most days, to prove him wrong. If I had to work myself to exhaustion to hear him say "I was wrong!" I was willing, even though I knew he had little interest in the evidence and even less in apologizing. The story varies from person to person, but millions tread a similar path. We find fuel in the insults of a dark mentor or rival, or in a bitter teacher. We stoke the anger that spurs great exertion.

Again, there are good reasons to work hard: rare skills, love of the work itself, or love of the cause it serves. Business leaders feel the weight of the people who depend on them for a paycheck. But all too often our overwork is sinful, driven by slavery to false gods. So let me ask: Do you labor to silence critical voices? Or is it enough for the Father to call you his beloved child? Do you toil to provide a secure financial future, to stave off every possible disaster? Or do you work hard enough, then entrust yourself to the Father's care? Are you willing to repent of your unbelief and throw down the idols that loiter near the workplace–prestige, privilege, and wealth?

Try this diagnostic question. What makes you say, "If I lose this, I don't want to live"? If you would rather die than lose your status, wealth, skills, or achievements, they are your gods and work is their lackey. Again, what reversals hit you harder than they should? If a minor problem crushes you, the threat to an idol may be the cause. If you suffer a dip in income and you crater, possessions or security are probably an idol. If times of low achievement bring high anxiety, achievement is an idol that you need to debunk and dethrone. There are good and bad reasons to work long and hard. A noble cause may require intense labor. But let's not fool ourselves and call our idols by any other name.[14]

14. Christian leaders are as susceptible to this as anyone. This is a metatheme in Bob Burns, Tasha D. Chapman, and Donald C. Guthrie, *Resilient Ministry: What Pastors Told Us about Surviving and Thriving* (Downers Grove, IL: InterVarsity Press, 2013).

| 8 |

A Man as Leader

Martin Luther once said, "Young fellows are tempted by girls, men who are thirty years old are tempted by gold, when they are forty years old they are tempted by honor and glory."[1] Luther understood that for many men, leadership is a temptation before it is a calling. Many of us associate leadership with higher pay, more respect, and a nicer office at work. Even in the church, we can link leadership with honor rather than character. Once, at a conference in a small town, I asked my host, obviously a respected leader, what made people respect a man in his town. He replied, "A man knows he's got it made when he has a good truck, a cabin on the river, and the office of elder in the church.... Of course, if he can kill a deer with a bow at fifty paces, that helps too." Valued skills, possessions, and positions are the currency that buys us social respect. But Luther knew, as we do, that Jesus defines leadership differently:

> You know that the rulers of the Gentiles lord it over them, and their high officials exercise authority over them. Not so with you. Instead, whoever wants to become great among you must be your servant, and whoever wants to be first must be your slave—just as the Son of Man did not come to be served, but to serve, and to give his life as a ransom for many. (Matt. 20:25–28)

Jesus demonstrated that true leaders serve—and suffer. Like Jesus, leaders will be blamed for things they did not do wrong.

1. Martin Luther, "Table Talk," in *Luther's Works*, trans. Theodore Tappert (St. Louis: Concordia, 1967), 158.

King David suffered attacks simply because someone wanted to "thrust him down from his high position" (Ps. 62:3–4 ESV). Leaders suffer pointless envy and irrational hate. Jesus said, "They hated me without a cause" (John 15:25 ESV). On the other hand, leaders are praised for work they did not perform. Their people favor them, serve them, and show frightening levels of devotion; consider the men who risked their lives to get David a drink of water from his favorite well (2 Sam. 23:14–17)! Still, leadership is hard. The work never ends. Leaders constantly plan and prepare. They field endless requests for assistance or endorsement. Whenever they propose a new initiative, those who favor the status quo line up to oppose them. Yet they are responsible to forge consensus, to make the right course of action seem obvious, and that can take a long time.

Even in the business world, leadership ought to be—perhaps it must be—hard work and service first, long before it ever leads to glory. Before he became famous, Sam Walton used to dress in blue jeans and a flannel shirt and walk, incognito, into his Wal-Mart stores to buy shampoo and toothpaste to evaluate the service. Walton understood that to lead you have to serve, and to serve you have to forego glory.

Beside its interest in servant leadership, the Bible stresses character-based leadership. The key text for that is 1 Timothy 3, Paul's description of a church elder. Of course, leadership in business and society is much broader than authority in the church. Nonetheless, Paul's principles apply to every kind of leadership.

The Character of a Christian Leader

If anyone sets his heart on being an overseer, he desires a noble task. Now the overseer must be above reproach, the husband of but one wife, temperate, self-controlled, respectable, hospitable, able to teach, not given to drunkenness, not violent but gentle, not quarrelsome, not a lover of money. He must manage his own family well and see that his children obey him with proper respect. (If anyone does not know how to manage his own family, how can he take care of God's church?) He must not be a recent convert, or he may become conceited and fall under the same judgment as the devil. He must also have a good reputation with outsiders, so that he will not fall into disgrace and into the devil's trap. (1 Tim. 3:1–7)[2]

Notice that Paul's list first describes the *character* of an elder, not his work. Paul begins, "An overseer must *be* . . ." not "An overseer must do . . ." Of course, all leaders must have skills and personal strength. Fittingly, Paul mentions the ability to teach and manage. But all other elements of Paul's list refer to personal qualities, not tasks. Thus, Paul calls oversight a "noble *task*," but he emphasizes the leader's character more than his skills. This is especially striking since Paul here calls the church leader an "overseer." *Overseer* is interchangeable with *elder* (Titus 1:5, 7), but it usually refers to a leader's *functions*, whereas *elder* refers to his maturity. Paul seems to say, "Your first 'function' is to be mature." For a Christian, it is not enough to do the work, we must also be the man. Paul explains three aspects of a leader's character in Timothy: his virtues, his family, and his reputation.

The Public Virtues of a Leader

At first glance, Paul's list of virtues has little in common with other New Testament virtue lists. We miss leading Christian virtues such as love, faith, righteousness, endurance. Of the fruit of the Spirit listed in Galatians 5:22–23, only one *word*, *self-control*, also appears in 1 Timothy 3. But if we look more closely, we see that, while the words differ, almost every *concept* from the fruit of the Spirit appears somewhere in the traits of a leader. Specifically, the list in 1 Timothy 3 describes the fruit of the Spirit as it expresses itself in public. The *public* behavior of a leader in family, church, and society proves that God is working in him privately, internally. The chart below compares the

---

2. This chapter takes 1 Timothy 3 as a foundational text for the study of Christian leadership. First Peter 5:1–4 is another worthy passage on the theme; I have published a study of it in *1 Peter*, Reformed Expository Commentary (Phillipsburg, NJ: P&R Publishing, 2014).

ninefold fruit of the Spirit (Gal 5:22–23) to the traits of an elder
(1 Tim. 3:1–7; Titus 1:5–9).

Fruit of the Spirit	Traits of an Elder
Love	Elders take care of family and church, which are expressions of love (1 Tim. 3:4–5).
Joy	Joyful people are contented, hence free from greed for money (3:3).
Peace	Elders are not violent or quarrelsome (3:3).
Patience	Elders are not quick-tempered (Titus 1:7). Patience aids teaching (1 Tim. 3:2; 2 Tim. 2:24–25).
Kindness	Hospitality (1 Tim. 3:2) publicly expresses kindness.
Goodness	Every term in the list is a form of goodness; Titus 1:8 says elders "love what is good."
Faithfulness	Elders are faithful to wives and children and to the faith (1 Tim. 3:2, 4–5, 9; Titus 1:6, 9).
Gentleness	Elders are temperate and gentle,* not violent or quick-tempered. Gentleness is also part of aptitude for teaching in 2 Timothy 2:24–25.
Self-control	This is the one word that appears in both passages.

*There are two words for gentleness. Galatians suggests gentle humility. Timothy suggests gentle mildness.

   The results are clear. Paul expects leaders to experience the fruit of the Spirit and to express that fruit publicly. But a leader must show his character in the world, not just the church. Paul shows that he knows this by placing several key *pagan* virtues in his list.

The Pagan Virtues of a Leader

   Three items from Paul's list of virtues also appear in the lists of virtues that pagans admired. They are temperance, self-control, and generosity. Paul recognizes that Greeks and Romans agreed with God's standards in important ways. In short, Christian and pagan virtues overlap. Of course, Greeks and Romans often lived by standards we find appalling. For entertainment, they watched gladiators fight to the death. In some temples, "worshipers" copulated with "sacred" prostitutes. In Ephesus, a brothel stood directly across the street from one of the ancient world's largest libraries. But not everyone was amoral. Pagan philosophers extolled the virtues of courage, justice, wisdom, and temperance. Everyone admired generosity, insight, and self-control.

Paul's description of a leader in 1 Timothy 3 shows that he treasured some of the same virtues that pagans valued. He mentions *temperance* and *self-control* in 3:2. He forbids elders to love money, and he enjoins hospitality (vv. 2–3), showing his approval of *generosity* and the popular view that wealth is to be shared, not hoarded. We conclude, therefore, that *elders must meet the valid pagan standards of the day.* That is, the public conduct of Christian leaders must be acceptable to pagans who, by God's grace, made some accurate moral judgments.

We must handle this principle carefully. Clearly, we don't *follow* pagan standards; we follow biblical standards, giving thanks when pagans accept them too. Nonetheless, in every generation some secular people admire many of the same moral qualities that we admire. Today, morally sensitive pagans have a high regard for honesty, financial integrity, marital fidelity, generosity, and hard work. Consider how much a godly Christian leader enhances his ministry by shining in these areas. And consider how much the cause of Christ has suffered when corrupted ministers expose themselves to society's proper disdain for fraud, greed, hypocrisy, and infidelity. For the sake of its credibility, church leaders should meet the valid pagan standards of the day!

Character Tested

Good leaders are strongest in times of testing. They are ready to fight where the battle rages. They engage the issues of the hour. When crises arise, they lead the way when others get lost. Thus Paul requires leaders to be strong where, in his day, false teachers were weak:

- False teachers were violent and quarrelsome (1 Tim. 6:3–5; see also 2 Tim. 2:23). But an elder teaches gently and kindly and avoids quarrels (1 Tim. 3:3; see also 2 Tim. 2:24–26).
- False teachers love money (1 Tim. 6:5, 10). But leaders are generous and hospitable. They love neither money nor dishonest gain (1 Tim. 3:3, 8; see also Acts 20:33; Titus 1:7).
- False teachers love speculation, breed controversy, and "do not know what they are talking about" (1 Tim. 1:4, 7). But leaders know what they believe and can teach it (1 Tim. 3:2, 9).

Leaders also persevere. Observe that the list in Titus describing those who *will be* elders and the list in Timothy describing those who *are* elders are virtually the same. This means that becoming a leader is not like cramming for an exam. True professionals—whether in medicine, law, finance, or technology—know they must keep improving their skills; they cannot study and forget. Likewise, Christian leaders cannot cram for character, then forget it. Paul's letter thwarts anyone who might think that way. He published the leader's character requirements. By announcing the list publicly, Paul lets the whole church, even the whole world, call leaders to account.

Leaders prove themselves *publicly* by their exemplary character. They also prove themselves *privately*, in their families. Jesus said, if someone is faithful over small things, he will entrust them with larger things. If a man cannot love and care for his own family—a few people, whom he knows best—how can he manage a larger family (the church)? He *knows* them less and *owes* them less. Leaders prove they can lead in a large arena by leading well in a smaller, easier arena, the family. Paul mentions both marriage and parenthood in his teaching about leaders in our passage. Both comments are short but rich.

The Marriage of an Elder: Loving a Wife

Paul's statement that an overseer must be "the husband of but one wife" seems clear, but there has been considerable debate about Paul's precise message. Literally, the Greek says an overseer must be "a one-woman man."[3] This short remark can mean one of four things:

Option 1: Paul believed overseers had to be married men. Of course, most Christian leaders are married, but why would Paul make this an absolute requirement? After all, he was single himself and *he* was an overseer of the church. Further, Jesus, the supreme leader of the church, was unmarried. Surely we don't want to say that Jesus lacked the necessary qualifications to lead (it's not a good idea to present leadership criteria that Jesus doesn't meet). Finally, Paul commended celibacy for those with the gift, because it increases freedom for service (1 Cor. 7).[4] So Paul must have meant something else.

Option 2: Paul believed overseers may marry only once in a lifetime. That is, any man who has divorced and remarried cannot be a Christian leader. Certainly, divorce is a great evil and the leadership potential of an adult Christian is damaged by it. But the problem with the once-in-a-lifetime view is that it also forbids widowers from marrying, and that seems like a gratuitous legalism. The Bible grants widows and victims of infidelity the right to remarry elsewhere (Matt. 19; Rom. 7; 1 Cor. 7), and Paul would not contradict that.

Option 3: Paul believed overseers must be monogamous. This is certainly true; polygamy was already illegal in the Roman Empire and very few practiced it at that time. Why would Paul

---

3. The Greek, *mias gunaikos andra*, means a "one-woman man."

4. If someone wants to read 1 Timothy 3:2 hyperliterally and demand that elders have one wife, then they should also *require* that elders have two or more children, since 3:4 says elders must keep their *children* in respectful submission.

bother to forbid a sin no one committed? Again, he must have had more in mind.

Option 4: Paul believed overseers must be faithful husbands. Leaders must be monogamous (above), but more, they should be exemplary husbands. This makes sense in both Paul's day and our own. A very similar passage in 1 Timothy 5:9 supports this view. There Paul says a widow who receives financial aid from the church should have been "the wife of one husband" (ESV). The Greek reads: "a one-man woman."[5] In context, this clearly means she was a *faithful* wife. Here, at last, a familiarity with country music promotes Christian thinking. Paul is describing what country music might call "a one-man woman," as in the saying, "I was a one-man woman, but he was a two-timin' man." When Paul requires a leader to be "the husband of but one wife," it means he should be a "one-woman man"; that is, a faithful man.

From time to time, a man sidles up to me and complains, "I just don't understand women," as if his ignorance of the female of the species accounts for his marital woes. But this is a mistake. Husbands, Paul does not ask you to understand "women" as if they were a field of academic study. You must first know, love, and serve *one woman,* your wife, working to understand her and use your knowledge to love her in every way. After that, perhaps we can try to understand, love, and serve the other women God places in our lives.

The Children of an Elder: Leading Children and Leading the World

Paul expects leaders to prove themselves again with their children, as they manage and take care of them (1 Tim. 3:4–5). To "manage" is to oversee, direct, and plan the things that shape his family. To "take care" is to lead by serving everyone, by nurturing the weak and forgotten, and by going last.

---

5. The Greek, *henos andras gunē,* means "a one-man woman."

Notice that Paul does not simply require leaders to have obedient children. The children should obey *with respect*, with dignity. That is, parents ought to *obtain* obedience without shouts, threats, or violence; and children ought to *render* obedience respectfully, without slouching, grumbling, or rolling their eyes.

Parents of teens may think this is like asking for a snowball fight in sub-Saharan Africa. But we can gain obedience with respect if we have a proper relationship with our children. Infants and little children submit to their parents out of necessity. They are utterly dependent on their parents, who are so big and strong that they often have no choice but to obey. If we tell a twenty-month-old, "Time for bed," and he yells, "No bed, no bed!" all we have to do is pick the boy up, put him in the crib, pull up the side, turn out the light, and shut the door. We win! But the older children get, the more independent they become.

Older children may still submit to unloving parents because they know they need their parents and because they fear punishment. If parents fail to show that love motivates the laws of the house, older children may yet obey. But if parents lead harshly, they can't expect older children to obey with a submissive, respectful spirit.

Mao Zedong was right when he said, "*Power* proceeds from the barrel of a gun" [emphasis mine]. That is, people will obey when someone points a gun at them. But what happens when the "gun"—the threat of punishment—is removed? People obey when compelled, but then they rebel as soon as they can. On the other hand, if leaders exercise *intimate* authority, people follow willingly. That is, teenagers and adults give obedience with respect when they respect both the *position* of the leader and the leader's *right* to it. We have the right to govern when God or man duly appoints us to a position, and when we use that position, gently and respectfully, for the good of others.

Children are much more likely to submit willingly if they know their parents lead with love and justice. Workers are willing to follow leaders who model commitment and excellence. Herb Kelleher, the founder and CEO of Southwest Airlines, won legendary loyalty from his employees by slinging luggage alongside his ground crews. Stephen Jobs had a passion to design elegant, "insanely great" products. His passion, along with his willingness to take risks, inspired the same traits in his design teams.[6] In contemporary companies, workers love it when the CEO's office and furnishings are only slightly nicer than theirs. They love it when everyone contributes, everyone has a voice, and everyone gets a vote, even if, somehow, the boss always has the decisive vote.[7]

Likewise, the effectiveness of church leaders depends more on the care they give than the power they wield. Church and family are so similar that if you cannot lead the family, you cannot lead the church. Both require the leader's direction and humble service. Good leaders neither shirk leadership, nor use it for selfish advantages.

Some husbands and fathers suffocate their wives and children through ungodly domination. Others abdicate their leadership role. Domination may be the greater error, but abdication is a husband's more common error. Too many men are too lazy, exhausted, or distracted to lead. (Some of these points also apply to church leaders.)

Children respond to parental authority when parents lead by example, when they give reasons for what they say, when they appeal to imagination, not just the rules. Then they obey with respect. Adults are similar. We respond when we see a servant at the helm, not just a boss. Of course, the boss can dress down and eat hot dogs to create a veneer of egalitarian concern. But many of them mean it. Christians, at least, take their cue from Jesus, who didn't just dress down for company picnics. He dressed down to wash his disciples' feet, even though he saw no immedi-

---

6. Jobs could be childish, demanding, and foolish, but his skill and zeal for excellence outweighed his flaws—for most of his people, at least. See Walter Isaacson, *Steve Jobs* (New York: Simon & Schuster, 2011).

7. David Brooks, *Bobos in Paradise: The New Upper Class and How They Got There*, (New York: Simon and Schuster, 2000), 127–33, 264–66.

ate rise in their productivity. He suffered himself to be dressed down further still by the Romans, at his crucifixion, though he gained no personal benefit from it. By his sacrifice he redefined leadership and stirred new levels of loyalty and obedience.

Years ago my family witnessed a remarkable example of Christlike, redefined leadership. My daughter Abby joined her high school's cross-country team the fall of her freshman year. The team was strong and she expected nothing more than an opportunity to meet people and get in shape. But as the season progressed, she surprised everyone by coming at the top of fresh-man races, then junior varsity races. In the last regular-season race, her time bested a couple of experienced varsity runners. With district and state championships coming up, the varsity runners asked the coaches for a team meeting and asked Abby to join it. One of the seniors told the coach, "We have all seen that Abby has been running really well lately, and we think she deserves to run on the varsity for districts." She paused and looked at Abby, then at the coach, caught her breath and concluded, "And she can have my place."

For the sake of the team, she gave up her last two varsity races. Coaches love to talk about seniors stepping up to leadership. But in this case, stepping down was leadership. Where would we be if Christian leaders were so secure in God's love, so sure of their identity in Christ, that they too could give up their place and put others first? When people know their leaders are willing to put *them* first, it becomes easier to follow. Spiritual authority depends more on care given than power wielded.

Like John the Baptist, true leaders know when to say, "He must increase, but I must decrease." As the hymn says:

> I would not have the restless will
> That hurries to and fro,
> Seeking for some great thing to do
> Or secret thing to know;
> . . . .

So I ask thee for the daily strength,
To none that ask denied,
. . . . [to be]
Content to fill a little space,
If thou be glorified.[8]

Reputation

Finally, Paul considers the public standing of a leader. For one thing, Paul forbids that an elder be a recent convert (1 Tim 3:6; literally, "a newly planted person"). Paul does not state how long someone must be a Christian before becoming a leader, but the metaphor of a growing plant suggests that maturation is a process that cannot be rushed. It is not the style of Paul or the Bible's way to specify a timetable for leadership. Still, we can say it ordinarily takes several years for someone to gain sufficient maturity to lead. Christians certainly find reasons to rush new converts into leadership: We don't have enough leaders. Our current leaders are weary. New Christians have enthusiasm. We want them to grow through service. But Paul says a hasty rise to prominence tempts us to pride and conceit. This leads to "the condemnation of the devil" and "the trap of the devil" (vv. 6–7 LEB). This can mean one of two things. Either pride will trap immature, conceited leaders so they share the condemnation the devil must endure. Or the devil will use the immature leaders' pride to trap and condemn them. Whichever Paul means, we should want no part of it.

It is better if people move toward leadership gradually. If someone has ability and humility, he will seek to *assist* first. If, as Jesus said, he proves faithful in small tasks, then he can take charge of more (Matt. 25:21–23). To put it differently, the best way to find new leaders is to locate people who are already leading quietly but effectively in a little noticed corner. There are exceptions, but if God has called and gifted someone to lead in an area, he has probably placed a desire for that work in his

---

8. Anna L. Waring, "Father, I Know That All My Life," 1850.

heart. Therefore, the person will find a way to become active in that area, even if no one recruits or rewards him. On the other hand, once someone becomes known, it is worthwhile to observe what others ask him to do. Communities are usually very good at reading the skills of their members. If someone is being asked to organize events over and over, they are probably good at organizing. We can discover the sphere where we may best lead by asking, "What do people most regularly invite or recruit me to do?"

Paul also requires leaders to have a good testimony or reputation with outsiders (1 Tim 3:7). This is fitting, since he already insisted that elders meet the valid pagan standards of the day. But why does Paul twice emphasize reputation? Above all, we must recognize that nothing undermines the church's witness faster than the loss of ethical rectitude. Secular people already have a certain antagonism toward the church for claiming high standards, for a perceived "holier than thou" attitude. We all know a Christian businessman—perhaps you are one of them—who cannot fit in with "the boys" when a work team travels out of town. The guys are out gambling or womanizing or drinking at a strip club, while he stays in his room, reading and watching TV. His wordless testimony may make them hostile, derisive, uncomfortable, or all three. Is he "holier than thou"? In a way, we cannot avoid the accusation. We do lay claim to a high standard. We do aspire to holiness, and if someone else cares nothing for holiness, then we do try to be "holier" than others. Of course, once we make the claim, others will do us the honor of holding us to it.

Years ago, an incoming president loudly proclaimed that he would restore the highest level of ethical integrity to an executive branch that had grown corrupt. He soon nominated a woman to be attorney general—the nation's highest law enforcement officer. She was married to a Yale law professor and enjoyed a great income. The public soon learned that she had hired an illegal immigrant to be her child's nanny—a special embarrassment since, as attorney general, she would oversee immigration. Further, she had (illegally) made no Social Security contributions for the nanny for two years. Finally, she had the gall to blame her errors on bad legal advice. Within days, the public outcry forced the president to withdraw his nomination.

The lesson is clear: those who *claim* a higher standard will be held to it. Because Christians claim a higher standard, our leaders *must* have a good reputation. To be sure, reputations can err. Yet, in the long run, we usually get the reputation that almost matches what we deserve. The inner man shows himself often enough that our deeds do represent our character.

Conclusion

In review, Paul's description of a Christian leader looks daunting. First, a godly leader should experience the fruit of the Spirit and, second, he should demonstrate that fruit publicly. Third, he should meet the valid pagan standards of the day. Fourth, he is strong wherever spiritual battles rage. Fifth, he is a dedicated husband. Sixth, his children render respectful obedience. Seventh, he has a good reputation in his community.

But we are all so flawed that we wonder, "If this is the standard, who deserves to lead?" But Paul does not seek to disqualify leaders. Rather, he describes who *is* qualified, whose life and aspirations make them leaders. In some ways the Bible is simply describing a Christian man with normal maturity. It just seems demanding because most of us fall so far short of God's ways.

So then, what does God require of the man who wants to be a fruitful servant and effective leader in his kingdom? He must be a Christian, must know his sin, must know Jesus is his only hope, now and forever. All leaders have certain gifts that they are willing to hone and use. Public leaders need gifts of mind and tongue and social relations. One must have a call, and the spirit to follow it. But I believe the Bible says, here, that what an elder needs most is the desire to serve. Gifts are important, but for the Christian leader there is no substitute for godliness and a willingness to work just where the work needs to be done.

Discussion Questions

1. Have you thought of leadership as something we do more than who we are? Why is Christian leadership more a matter of character than deeds?

2. Are you a godly leader in the home? A one-woman man? Do you lead and care for your children?

3. Explain the difference between authority and power, in the work of leadership.

4. Are you mature enough to lead? Is your reputation good enough? (Why does that matter?) Is your faith deep and long enough? Do you aspire to godly leadership? For the right reasons?

5. Do you lead in the social or public spheres? Do you serve in difficult places? If not, what prevents you from expressing your faith in public arenas?

| 9 |

A Man and His Wealth

National economies rise and fall; personal incomes do the same. In the West, each generation worries that it will be the first to enjoy less wealth than their parents as their national economies struggle and power seems to shift to other parts of the globe. In most of the world—including large segments of Western societies—concerns are more immediate. People wonder where they will live, and worry that they may not have enough money to survive the next weeks or months. There are other tensions. Men struggle as an increasing number of jobs seem to require skills that greater numbers of women possess. Will middle-class jobs for men disappear? Will men lose the ability to provide for their families?

In a different vein, if populations and desires continue to grow, will the earth be able to supply all that people demand? Or will all our eating, mining, and manufacturing make the world a less and less habitable home? To pick one example, in recent years the Atlantic Ocean seems to generate storms of greater size and destructive power. But scientists believe that human activity has destroyed much of the God-given buffer that protected coastlines—coral reefs, wetlands, and oyster beds. All three reduce the power of waves and storm surges, but all three have suffered long decline due to pollution from the runoff of farm sediments, heavy metals, and pesticide. In addition, wetlands are drained and converted to roads or farmland. Oysters were harvested—eaten—almost to the point of extinction, and pollution finished the job around New York City. Coral reefs also suffer from overfishing and, most scientists believe, a rise in ocean temperatures and acidity.[1] This is a small aspect of the great question of creation care.

Creation care is one of many questions we have that connect to the topic of wealth. What would happen if the whole world achieved a lifestyle like Western nations? Is it a problem if wives earn more than their husbands? Many in the rising generation would prefer to have less wealth if they had more time for leisure and relationships. Is that wise or foolish? What would happen if the rising generation did indeed gather less wealth than its parents? We can't answer all these questions, but we can gain a biblical perspective on wealth. If we have a clear grasp of that, we can sort out our more specific questions.

Jesus knows something profound about people and wealth. Whoever they are, whether rich or poor, most people do want *more*. Because most people care deeply about wealth and security, he addressed it often, sometimes at their request.

A Question of Money

One day, Jesus was teaching a crowd about the cost of discipleship. Apparently Jesus paused for a moment, allowing a man in the crowd to interrupt. "Teacher," he blurted, half pleading, half demanding, "tell my brother to divide the inheritance with me" (Luke 12:13). We do not know if this man actually suffered an injustice. But he believed his brother had taken too much.[2]

Jesus replied brusquely, "Man, who appointed me a judge or an arbiter between you?" (v. 14). In fact, the man did have reason to call on Jesus. He correctly viewed Jesus as a teacher; and Israelites turned to teachers, not lawyers, to resolves their disputes. But Jesus declined to play the judge. It was not his mission to settle family disputes; indeed, sometimes he causes them

---

1. See, for example, Paul Greenberg, *Four Fish* (New York: Penguin, 2011).
2. With two sons, the older inherited two-thirds and the younger one-third. But death and divorce complicated matters. Also, someone might have no male heirs or too many heirs (Num. 27:1–11; 36:7–9; Deut. 21:15–17).

(vv. 51–53). Jesus refused to give the man what he *asked*, but he offered what he *needed*: a better understanding of possessions.

The Danger of Greed

Jesus began with a double warning: "Watch out! Be on guard against all kinds of greed; a man's life does not consist in the abundance of his possessions" (Luke 12:15). Twice the Lord says to beware, for greed is a subtle thing. Whether we have much or little, even if we have shunned the paths that lead to a large income, greed can slip into our hearts. We can become greedy if our neighbors have more than we do or if we meet an old friend who has done a bit too well. We all have days when possessions seem very important.

Imagine the life of Leonard, a college freshman whose year has come and nearly gone without a single solo encounter with a young lady. Pondering his plight, he decides the problem is transportation. "If only I had a car," he thinks, "I would have a social life." Since Leonard is a Christian, he prays for a car, and God answers—with a clunker. The car is neither fashionable nor reliable; what girl wants to go out on a date knowing there is a realistic chance of walking back? Frustrated, Leonard prays again, "Lord, thanks for the car, but I need something more dependable." Again God provides—a twelve-year-old economy car. It runs, but the previous owners' children were known to dump milk in the air vents. Mix this with the aroma of partially burned oil circulating through the rust holes in the back, and Leonard still has no social life. He prays again, "Lord, thank you for providing, but I know I could find the girl of my dreams if I had something a little more sporty." This time he finds a ten-year-old sports car. It *is* sharp, but it gets seven miles per gallon and the insurance payments are mountainous, so he can't afford to drive it. Resolute, Leonard prays again, "Lord, now I realize that I need a newer, more economical car." You get the point. Leonard has slipped into believing that possessions do grant the good life.

Mature men rarely fix on one thing they must have. They focus on the income stream that provides every need and an array of desires—finer food and clothes, more exotic vacations. Thus we think, "If only my boss paid me what I am worth, if my business were more profitable, if the stock market were more stable, then I could afford a bigger house, a real vacation, a nicer neighborhood. Then we would be content." Indeed, financial security makes us feel peaceful, and the increase of possessions brings a temporary lift.

Yet as income increases so does outgo. Whatever we have, we always crave more. Ecclesiastes says, "Whoever loves money never has money enough; whoever loves wealth is never satisfied with his income" (5:10). Gathering possessions to find contentment is like drinking water to satisfy hunger; it stops the aching for a while, but cannot solve the root problem. Still hungry, we crave more, but since we choose the wrong remedy, our appetite remains. "The eye never has enough of seeing, nor the ear its fill of hearing" (Eccl. 1:8). Wealth cannot satisfy our deepest longings. As Solomon says, "I denied myself nothing my eyes desired; I refused my heart no pleasure.... Yet when I surveyed all that my hands had done ... everything was meaningless" (Eccl. 2:10–11).

Once, after I gave a talk on money, a middle-aged man approached me, smiling sadly. He came to confess something, "I am making *twice as much money as I ever dreamed possible*, but I find that it still isn't enough." Jesus understands that. He knows the subtle threat of greed, and told a parable to show that life does not consist in the abundance of possessions:

> The ground of a certain rich man produced a good crop. He thought to himself, "What shall I do? I have no place to store my crops." Then he said, "This is what I'll do. I will tear down my barns and build bigger ones, and there I will store all my grain and my goods. And I'll say to myself, 'You have plenty of good things laid up for many years. Take life easy; eat, drink and be merry.'" But God said to him, "You fool! This very night your life will be demanded from you. Then who will get what

you have prepared for yourself?" This is how it will be with anyone who stores up things for himself but is not rich toward God. (Luke 12:16–21)

A Fool and His Money

At first glance this parable seems poorly matched to the concerns of the man who worried about his inheritance. Outwardly, the man in the crowd and the man in the parable are opposites. One does not have enough possessions, the other has too many. But inwardly, they share a hidden commonality, a solidarity discovered by listening carefully to the farmer of Jesus' parable.

At first, Jesus' farmer looks like an honest man. Since God gives fruitfulness to the earth, his wealth seems to be a token of God's blessing. His ground produced a crop so bountiful that he had a storage problem. Surveying his crop, he proposed a solution, "I will build bigger barns." He will make an investment to protect his assets; that looks like good stewardship.

But after he makes his plans, he dreams his dreams, and we see another side, one that is not so innocent. Once those new barns are complete, he will "take life easy, eat, drink and be merry." Alert readers notice that he nearly mouths the hedonist credo, "Eat, drink and be merry, for tomorrow we die." The farmer's hedonism is rather obvious, but he has a second problem that emerges if we retranslate his speech, emphasizing the pronouns:

He thought to *himself*, "What shall *I* do? *I* have no place to store *my* crops." Then he said, "This is what *I* will do. *I* will tear down *my* barns and *I* will build bigger ones, and there *I* will store all *my* grain and *my* goods. And *I* will say to *myself*, '*Self*, *you* have plenty of good things laid up for many years. *You* take life easy. *You* eat, *you* drink, *you* be merry.'"

This strange-looking translation follows the original, where eighteen of the farmer's fifty-four words are to or about himself.[3] Notice too, that the bulk of the parable is a mono-logue. This also seems innocent, until we notice whom he does *not* consult. The farmer does not pray about his wealth, to thank God or seek direction. He confers with neither friends nor family about his possessions. He has no thought of sharing with the poor. He talks *to* himself, *about* himself, which is suspect in itself.[4]

The farmer thinks he has a storage problem. He proposes an architectural solution—bigger barns. He hopes that will guarantee that he will enjoy his possessions for many years. Indeed, the farmer believes life *does* consist in abundant possessions. In his soliloquy, he plans to keep his wealth for himself. He thinks he is alone in his room, but to his surprise, someone else is there—God—and God interrupts the farmer's plans.

God calls the farmer "You fool," not because the farmer is stupid, but because he says in his heart, "There is no God" (Ps. 14:1; 53:1). The fool need not be a philosophical atheist who believes he can disprove the existence of God. As long as he is a practical atheist, a fool may vacillate on the *existence* of God. Practical atheists do not care if God exists or not because, they think, even if God does exist, he sees, knows, cares about, and does nothing.

The fool anticipated many years of ease, but he forgot God, forgot the day of reckoning. He trusted a dead god, money, and it killed him. Now the living God speaks (Luke 12:20): "This very night your life will be *demanded* from you. Then who will get what you have prepared for yourself?" The farmer wanted to guarantee his possessions for himself, but he forgot this: "Naked a man comes from his mother's womb, and as he comes, so he departs. He takes nothing from his labor that he can carry in his hand" (Eccl. 5:15; see also Job 1:21). A day of reckoning, before God,

---

3. Of fifty-four Greek words, thirteen have "I," "my," or "myself," and he addresses himself five times.

4. Seven of Luke's parables feature internal dialogue. Self-interest or self-promotion is prominent in five of them: 12:17–20, 45; 16:3–4; 18:4–5, 11 (contra 15:17–19; 20:13).

will arrive. We will account for the use of our material wealth as well as our God-given capacities—of mind, energy, and skills. The word translated *demanded* (Greek *apaiteo*) in Luke 12:20 deserves our attention. It means to *recall* or *ask back* something that was stolen or loaned out. That is, God will *recall* our lives as a lender recalls a loan. Our lives and possessions are not truly *ours*, but a loan.

On Loan from God

We typically view both our wealth and our abilities as *our own* possessions. We think of *my* organizational skills or people skills; *my* intellect, artistic ability, or physical strength; *my* knowledge of engineering or finance. When I exercise them well, I earn *my* money. In a way, our abilities do belong to us. But surely we know that most of them were bestowed at birth. Yes, we hone skills and practice them, but who implanted a desire to hone them? Who sent a mentor to direct our development? Deep within, we know all our abilities are gifts and loans from the Lord, given for his pleasure as well as our pleasure.

Let me speak personally. Like most professors, like most teachers and preachers, I believe the Lord gave me a good mind, a love of ideas, some ability to organize ideas, and enough capacity to read people that I can tell when I am losing or boring them, so that I need to shake things up. I inherited a strong voice and physical health from both grandfathers, and other relatives and friends instilled a respect for hard work. Everything I do, every job I have performed, every dollar I have earned is a result of these gifts—and they are *gifts*. Most are genetic. The rest were in the air I breathed; I could hardly have escaped their influence.

Are you willing to draw up an inventory of your skills? If you are honest, you will see that God gave or loaned you all of your abilities. Each of us has capacities that are simply *there*. They earn us praise or wealth, but they are God's more than ours. Since our gifts are his loans, we should be "rich toward God" (as in Luke 12:21) with all we receive for exercising them. Jesus tells us *how* to do that: "Give to the poor" and put your "treasure in heaven" (Luke 12:33–34). Being rich toward God means things like this:

- Tithing to your local church so it can fulfill its mission.
- Supporting an inner-city church plant, so it can assist the needy in its neighborhood.
- Giving Bibles and reference works to students in third-world Bible colleges, when you learn that they are too poor to buy them for themselves.
- Putting off a renovation in your house so you can support an orphaned or abandoned child, whether in your own nation or abroad.

Being rich toward God means gently leading your wife and children to see that an old car can be viewed as an embarrassment or as a gift to the kingdom. If you have $50,000, which is the nobler use: to purchase one "cool" vehicle or to provide a *century* of food, clothing, and Christian education for impoverished children overseas (ten children for ten years each)? Being rich toward God means deferring or eliminating some expenses so you can tithe, and more than tithe. It means celebrating when you reach 15 or 20 percent. It means fixing our eyes on the things that matter to God, even if they have no publicity office.

The farmer understood none of this. Because he saw only *his* possessions, it seemed logical to spend them on self-indulgence. This is precisely how most people—even Christians—think: "My skills and my hard work earned me my money." But God says the skills and the funds are both his, loaned to us for a season.

This is no attack on the rich, for Jesus targeted wealthy and poor alike. The man in the crowd and the rich farmer are *financial opposites* but *spiritual twins*. One had too little and one had too much, but both believed life *does* consist in abundant possessions. Both are fools. Both need to be rich toward God. Yet neither can do so, for each loves money rather than God. Only a man after God's own heart can use money God's way. Wealth is a rival deity, as Jesus says. "No one can serve two masters. . . . You cannot serve both God and Money" (Matt. 6:24).

> Do not store up for yourselves treasures on earth, where moth and rust destroy, and where thieves break in and steal. But store up for yourselves treasures in heaven, where moth and rust do not destroy, and where thieves do not break in and steal. For where your treasure is, there your heart will be also.
> The eye is the lamp of the body. If your eyes are good, your whole body will be full of light. But if your eyes are bad, your whole body will be full of darkness. If then the light within you is darkness, how great is that darkness!
> No one can serve two masters. Either he will hate the one and love the other, or he will be devoted to the one and despise the other. You cannot serve both God and Money. (Matt. 6:19–24)

Whom Do You Love?

The teaching of Matthew 6 stands near the climax of the Sermon on the Mount. There Jesus describes the life of discipleship, and idols such as reputation and money as they try to displace the Lord. The statement, "Store treasure in heaven, not earth," is both command and battle cry. The command is, "Don't store treasure on earth, because here it rots, and in heaven it is worthless." The battle cry is, "Depose the blasphemous deities!"

Indeed, everything does decay under the assault of moths, rust, water damage, and inflation. Therefore, we should store treasure in heaven, where it is safe, guarded by the God who also guards us. Placing treasure in heaven means investing in God's causes and God's people. Do that and your heart will follow, so that *both* heart and treasure are safe with God.

Pagans cannot grasp this. Atheists *cannot* store treasure in heaven. If there is no God and no heaven, it is nonsense to store anything there. Secular people *inevitably* store their treasures on earth. How could it be otherwise? They cannot trust God to reward them when they deny his existence. Unbelief destroys the capacity to obey.[5]

Soon, Jesus drops talk of treasure and heaven and speaks of eyes and light. The theme seems new, but actually it is a new perspective on the same issue. In the Bible, the "eye" and the "heart" can both refer to that inner core of a person that sets his life's direction.[6] When Jesus says the eye is the lamp, he means we find our way through life by the direction it gives, whether good or ill.

Jesus diagnoses our condition: "If you cannot take your eye off your wealth, if you live for it, it is because your eye—your heart—is corrupt!" If our eyes are dark, there is no hope, unless God grants renewal. No one can *do* what is right unless he can *see* what is right. The unbeliever inevitably hoards treasure on earth because he neither sees nor knows the Father in heaven. Therefore, Jesus does not tell the unbeliever, "Try harder to store treasure in heaven." He says, "Examine your heart, your eyes."

In Matthew 6, Jesus addresses unbelievers, but he warns disciples about greed, too. We see this in the specific Greek words used for the good and bad eye. Literally, "If your eyes are bad" reads, "If your eye is *evil*." Literally, "If your eyes are good" (as in Matt. 6:22) reads "If your eye is *simple*."[7] In biblical times, an "evil eye" signified a jealous eye, a coveting eye. Thus, while Jesus tells unbelievers to examine their eyes, he warns disciples against jealous eyes. Instead of jealous eyes, we should have simple eyes. A simple eye is clear; it does not see and covet, it simply sees. A simple eye is generous, because it is not always looking for an angle. When it gives, it just gives. It does not give *and* ask what

---

5. Daniel Doriani, *Putting the Truth to Work* (Phillipsburg, NJ: P&R Publishing, 2001), chapter 6.

6. *Eye* and *heart* are used interchangeably here and in Psalm 119:10, 18; 119:36–37.

7. The Greek idiom, the "evil eye" (*pongros ophthalmos*), meant a greedy or stingy disposition (Matt. 6:23; 20:15; Mark 7:22; Luke 11:34; Deut. 15:9; see also Deut. 28:54, 56; Prov. 23:6). A good eye (*agathos ophthalmos*) is generous (Matt. 20:15). (Deuteronomy and Proverbs citations refer to the LXX [or "Septuagint"], the Greek translation of the Old Testament that shaped New Testament vocabulary.)

is gained by the gift, what favor may be returned. It has neither ulterior motives nor side motives.

We must be careful where we set our eyes. When visiting a prosperous friend, watch your eye as you scan his house. At home, shun mail-order catalogs, with their exquisitely textured casual clothes. When car advertisements find you, *don't* picture yourself behind the wheel. Beware of gracious living magazines; they may provoke jealous schemes to get everything in them. The graphic display of the body to promote sensual lust is called pornography. Perhaps we also need a word for graphic displays of wealth designed to promote materialist lusts. Since *plutos* means *wealth* in Greek, we could call it *plutography*.

To unbelievers, Jesus asks, "If you cannot control your eyes, what is the reason for your inability? Go to the root of the matter—your allegiance to other gods." To believers, he warns, "Be careful little eyes, what you see." He concludes, "No one can serve two masters. *Either* he will hate the one and love the other, *or* he will be devoted to the one and despise the other. You cannot serve both God and Money [or Mammon]" (Matt. 6:24).

Money is capitalized here because Jesus labels it a god. He calls it *Mammon*, which means *that in which one trusts*. Indeed, we are prone to trust money. Remember the prayer, "Give me neither poverty nor riches. . . . Otherwise, I may have too much and disown you and say, 'Who is the LORD?'" (Prov. 30:8–9; see also Hos. 13:6). Jeremiah commands, "Let not . . . the rich man boast of his riches" (9:23), and Ezekiel accuses, "Because of your wealth your heart has grown proud" (28:5). Job knows a man can speak to gold and say, "You are my security" (31:24). David sings, "Though your riches increase, do not set your heart on them" (Ps. 62:10).

Yet we do trust in riches. Our words prove it. The United States' national retirement plan is called "Social *Security*." We call our investments "securities" and "trusts," as if we can trust them for a secure future. We make money a god in additional ways. We give it the title of deity: "the Almighty Dollar." We make money a judge. When someone asks, "What is he worth?" it means, "How much money, how many assets, does he have?" We speak as if a man's financial assets determine his worth.[8] Of course, money is not the kind of god that explicitly demands exclusive worship. No one needs to get on his knees, for money is a *polytheistic* deity. It merely wants a shrine somewhere in the pantheon, one with room for other demigods, such as status, power, and pleasure. It even lets its worshipers be Christians too.

These ideas baffle some people. They cannot see why they must choose between God and money. They think it quite feasible to serve two masters, for they do it themselves. They honor God for part of Sunday, serve Mammon Monday to Friday, and reserve Saturday for themselves. They may even think that God and prosperity go hand in hand. But they are thinking of faith as a hobby, like gardening. Or they regard God as an employer, not a master. Surely a man can *work* for two employers, schedule permitting. But no one can *belong* to two masters. No slave can be the property of two owners, "for single ownership and full-time service are of the essence of slavery."[9] We serve God or Mammon.

The Rich Exterminator

Few people openly live for money, but I did encounter one who did while in grad school. Hoping to find a summer job to cover the next year's tuition, I searched for seasonal work that was unpalatable enough to pay well and chose pest exterminating. After calling several businesses, I got an interview with a young and energetic owner. He shook my hand, sat me down, then asked, "What is your purpose in life?" Momentarily stunned, I quickly seized this surprising chance to share

8. For a cultural analysis of money, see Jacques Ellul, *Money and Power* (Grand Rapids: Eerdmans, 1984).

9. R. V. G. Tasker, *The Gospel according to St. Matthew* (Carol Stream, IL: Tyndale, 1961), 76.

my faith and a Christian's life purpose. Within a minute, the exterminator interrupted, "Listen, my purpose in life is to make money, and I want to know if you want to make money." At one level, I understood him. After all, does anyone start a rat and cockroach control business in Philadelphia out of generalized love of humanity?

The exterminator had exceptional clarity, not exceptional convictions. Candid and self-aware, he announced, "I live for Mammon." Many people do, but they prefer to mask it. They like shades of gray, not black and white. The gray palette lets them say, "I look at my house, my car, and my furnishings as investments" and "I simply want to provide the *best* things for my children."

Jesus presents a stark choice between two ways of life. Will we store treasure on earth or in heaven? Will our eyes be light or dark? Will we serve God or Mammon? He addresses both rich and poor, for both want "just a little more." Both seek security in material wealth. Rich or poor, Christian or pagan, all are susceptible to greed.

Sadly, most Christians live roughly like their peers, even if those peers are secular. If the careers and income are the same, the lifestyle is probably the same, too—the same hours of work, the same use of money, the same overstuffed schedules. Our vision of the good life owes more to society than to Scripture.

We can always explain our behavior away: "We work hard and only want our due. Others have much more. God wants to give gifts to his children. We will be good stewards of our possessions," and so on.

The poor strive to get what they can. The rich spend or hoard to guarantee their future security. We are nearly the richest people on earth, but studies show that American Christians give about 3 percent of their income to charity. Sadly, as they grow richer, people usually donate *lower* percentages of their wealth. Somehow, we convince ourselves that we are deprived whenever we cannot get what we want. We compare ourselves to someone who has more. We run after possessions like the pagans, but nothing satisfies for long.

Rich toward God

The cure for the malady of materialism is generosity toward God, starting with the heart, then moving to actions. Generosity of heart starts with trusting God, rather than worrying about food or clothes. Jesus supplies four reasons not to worry (Luke 12:23–31). First, God feeds birds, and we are more valuable than they (v. 24). Second, worrying is futile. Worrying cannot add one hour to our lives (vv. 25–26). Third, God clothes wildflowers and grasses with beauty, though they last but a day, and we are more valuable than they (vv. 27–28). Fourth, God knows our needs and will supply them, if we seek his kingdom first (vv. 29–31). Knowing this, disciples can sell their possessions and give to the poor (vv. 32–33). As one scholar said, "Serious application of this principle to contemporary churches would require such radical transformation of most Christian fellowships that few seem willing even to begin." But great journeys start with a single step. Some fear schemes to redistribute wealth, but we could travel far down that road "before anyone suspected us of extreme obedience."[10]

Four Ways to Be Rich toward God

1. Use money as God directs. Paul lists three proper uses of money in 1 Timothy 6. First, meet basic needs for food, clothing, and shelter. "If we have food and clothing, we will be content with that" (v. 8). Second, enjoy God's good creation.[11] "God . . . richly provides us with everything for our enjoyment" (v. 17). Third, give generously. "Those who are rich in this present world [should] be generous and willing to share" (vv. 17–18).

2. Develop a godly career. A few laws govern our careers. First, we must work to supply our needs (2 Thess. 3:6–10). Second, our

10. Craig Blomberg, *Neither Poverty nor Riches* (Grand Rapids: Eerdmans, 1999), 132.
11. This chapter stresses generosity more than enjoyment of creation. We'll consider enjoyment in chapters 10–12. See also Joe Rigney, *The Things of Earth* (Crossway, 2015).

work should be constructive and lawful. No Christian should work as a thief, gambler, or pornographer. Third, we should do good to all, offering them something of value.

More than laws, we need godly goals for our careers. We should offer our work to God, governing our corner of creation for him, using the gifts he bestows. One day we will stand before the Lord and render an account. Who wants to say, "Lord, I used my business skills to market fake fireplaces." Instead, let us strive to use the highest gifts God grants us. Yet we must guard against overwork, organizing our life and career so we have time for family, friends, church, and godly pleasures. We must refuse to work endlessly, simply to support expensive tastes.

3. See wealth as God does. "Everything God created is good" and to be "received with thanksgiving" (1 Tim. 4:4–5). Yet Christians should never be engrossed with money (1 Cor. 7:31–35). The Bible never condemns those who *are* rich. Abraham, Joseph, David, Solomon, Jehoshaphat, Josiah, Job, and Joseph of Arimathea were all rich and blessed. But it often warns against making it your life goal to get rich. "The love of money is a root of all kinds of evil" (1 Tim 6:10). People who live to get rich love this world, not God. They fall into temptations, traps, and snares. If our gifts and efforts lead to riches, more or less by accident, praise God. But we should not choose a career just to *get* rich (James 4:1–4; 1 Tim. 6:6–10). Riches are a good servant, but a bad master. As Paul says, "Godliness with contentment is great gain" (1 Tim. 6:6).

4. Pray for a generous heart. My wife and I learned in seminary that one need not be rich to be rich toward God. We arrived in January with no job. After paying tuition and rent, our wallets were as barren as the winter landscape outside. Our meager savings dwindled for five weeks as neither of us found work. It could have been frightening, but God sent a seminary couple with generous hearts. She was a secretary. We knew them from college, and when we arrived, they invited us to dinner. When they learned that we had no income, they invited us to dinner again, days later. Every few days, they invited us again. When we asked them to a meal, they laughed, "Not now, invite us over when Debbie gets her job." Objectively, they didn't give us much. Seven meals in five weeks cannot stave off bankruptcy. But when we lay in bed at night, wondering, our friends' generosity looked like manna, like God's sign from heaven. One of us asked, "Will we go hungry?" The other replied, "No, God will take care of us. He already sent us Mark and Adele." Small gifts, given with liberality, accomplish great things.

Large gifts are strategic, too. Generosity is a spiritual gift (Rom. 12:8). Generous people understand that quotas, like tithing, can impede true generosity. If people tithe to keep a legal formula, they may think, "I gave my due, now I'm done." But Jesus is the model for giving, and he gave all, not 10 percent. Generous people *love* to give. They taste the splendor of Christ's kingdom, its world-changing power. They see Jesus restraining the work of the evil one. They delight to support God's work in areas where money can make a difference.

Conclusion

This age keeps its eye on money, but the man after God's heart keeps his eye on God and his kingdom. He knows he cannot serve both God and Mammon. He realizes that all he has is a loan. Beyond the tithe, he sets the generosity of Jesus as his model. Because his heart is right, God's man is free to be generous. Generosity is a spiritual gift, but because we love God we can shake off greed and possessiveness and act generously. If first we are rich toward God with heart and mind, generosity with our wealth follows.

Discussion Questions

1. Why are we prone to think that life does consist in having the right possessions?

2. What was the rich farmer's basic problem? How does that problem manifest itself today? What forms do "bigger barns" take today? How might we hoard money for our selfish indulgence? Where might the "Eat, drink, and be merry" credo show itself?

3. Why do so many people think you *can* serve God and Mammon? What would you say to someone who seemed to be trying to serve both masters?

4. How can you show, by concrete action, that you see your money and gifts as a loan from God?

A Man and His Body: A Proper Concern for Our Flesh and Blood

Western culture makes it hard to be a good steward of the body. Foods abounding in sugar, salt, and fat lie all around us. We arrange our cities so that travel by foot or bicycle is almost impossible. For the sake of economic efficiency, noble manual labor becomes ever more rare. God created mankind as a body-soul unity, but more and more of our work is mental. We sit through meetings, stand at counters, talk on the phone, or pound a computer keyboard all day. Hours of crises and deadlines load stress onto our shoulders, and our energy flags. To fight off our weariness, we reach for caffeine. After a journey home through harrowing traffic, we wonder if our jangled nerves need a pill or a drink so we can relax.

Some people, alarmed by this lifestyle, run the other way. The growth of obesity and diabetes makes them reject coffee, cakes, and muffins. After purging processed foods, they follow the trajectory to a vegetarian life. Fearing softness and lethargy, they get fit, very fit. Men and women train, getting leaner and meaner as young adults, and they keep at it into their forties, fifties, or sixties. Men run, cycle, and lift weights until what was once leisure looks like a schedule-dominating obsession. Some of us train and play so hard that we lose the time we need for relationships or professional growth. Older adults, trying to stay strong, seem oblivious to the realities of aging.

I face the same problems. I sit at a desk many hours each day. I have walking meetings when I can, but I still turn to caffeine when my energy flags. I exercise hard most days; and my weight, pulse, and pull-up and push-up count are nearly the same as when I finished college decades ago, but that has brought sore muscles and stress fractures. So I wonder—am I a good steward of my body or an old fool?

Our culture lives with contradictions. We see rising obesity *and* a rising obsession with body image. We celebrate food and drink and we diet constantly. Technology lets us keep track of every step, every bite, every heartbeat; does that make us healthy or obsessive? Or go to a rock concert and notice the inconsistent rules. There is no smoking inside, so people suck their last cigarette by the door. No one would inflict secondhand smoke on the crowd! But inside the venue, clouds of smoke from pot are so thick they threaten to obscure the band. Ticket takers confiscate water bottles, but inside beer is everywhere. So they forbid cigarettes, which are legal, but tolerate pot, which is illegal. They forbid water, but promote alcohol, although drunkenness causes problems at concerts. Clearly, we're confused.

The church has its own problems. Christian leaders tend to *neglect* the body, possibly as a result of the ancient tendency to split life into two realms: sacred, spiritual things, which matter to God, and secular, physical matters, which supposedly do not. That is nonsense. God created and sustains *all things*, including our bodies, so he certainly takes interest in our physical life. Most Christian leaders know this. Large churches may even have a gym! Still, we don't give sustained thought to bodily life, nor do many people take physical disciplines seriously.

There are reasons for our neglect. Until the last few decades, starvation was a greater risk than obesity. And we were more likely to toil until exhaustion than we were to do nothing and get flabby. But it is time to start writing position papers and songs and statements of faith about the body. And we need to do what we say. We need to get serious about integrity in the body.

Jesus certainly took the body seriously. Paul's poetic confession of "the mystery of godliness" begins with Jesus' body: "He was manifested in the flesh" (1 Tim. 3:16 ESV). This could inspire our own confession of faith lived in the body:

> In the incarnation, Jesus took our flesh and blood (Heb. 2:14). As a child, he learned to use his hands, feet, and tongue (Luke 2:52). As a man, he worked with his hands (Mark 6:3). He ate and drank joyfully, touched gently, slept peacefully, and resisted temptation faithfully (Matt. 8:3, 15; 9:29; 11:18; 20:34; Luke 8:23; John 2:1–12; Heb. 4:15). As Messiah, his body was an instrument of righteousness (Rom. 6:13) As prophet, he taught and healed with authority (Matt. 7:28; 8:8–9). As king, he ruled over disease, death, even nature itself (Luke 8:22–56). As priest, he suffered in his body, in his flesh, for our sins (Mark 15:19–24; Col. 1:22; 1 Peter 2:24). As Lord, he rose, flesh and bones (Luke 24:39), demonstrating with power that he is Lord and Son of God (Rom. 1:4).
>
> In all this, except his atoning death and resurrection, he left us an example (1 Peter 2:22). So, even though we can't offer ourselves as an atoning sacrifice or perform miracles, we *can* work with our hands, eat and drink joyfully, touch gently, sleep peacefully, resist temptation faithfully, and present our bodies to the Lord as instruments of justice and righteousness.

Many of us grew up in churches that treated the body as something we leave behind when we "die and go to heaven." But that idea owes more to Plato than to the Bible. Scripture says we will have resurrection bodies, like Jesus. We will have perfected flesh and bones forever.

Why do Christians act as if the body is unimportant? Do we think it's just a house for what really matters—the soul? The incarnation and resurrection point us in the opposite direction. God created mankind as a body-soul unity. It's almost impossible to think of ourselves apart from our bodies. Everything we do, we do in the body. My face, voice, shoulders, and arms are more than my body parts. I cannot separate myself from my body, and all that I do in the body matters to the Lord.

Why then do we neglect the body? Do we simply follow our traditions? Maybe we worry about the gap between rhetoric and practice; it's hard to teach about self-discipline when our seams are bulging.

If we are spiritually minded, we should at least care for our bodily lives because so many sins and idols are physical. We turn to food, sleep, and drink for comfort. Sex and sports promise excitement and significance. The quest for pleasure and adventure can supplant the devotion we owe to God. In the body, we steal and fornicate. The sins we commit harm the bodies of others. Oppression impoverishes people, they feel it in their bodies. We also feel the effects of sin in *our* bodies. After the fall, work becomes toil, and birth becomes pain (Gen. 3:14–19).[1] And even if we never harm anyone or commit great physical sins, failure to care for the body compromises our ability to serve God and neighbor. So we should want to use our bodies rightly.

If we want to use our bodies well, we need to view our bodies correctly. So let's spend a few pages summarizing the biblical teaching on the body. We will begin with God's original plan, then the fallen body, the redeemed body, and the body in the age to come. Our labels will be God's design at creation, the status of the fallen body (with a word about secular views of the body), the body redeemed, and the body in glory.

God's Design for the Body at Creation

God created mankind as a body-soul unity. We are not angels—minds without bodies. Nor are we mere animals—bodies without a mind's spiritual self-awareness. We have eternity in our hearts (Eccl. 3:11); ants, dung beetles, worms, birds, and dogs (no matter how we love them) do not.

---

1. Thanks to my editor, Julia Craig, for this point.

Genesis 2:7 says "the LORD God formed the man from the dust of the ground and breathed into his nostrils the breath of life, and the man became a living being." Since our creation, we live in dusty bodies. Flesh, blood, heart, and mind are interdependent. Our bodies are *us*. When we see a friend, we don't say "I see *Mark's body*," we say, "I see Mark."

In the beginning, our bodies were good. Whether Adam and Eve had navels, whether they rippled with muscle or not, we do not know. We *do* know that God tuned our bodies for this world. He equipped the human body to fulfill the creation mandates. God commanded Adam and Eve to marry, have children, work, and rest and then designed our bodies to fulfill these mandates. The Lord created mankind male and female so we could marry, have children, and nurture them (Gen. 1:27–28). He gave us strength to work and fill the earth. That is why Moses can say "Love the Lord your God with all your heart, and with all your soul, and with all your strength" (Deut. 6:5, echoed by Jesus in Matt. 22:37). "All your strength" means we love God with our bodies.

The Status of the Body after the Fall

The fallenness of the body shows itself in two principal ways: in sin and in disease and death. The body isn't just weak or diseased, it bubbles with unruly impulses. We feel strong cravings and destructive desires. The appetite for food, drink, sleep, and sex are good in themselves, but we want them in the wrong place, at the wrong time, in the wrong quantity. Working, sleeping, and eating are good, but we spoil them by doing them too much or too little. One toils and toils, another slouches through life, getting weak and lazy.

We *choose* some bodily sins, but we slip into others. Sexual sin is more common today because we live in a sexualized society. We are *prone* to lust because clothes, advertisements, and pornography *promote* lust. We commit sexual sin because the human sex drive is the same as always, but young adults delay marriage and adults of all ages question the very idea of marriage.

Social and economic forces make it easier to eat foolishly too. The food industry is willing to profit from our flawed tastes. They will supply whatever we demand, if it brings revenue. Taste experts set the portions of fat, sugar, and salt so that the body wants to consume more. Junk food goes into the mouth and down the gullet so easily that it barely registers, in the stomach, that this might be food. French fries, potato chips, and donuts have so little texture and nutrition that they are calorie delivery systems, not real food. The same yearnings that lead us to sweets and caffeine can leap onward to drugs, including nicotine, and drunkenness.

Genesis 3 says physical decay and death entered this world when Adam and Eve rebelled. We certainly see the fall in bodily disease and death. Fevers, aches, and small injuries are so common that we forget that they violate God's original plan. We get common colds and terrible tumors. Bones break, muscles tear, we age, and we die. We wonder why the good die young while our lonely forebears live on and on as twilight fades to black. We groan—and await the redemption of our bodies (Rom. 8:23).

If we want to change the way our culture accelerates the effects of the fall on the body, we need to do more than enumerate and lament our civilization's problems. We can resist social pressures. We can foster better ideas and practices. First, however, we should identify the secular views that drive godless habits.

Secular Views of the Body

As far back as records go, humans have liked alcohol and sex, but certain ancient philosophers thought that moments of pleasure merely interrupt a life dominated by pain. Classical Buddhism says extinction of desire and even of the self is good, since human life is filled with suffering. In Greece, Plato called the body the *prison house* of the soul. Since death releases the soul from bodily pains, we should welcome it.

Later, Plutarch wrote an essay entitled "That Epicurus Actually Makes a Pleasant Life Impossible."[2] Plutarch wrote before the advent of pain relievers, when food was scarce. He observed that hunger goes on and on, but the pleasure of eating lasts only until one is full. Likewise, a bad tooth keeps on hurting, but we don't feel a good one. Whatever pleasure we find, just one part of the body is touched by it. But fire, sword, scourges, aches, heat, cold, and fevers sink into the whole body. Since pleasures are fleeting and pains go on and on, pleasure can never outweigh pain.[3]

The Stoics, of the same era, shared Plutarch's pessimism and had a strategy for it. They resolved to remain unmoved by suffering, so life's inevitable griefs and pains wouldn't trouble them. They kept expectations low and anticipated disappointment. That, they believed, would make life endurable.

Still, some were hopeful. Plato said the body was the soul's *prison house*, but the Neo-Platonists, said the body is the *house* of the soul. Since it is our house, they reasoned, we should treat it well. That thought ultimately leads to hedonism, which commands, "Eat, drink, and be merry, for tomorrow we die" (partially quoted in 1 Cor. 15:32).

Hedonists pursued pleasure, but most Greeks knew the headlong pursuit of pleasure leads to hangovers, dissipation, boredom, and disease. The Epicureans saw this and said the pursuit of pleasure should be *sustainable*. They wanted to eat,

---

2. Plutarch, "That Epicurus Actually Makes a Pleasant Life Impossible," in *Plutarch's Moralia*, vol. 14, trans. Benedict Einarson and Phillip de Lacy (Cambridge, MA: Harvard University Press, 1967), 14:21–27.

3. Plutarch still wanted his pleasures and promoted them, sometimes in strange ways. In a wedding speech, he spent some time justifying the new husband's possible infidelity. Persian kings, he said, eat dinner with their wives. As the meal progresses, the kings get drunk, dismiss their wives and *then* send for the courtesans "This is right because they do not concede any share in their licentiousness and debauchery to their wedded wives." So if a dissolute husband dallies with a paramour or maidservant, "it is respect for her which leads him to share his debauchery, licentiousness and wantonness with another woman." See Plutarch, "Advice to Bride and Groom," in *Plutarch's Moralia*, vol. 2, trans. Frank Cole Babbit (Cambridge, MA: Harvard University Press; London: W. Heinemann, 1927–69), 2:309.

drink, and be merry in moderation so they would *not* die but enjoy pleasure for years.

Still, Stoics, hedonists, and Epicureans had the same goal— the most pleasant life possible. One said, "Seek pleasure"; another said, "Avoid pain"; but they agreed on the centrality of the pleasure/pain calculus. Epicureans judged that some self-denial today could lead to greater pleasure tomorrow. One way or another, each philosophy tried to promote pleasure or manage pain. The terms are different, but this is still the way people think. We can see it in contemporary movies. Anyone could make a list of hedonistic or Epicurean films, but Stoicism is common too. Take *The Princess Bride*, which opens with Westley, a love-smitten farm boy who goes to seek his fortune so he can marry the lovely Buttercup. He becomes a protégé of the Dread Pirate Roberts (a real man, in fact), who teaches Westley martial arts and, apparently, Stoicism.

When, years later, he sees Buttercup, he tells her, "Life is pain, Highness. Anyone who tells you differently is selling something."

And in his great sword fight with Inigo Montoya, Inigo, stunned by Westley's skills, interrupts the conflict to ask, "Who *are* you?

Westley: "No one of consequence."

Inigo: "I must know."

Westley: "Get used to disappointment."

"Get used to disappointment" is popular Stoicism. This is the logic: if we accept disappointment, it won't trouble us and we can live in peace. Greek ideas are common today: hedonists still live for pleasure. They say, "Let's get drunk and go crazy! Who cares about tomorrow?" Epicureans still live for the finer things. They say, "Let's buy some fine wine and let it age." Stoics think, "Life is hard and grief is coming, so prepare."

I recently summarized this for my favorite lay philosopher (my wife). She said, "I see both points. I like pleasure and merriment, like the Epicureans, but I also like to manage disappointment, like the Stoics."

Whether you lean toward pain management or the quest for pleasure, there is more to life than calculations of pain and pleasure. Pleasure, like friendship, finds us when we aren't looking for it, when we're busy at other things. Moreover, our deepest satisfactions often come after intense sacrifice and physical or spiritual pain. We'll never taste the great joys of life if we try to avoid pain. The straight quest for pleasure often leads to disappointment. And if we always try to avoid pain, we will miss life's great achievements. Jesus' way of life is a pattern for us (John 13:16; 15:20). Because he endured great grief, he tasted great glory by redeeming his sons and daughters. That redemption touches our bodily lives, even now.

The Body Redeemed (in This Age)

Christians await "the redemption of our bodies" (Rom. 8:23), but we have tastes of our redemption even now, in the body. Genesis says the body was good when God created it. Since then, Jesus upholds creation "by his powerful word," so we can count on it (Heb. 1:3; see also Col. 1:17). Paul says the Lord is "*for* the body" (1 Cor. 6:13). So our bodies ordinarily work well. Because Jesus sustains the body, hearts beat, muscles contract, and by training we can gain skill and strength.

The Lord also made the body with a capacity for honest pleasures. He wants his people to enjoy bodily life, including food, drink, sex, and exercise. He designed us to eat, drink, run, and play—and to take pleasure in it. Paul spoke about running and wrestling so often that some suppose he must have loved sports.

God wants us to enjoy bodily life. In Genesis, God gave mankind freedom to eat fruits, vegetables, grains, and meat. He told Noah, "I give you everything" (Gen. 9:3 esv). In the Old Testament, some foods were off-limits, but since Jesus came, "all food is clean" (Rom. 14:20; see also Acts 10:15). He *commanded* his people to celebrate their redemption with feasts where they eat and drink "whatever you desire—oxen or sheep or wine or strong drink.... Eat there before the Lord your God and rejoice"

(Deut. 14:26 ESV). Psalm 104 says God supplies needs, then adds pleasures: "wine that gladdens the heart of man, oil to make his face shine" (104:15). Jesus even promises a day when we will eat and drink with him in his kingdom (Luke 22:14–18; Rev. 19:7–9). Solomon blessed laborers who eat and drink joyfully and sleep in peace (Eccl. 5:12, 18). The psalmist and Jeremiah also delight in the way sea creatures and cattle frolic (Ps. 104:26; Jer. 50:11). The Lord also smiles on marriage and sexuality. At creation, Adam and Eve were naked and unashamed, and God told them to have children. Need we say more? Yet Scripture does say more. The Song of Songs *celebrates* romantic love. The woman says, "Let him kiss me with the kisses of his mouth—for your love is more delightful than wine" (1:2). She praises him, head to toe (5:10–16), and delights in his lips, his embrace (2:6; 5:13). He praises her face, body, lips, and smell (4:1–16; 7:1–9).

Here we can lay down two guiding principles—freedom and self-control. We have freedom to eat, drink, sleep, and play. At the same time, we must exercise self-control so that we do these things in the right place, at the right time. So we are free to enjoy sleep, but we exercise self-control by staying awake at work, especially in meetings. Again, we enjoy our God-given sexuality (freedom) within marriage (self-control). (We'll discuss specific ideas for food, drink, exercise, and sleep in the next chapter.)

Religious leaders often call for self-denial. They forbid marriage and restrict food, drink, clothing, and sleep, dreaming that this will gain them God's favor. Paul calls this a "self-made religion" that has "no value" in preventing sin or pleasing God (Col. 2:23 ESV). He condemns those who "forbid people to marry and order them to abstain from certain foods, which God created to be received with thanksgiving by those who believe and who know the truth" (1 Tim. 4:3). We should realize, Paul says, that "everything created by God is good, and nothing is to be rejected if it is received with thanksgiving" (v. 4). We thank God as we eat, drink, and marry, and enjoy the physical gifts God has given us.

I write these words in an early autumn weekend. One morning, my wife and I hiked a hilly trail under a canopy of leaves, capped by a cerulean blue sky. Later, I played tennis with a group of friends from my league. We are mostly in our fifties, but some of us can still hit a ball about one hundred miles per hour. We marvel that our bodies let us play so hard at our age; I take each match as God's gift. That evening, we celebrated the wedding of a deliriously happy bride and groom. The next evening, we shared a meal with friends on our porch. As we ate savory fish and the last of our garden vegetables, we surveyed a dozen varieties of flowers still in bloom—zinnias, roses, canna and stella d'oro lilies, lantana, black-eyed Susans, liriope, and more—and gave thanks for God's bounty. We enjoy it all because "the earth is the Lord's" (Ps. 24:1). Everything in it is good, unless sin corrupts it.

The principle for the right use of God's bounty is simple: "Whether you eat or drink, or whatever you do, do all to the glory of God" (1 Cor. 10:31 ESV). That principle is also a test: As we prepare to eat or drink or enjoy another created gift, let us ask, "Can I offer this act to the Lord? Can I do this to the glory of God?"

These are good questions, because they teach us to thank and praise God throughout life. They are also diagnostic questions, because they keep us from self-indulgence. Wine makes the heart glad (Ps. 104:15), but it can also lead to drunkenness, a sin the Bible condemns many times. Joyful eating can cause gluttony, a lust for more, and a greed for the wealth that finances luxury. So we need to join freedom and self-control.

Jesus shows us how to live with both self-discipline and pleasure. He wasn't prosperous, but for his first miracle, he produced over 150 gallons of fine wine for a wedding feast (John 2:1–11). And he ate and drank so freely that his foes (unjustly) called him a glutton and a drunkard (Matt. 11:19). God designed life's bodily pleasures; we don't *steal* them from him. He designed them for us, and grants them to us with a smile. Our pleasure gives him pleasure.

Of course, our actual bodies falter in many ways. The body is our home (2 Cor. 5:1–10), but the building tilts and leaks. After the banquet comes the bellyache; after the athletic conquest, the sore muscles; after youth, middle age. But God says something better is coming (Rom. 8:22–23; 1 Cor. 15:35–57; 2 Peter 1:13).[4] Jesus came *in* a body and promised to *restore* us, soul and body. We await that day, but until then Jesus has given us signs of our future. By his power and compassion, the blind saw, the lame walked, lepers were cleansed, the deaf heard, and the dead rose (Matt. 11:5). Each miracle gave a glimpse of the future, when brokenness and death end. May we let the pains of the body teach us to yearn for that day.

The Body Redeemed (the Resurrection)

The human body eventually weakens and dies. When the redeemed die, we enter the Lord's presence and await the day when we rise and receive an imperishable body, like his (2 Cor. 5:8). Jesus' resurrection body was recognizable and solid to the touch, yet different, so the disciples didn't recognize him at once (John 20:11–18; 1 Cor. 15:20–28, 42–55).[5] He had scars from the crucifixion and he ate food, but he could pass through walls. We can expect a body like his: powerful; immune from disease, death, or deformity; free from sin and its effects; energetic; and perfectly suited to new life. We will walk, touch, eat, worship, and, most likely, play.[6]

In 1150, Hugh of St. Victor pegged thirty years as the ideal age, when the body is strong, mature, and healthy. Indeed, the body's strength and resilience starts to decline in our thirties (as the rosters of professional athletic teams show). Can you

---

4. Translations of the Greek *skenoma* vary considerably. The ESV, "this body"; the NASB, "this earthly dwelling"; and the NIV, "the tent of this body," are all plausible.

5. The great Italian painter Caravaggio attempted to convey this by giving the risen Lord a face that looked a bit plump next to the gaunt face of Jesus from the hours before his death.

6. Jeffrey Burton Russell, *A History of Heaven: The Singing Silence* (Princeton: Princeton University Press, 1997), 119.

picture bodily life in the new creation? Everyone we see, even our grandparents and grandchildren, will seem to be thirty years old forever. Every eye is clear, every tooth straight, every head lush with hair, every muscle strong, every sinew responsive to the wish of the mind (although there may still be a place for practice, since growth and progress are not evil).

A volleyball enthusiast once asked me a question that might aid the imagination. He asked, "Will there be volleyball in heaven?" How might a game go? Flawless bodies and minds will generate high-caliber play. The first point begins with a jump serve, rocketing over the net, curving toward a corner. The receiving team counters with a flawless dig, a perfect set, and a thunderous spike. But the serving team sees it coming. They block, set, and spike in turn. And so on. After 407 hours, someone shouts, "I want to visit a friend, but maybe I'll be back before you finish the point."

It makes the head spin, but in a delightful way. Again, a little boy once asked his mother, "Will there be pears in heaven?" She answered, "Honey, if you want pears, there will be pears." The answer is wise because it conveys the essential truth: We will no longer suffer misguided desires. Everything we *do* want will be something we *should* want, since all our desires will be good. So *if we want something*—pears or volleyball or sex—then we will have it. If sex, pears, and volleyball are no part of the new creation, we won't miss them—Revelation 21:4 promises the end of sorrow. Instead, we will *want and have* something better. Best of all, like Jesus, our character, will, desires, and actions will be in harmony, causing continual joy and peace (Ps. 16:11).

Questions remain: Will we take naps, not from need, but because they feel good? Will we eat? In fact, Jesus says we will eat and drink when in his kingdom (Matt. 8:11; Luke 22:18), and Revelation blesses "those who are invited to the marriage supper of the Lamb" (Rev. 19:9 ESV). Now feasts mean food, and that may prompt someone to recall something Paul says: "'Food is meant for the stomach and the stomach is meant for food'—and

God will destroy both one and the other" (1 Cor. 6:13 ESV). How can we have a feast without a stomach? The original has a clue. The New Testament has two words that can be translated *stomach*. *Stomachos* means the stomach as the organ that takes in food. *Koilia* is the seat of our cravings for food, drink, and sex (Rom. 16:18; 1 Cor. 6:13; Phil. 3:19). Paul says the *koilia* will be destroyed, not the *stomachos*. So a proper appetite for food and its pleasure, felt by the stomach (*stomachos*), will remain. But the disorderly cravings of the belly (*koilia*) will end. We can expect the pleasures of food, but we will no longer battle gluttony.

Faithful Life in the Body Today

Let's end our thinking about the body with an outline of the Christian life found in Romans 1–8. That outline mentions the body in each major section and describes the way our life in the body reflects our relationship to Jesus and the gospel.

First, Romans 1:18–3:20 describes humanity's sin and rebellion against God. Most specifically, Romans 1:24–26 says the godless dishonor their bodies and indulge "dishonorable passions" (ESV).

Second, Romans 3:21–6:23 describes Jesus' atonement and the renewed life that follows. Romans 6:12–13 says sin once enslaved us, but it reigns over us no more. That change must show in our bodies: "Let not sin therefore reign in your mortal body. . . . Do not present your members to sin as instruments for unrighteousness, but present yourselves to God as those who have been brought from death to life, and your members to God as instruments for righteousness" (ESV).

The word translated *instruments*, *hopla*, ordinarily means *weapons*. That is a potent image. Our bodies, ruled by sin, were weapons for evil. But once redeemed, we can resist sin. As we present our bodies and their powers to God, we become tools or weapons for justice in God's arsenal.

Third, Romans 7 and 8 describe the ongoing struggle with sin. We feel that struggle in the body. Paul says that if the Spirit, "who raised Jesus from the dead dwells in you, he . . . will also give life to your mortal bodies" (8.10-11 ESV). So the body suffers the consequences of sin, but the Spirit renews our bodies. Later, Paul tells us that since we *are alive* by the gift of God's Spirit, we need to act like it, even in the body: "For if you live according to the flesh you will die, but if by the Spirit you put to death the deeds of the body, you will live. For all who are led by the Spirit of God are sons of God" (8:13–14 ESV). Paul knows that even the noblest disciples commit sins, both in and with their bodies. Paul himself says, "I do not do what I want, but I do the very thing I hate" (7:15 ESV). He cries, "Wretched man that I am! Who will deliver me from this body of death?" Jesus will, for there is "no condemnation for those who are in Christ Jesus" (7:24–8:1 ESV). Therefore, even as we groan over our sins, we also "wait eagerly for . . . the redemption of our bodies" (8:23 ESV).

Romans 7 says something essential—it is hard to escape sin, including the sins of the body. The sins we commit in the body readily become patterns or controlling habits. Gluttony and sensuality get a grip on us. Wine can lead from festivity to drunkenness to alcoholism. Sexual thrills, alcohol, tobacco, and drugs become addictions. We need Jesus both to forgive us and to liberate us. He does both, although the liberation may be slow and filled with reversals. As a result, we *can* present our bodies to him. That is a fitting response, since he gave his body for us. We can serve our King with our bodies and so please him (Rom. 12:1). But the consecration of our bodies will always be imperfect.

Jesus is Lord and King over all things, including our bodies. While we want to yield, we need the King's mercy, since our service is always imperfect. If we face our failures, we have made a good start. Jesus said, "Blessed are the poor in spirit" (Matt. 5:3). He blesses those who know their need and take that need to him, asking for grace.

Discussion Questions

1. Why is it hard for you to take care of your body the way you wish? Consider your habits and family history as well as factors at work and in the culture. How can you counteract them?
2. What can you learn about the value and use of your body by meditating on the physical life of Jesus?
3. How do you view the legitimate physical pleasures of life? As something "secular"? As something God doesn't care about, or even disapproves? As the gift of a loving Father? What difference does this make?
4. How does the hope of a resurrection body give you hope? How does it shape your practices today?
5. If you could change one aspect of your daily physical life, what would it be? What resources do you have from your faith—the gospel, the will and the character of God—that could help you make constructive changes?

| 11 |

A Man and His Body: Living Faithfully in Our Skin

In the last chapter, we considered what we ought to *think* about our bodies. Now I want to talk about what we *do*, how we live, in the body. To be human is to have an *embodied* soul or mind. I can hardly think of myself apart from my gender, my voice, my face. What my body does, *I* do. No one says, "My body ran well this morning"; we say, "I ran well." What happens to my body, happens to *me*. No one says, "My body has cancer"; we say, "I have cancer." What is true of my body is true of me. If I cut my finger, I cut *myself*. If my body is exhausted, *I'm* exhausted. If my body feels great, *I* feel great. If my body bubbles with energy, so do I. Life is a body-soul-in-union experience. Since we can't separate ourselves from our bodies, our physical practices change us, whether we realize it or not. When we laze around, eat junk food, take crazy risks, deprive ourselves of sleep, and compensate by pumping ourselves with stimulants, we don't just neglect our bodies, we hurt *ourselves*.

Many passages in the Bible speak of the body when they mean the whole person.[1] When a godly woman poured perfumed ointment on Jesus shortly before his death, he said, "When she poured this perfume on *my body*, she did it to prepare *me* for burial" (Matt. 26:12). To anoint Jesus' *body* is to anoint *him*. Similarly, when Jesus says, "If your eyes are good, your whole *body* will be full of light" (Matt. 6:22), he means the whole *person*, body and

1. See Matthew 6:22–23; 26:12; Luke 11:34–36; 12:4; Acts 9:40; Romans 1:24; 12:1; 1 Corinthians 13:3.

soul, will see clearly. When Paul says, "Present your bodies as a living sacrifice, holy and acceptable to God" (Rom. 12:1 ESV), he charges us to practice genuine devotion the only way we can—in the flesh. To give our bodies to God is to give ourselves to him concretely in daily life. We offer him the acts of mouth, hands, feet, and everything else, head to toe. If, by the mercies of God, we give *ourselves* to the Lord, we give our *bodies* to him.

It's easy to get negative about the body, condemning carelessness (munching chips) and sin (drunkenness), but we should be optimistic. We're *sober* because our bodies break down and we're liable to unruly desires. But we're *optimists* because God created our bodies. Whatever the fall has done to the body, it remains a masterpiece, loaded with potential. By God's design, the body rewards self-discipline and practice. We creak, groan, and die, but Jesus touches our bodies. They will be perfect one day, but even now we can enjoy the physical gifts of food and drink, exercise and fitness, sex and sleep.

Paul says, "So whether you eat or drink or whatever you do, do it all for the glory of God" (1 Cor. 10:31). Again, "Everything created by God is good, and nothing is to be rejected if it is received with thanksgiving" (1 Tim. 4:4 ESV). The goal is *enjoyment without self-indulgence.*

I just spent two weeks in Singapore, a multiethnic country, with fiery and fascinating food from many people groups. I am free to sample every cuisine, but I need to exercise self-control so I don't burn my tender stomach and tongue (which turned black one night, then stung for three days). We *are* free to enjoy food and drink, sex, sleep, exercise, and other physical goods as long as we don't burn ourselves by self-indulgence. We already considered love, marriage, and sex in chapter 4. Now, as we consider other bodily gifts and powers, we begin with exercise and fitness.

Exercise and Fitness

Men like to feel capable and strong. The Lord wants us to be strong too. Unfortunately, men who were tough and athletic in their youth often lapse into weakness and obesity as adults. Most of us have sedentary jobs that demand sitting, talking, thinking, typing, and reading, not physical exertion. Our work doesn't require us to be powerful. And if we own a car, we probably don't *need* to be fit. Our bodies don't have the muscle and skill we rightly desire. A great number of men feel alienated from their own flesh. We don't like the way we look or feel. We want our bodies to look better, hurt less, and function with greater accuracy, speed, and endurance. Does Scripture say anything about this? If so, is exercise and fitness a good idea or a mandate? And what is God's will for those who can't exercise?

I would like to mandate exercise, but perhaps I am biased. I love athletic competition and I need to exercise. Without it, energy flags, concentration lags, and I can get irritable. But I don't want to turn *my* preferences and practices into *your* law, so let me be precise: Scripture doesn't *command* exercise and fitness, but it does *commend* strength and physical self-discipline, including athletic discipline.

In fact, God often commands men to be strong before they enter combat: "The LORD commissioned Joshua the son of Nun and said, 'Be strong and courageous, for you shall bring the people of Israel into the land that I swore to give them'" (Deut. 31:23 ESV). He repeats the command "Be strong and courageous" several times (Deut. 31:7; Josh. 1:6, 7, 9, 18).

It is obvious that men need to be strong when they enter physical battle, but I want to show that it is *normal and good* for men to be potent and fit. Above all, God himself is strong. God the Father has no physical body, of course, but he acts with power in the physical world. The psalms often declare that God is strong (e.g., Ps. 29:1; 81:1; 93:1; 96:6–7; 118:14; 140:7). He also gives his people strength (e.g., Ps. 18:32–39; 28:7–8; 29:11; 68:35). Because God gave David physical strength, he crushed his foes (1 Sam. 17; Ps. 18:32–42). Since God made mankind in his image, we should share his strength.

Further, physical potency is a blessing. Proverbs 20:29 says, "The glory of young men is their strength." When aged Caleb declares himself ready to help conquer Canaan, four decades after he scouted the land for Moses (Num. 13–14), we hear his pleasure when he says, "I am still as strong today as I was in the day that Moses sent me; my strength now is as my strength was then" (Josh. 14:11 ESV). It is good to be strong, whether young or old. We stay that way, as the years pass, by regular physical exertion. As we just saw, God commanded Israel, "Be strong and courageous." We tend to take this as a metaphor for moral or spiritual endurance. But physical capacity is prominent, especially as men prepare to *fight* in Canaan. Moses makes it clear that the people can be strong and courageous because God goes with them (Deut. 31:7–8; Josh. 1:9).

Clearly, "Be strong and courageous" can have a spiritual sense. David commanded Solomon, and Hezekiah charged all Israel, to "be strong and courageous" when great tasks lay before them (1 Chron. 22:13; 28:20; 2 Chron. 32:7; see also Ps. 31:24). But we usually read "Be strong" before *battle*. If a man hoped to be courageous in battle, it helped to be literally, *physically* mighty and capable. To be sure, the Lord can cause panic in heathen armies (Judg. 8; 2 Kings 7), but that doesn't always happen. David's mighty men had both spiritual courage *and* physical strength to fight lions, giants, and vast armies (2 Sam. 23:8–23). Men trusted God *and* expected to fight hard (2 Sam. 10). In Israel's citizen army, mature men were expected to have both faith and vigor to go to battle.

Someone will say, "That's ancient history. Men don't need strength for work or warfare any more. We just read monitors and press buttons." But anyone can see that God created men with a capacity for strength. The body readily becomes stronger and faster with regular exercise. Both men and women respect strength and are drawn to it. Again, "the glory of young men is their strength" (Prov. 20:29). Proverbs 31:17 also praises the strong and dexterous woman: "She dresses herself with strength and makes her arms strong" (ESV). Yes, we can put too much stock in physical strength. That's why Jeremiah 9:23 warns, "Let not . . . the strong man boast of his strength." *But the very warning testifies that strength is desirable.*

Paul respects strength. He compares believers to soldiers (2 Tim. 2:3–4). He compares the Christian life to a battle: "Fight the good fight of the faith" (1 Tim. 6:12; see also 1:18). Some dismiss Paul's references to fights, races, and training as a matter of taste, as if Paul simply liked athletics. But Paul says, "Physical training is of some value" (1 Tim. 4:8)—not supreme value, but *some value.* We should want to do things God calls valuable.

David, Israel's model king, was powerful. While tending his father's flocks, he killed a bear and a lion with his two hands (1 Sam. 17:34–37). Paul's journeys demonstrate his physical capacity. He traveled 8,700 miles by land, on foot, during his known missionary journeys.[2] He had to be tough to endure his treks, beatings, and deprivations (2 Cor. 11:24–27). Jesus was a carpenter (Mark 6:3), so he had skilled hands. The term translated *carpenter* covers men who worked with wood, stone, and metal. If Jesus worked with heavy materials all day, he had to be muscular.

Even if no law *mandates* exercise, it's wise to be strong. Studies show that exercise increases our energy, eases our sleep, releases tension, and sharpens the mind. We typically think, sleep, and work better when we exercise. Exercise probably even enhances endurance at a desk. Furthermore, we can use our strength for the good of others. Suppose we see someone who is injured. We feel like a *man* if we have the stamina to run a mile (*now*, in street clothes) to get help or have the power to carry that person to safety.

Our sedentary habits stand in the way, but the goal is within reach. Our bodies harden when we push them. Most men can jump to a fair number of push-ups and pull-ups each day if they keep at it. A simple pull-up/push-up bar lets us do exercises that fortify most arm muscles in a few minutes. It's easy to add

2. Eckhard Schnabel, *Paul the Missionary* (Downers Grove, IL: InterVarsity Press, 2008), 122.

exercises for core strength. If we work out at a gym, we can make new friends there. If someone wants to change and isn't sure how to start, he can begin modestly, walking ten or twenty minutes, and go from there. We should find a way to move toward health for the whole person—body, soul, mind, and strength.

Sadly, injury, illness, and congenital problems make exercise impossible for some men and women. If this is your condition, I grieve with you. The Lord knows our sorrows; may you know his consolation. Others may think that age or injury or bad habits leave them no hope. But if you can still walk, improved cardiovascular health is in reach. Some of us may never feel *great*, but most of us can exercise and at least move in the right direction.

So then, Scripture doesn't require fitness, but bodily strength is good and it is normal and wise to pursue it. If we sit all day, we can lose contact with the body God gave us. Exercise helps us recover our whole selves, so we can be strong and courageous.

These are personal matters, so I will speak personally. I am sixty and I exercise hard enough, most days, to elevate my pulse and strengthen my core and upper body by lifting weights or doing pull-ups, push-ups, and whatnot. I still play tennis on competitive teams, even if body parts ache or burn after most matches.[3] At six feet and 180 pounds, I inherited a metabolism that lets me eat as I please, but "as I please" includes lots of fruit and vegetables and no donuts, which, in my view, belong at the less alarming end of a scale that also includes cigarettes and cocaine.

Harmful Things People Voluntarily Ingest		
Not so bad, but still …	Pretty bad	Are you insane?
Fries Cake Chips Donuts	Spam Cigars Cigarettes	Cocaine LSD Methamphetamines

3. Tennis players will want to know that my rank is normally 4.0 but sometimes 4.5.

I belong to an accountability group with about fifteen Christian leaders who are roughly my age. These are good and godly men, and we try to stay faithful together. We work hard and carry the privileges and burdens of leadership. Some of us were once athletes; others were not. When we meet, we discuss our ministries, social trends, and important books, but we also report on our families, our emotions, and our bodies. When our bodies betray us, we ask if our problems stem from nature or nurture. Most of us exercise faithfully. Some could run ten kilometers at a moment's notice. Most have stayed in shape, but some have not.

We all see a connection between health, exercise, sleep, and habits with food, drink, and tobacco. We also know the connection is loose. One pastor ran daily but suffered a heart attack at fifty. Another had to give up his favorite sport due to chronic pain. Had he pushed himself too hard? Good habits don't guarantee health and vigor, but the men who neglected their bodies have suffered. A couple of them have type 2 diabetes; another almost succumbed to an addiction. "Jack," a wonderfully talented and dedicated pastor said, "I feel guilty when I exercise. It takes me from God's work, from my calling, and from family and friends for the sake of self-centered, solitary activity." He ate poorly, gained weight, and got diabetes. Eventually, he so compromised his immune system that he nearly died of complications from a common cold when in his late fifties. Stricken to think that we nearly lost him, we chided him for failing to care for himself.

"God didn't give you a body by accident. You are more than a brain attached to vocal cords. Neglect of your body almost killed you. Your lifestyle implies that you think God made a mistake when he gave you a body. He created us with spirit and flesh and designed body and mind to work in harmony."

Jack listened and changed his habits. Now he walks fast and lifts weights. He works less, sleeps more, and feels better. "Mike" is at the other extreme. He runs several miles a day in the hills near his house, lifts weights, chops the wood that heats his home, and plays competitive softball. He describes what he sees in certain fellow professors: "Our work is essentially sedentary, and conference travel and publishing deadlines make life stressful. It's easy to sit at a desk all day, hardly moving, except to get coffee or walk to class. When older professors neglect their bodies, we look pale and lethargic. Without exercise, the mind grows dull too, and scholarly productivity drops off."

Most of us probably hope to fit somewhere between Jack and Mike. Again, disease, accidents, and genetic problems rule out vigorous activity for some children and adults. But almost everyone can at least walk. "Kate" is a professional woman who never played sports or exercised until she reached middle age. She decided to start walking; within a few weeks, she was walking several miles every morning. It keeps her mind sharp and pushes her weight down. She commented, "In these walks, I've been praying. This time of prayer has made the entire process delightful and addictive." Our bodies do tend to respond, once we tell them what we expect.

Let's compare the experiences of Jack, Mike, and Kate. Jack used to feel guilty when he stopped working, but he takes more time for himself and his family now. Mike is a gifted athlete who still loves a strenuous workout. Few of us will try to keep up with him, but we can admire his stamina. Kate exercises moderately, but she and Mike agree that God created us with two natures, the physical and the spiritual, in close union. Whether male or female, whether we love punishing workouts or light routines with friends, we *feel better and serve better* when we eat, drink, and exercise in ways that promote physical health. God designed our bodies to work better and life to go better that way.

No one can say exercise is mandatory. Again, physical discipline has "some value," but not *great* value (1 Tim. 4:8). If you love to exercise, the Lord is pleased. But sports and exercise can become an addiction or an idol. If you think, "Without sports, my life is empty" or "If I can't exercise, I'll die," then sports and exercise are probably an idol.

Athletes should ask themselves: How many hours do I devote each week to training and exercise? Am I as focused on serving God in my work as I am focused on myself in my sports? How many hours do I give to sports? How many to prayer, worship, discipleship, and Christian service? Since spiritual fitness is more important than physical fitness, our schedules should show it. Physical discipline has its great benefit in *this* life, but godliness has everlasting benefits. If getting in shape feels like a losing battle to you, you may be relieved to know that fitness is not *extremely* important. But it is right to care for the body. It is good to keep heart and lungs, arms, legs, and torso strong.

Therefore, unless we are professional athletes, we probably shouldn't spend hours and hours sculpting and training. Still, we should do more than walk to the car or play darts once a month. It is wise to shape our lives so that we demand something of our bodies. Farmers, ranchers, and construction workers have an advantage over desk-bound folk, who should make a habit of exercise, so that they miss it if they skip a couple days. When we exercise regularly, the exertion (normally) feels good. If running is drudgery or the gym is a burden, try a sport or walk briskly. Whatever we do, we should consecrate it to the Lord and enjoy it. If we say God was wise to give us bodies, let's act like it.

Food and Drink

In the last chapter, we said the Bible promotes both joyful freedom and sober self-control as we enjoy things like sex, food, and drink. As we know, Jesus was always willing to attend a dinner party, whether the host was a saintly Pharisee or a flagrant sinner (Luke 14:1; 15:2). Indeed, Jesus so enjoyed a good banquet that his friends asked him why he didn't fast, and his foes called him "a glutton and a drunkard" (Matt. 11:19; see also 9:10–17). We also remember that Jesus created over 150 *gallons* of fine wine to enhance a wedding celebration in John 2:1–12. John's account seems to allude to the prophets, who foretold a day of abundance, when "the mountains will drip new wine, and the hills will flow with milk" (Joel 3:18; see also Amos 9:13). Behind the promise lies the premise that God supplies "wine that gladdens the heart of man, oil to make his face shine, and bread that sustains [or strengthens] his heart" (Ps. 104:15). To be sure, God opposes gluttony and drunkenness. In the law of Moses they are signs of rebellion (Deut. 21:20). Solomon advised the man with a big appetite to "put a knife to your throat" to keep from eating too much (Prov. 23:2). As for drink, "Wine is a mocker and beer a brawler; whoever is led astray by them is not wise" (20:1). Indeed, he said, "The drunkard and the glutton will come to poverty" (23:21 ESV). Scripture condemns drunkenness dozens of times (e.g., Luke 21:34; Rom. 13:13; 1 Peter 4:3).

Isaiah calls out, "Woe to those who are heroes at drinking wine" (Isa. 5:22; see also 5:11–12), yet God's Word never requires total abstinence. Indeed, well-aged wine is a mark of the messianic age (Isa. 25:6). There is no virtue in self-imposed discipline that says, "Do not taste! Do not touch!" (Col. 2:21). It is senseless to abstain from foods God created, "for everything created by God is good," and we should receive it "with thanksgiving" (1 Tim. 4:4–5). But excess spoils everything. "Enemies of the cross" live to sate every appetite. Paul says, "Their end is destruction, their god is their belly" (Phil. 3:18–19 ESV).

Paul links freedom and self-control in Romans 14, where he addresses a debate about food. When he says, "All food is clean," he grants us freedom to eat meat or to abstain, to drink wine or to abstain (vv. 20–21). But if we eat meat, we must do so in faith, convinced that we have a right to do so, thanking God for the meal. If I drink wine, I shouldn't think I'm sneaking something past God. He takes pleasure in our pleasure (vv. 1–23).

But there are limits on our freedom. It may be fine in principle to drink a beer after a basketball game, but if a teammate is an alcoholic, I may choose not to drink in his presence, if that could cause him to stumble and fall (Rom. 14:13–22). Our love for others tempers our freedom (Gal. 5:23; 1 Tim. 3:2).[4]

Similarly, wealth is good in itself, but we are not free to heap up houses, orchards, and vineyards while forgetting the poor (Eccl. 2:1–23; 1 Tim. 5:6). Because our appetites can get the best of us, we need to practice self-denial on occasion. Solomon knew that marriage is good and physical union is good within marriage (Prov. 5:15–20). He should also have known that it's preposterous to have seven hundred wives (1 Kings 11:3–8). Leaders may also choose not to exercise their rights:

> It is not for kings, O Lemuel—
>> not for kings to drink wine,
>> nor for rulers to crave beer,
> lest they drink and forget what the law decrees,
>> and deprive all the oppressed of their rights. (Prov. 31:4–5)

Rest and Sleep

Sleep is sweet and necessary. What bliss to take a cozy nap on a rainy Sunday afternoon; what relief to fall into a warm bed at the end of a hard winter day. Sadly, even simple pleasures like sleep get complicated. If we sleep too much or too little, it becomes a problem. We fall asleep at the wrong times—at work, in class, in worship, at a movie—only to find that we can't sleep at night. Or we lie down at the end of a long, exhausting day and start to relax . . . until an unfinished task comes to mind. Next we recall an emotionally charged conversation. Soon our hearts are thumping and we're wide awake.

> Not to bed, not to sleep, not just yet.
> Duty can wring a final drop of adrenaline from the body's stores.
> So much to do in forty final ticks of frenzy—

---

4. Self-control is also commended in Proverbs 25:28; Acts 24:25; 1 Corinthians 7:5; 2 Timothy 3:3; Titus 1:8; 2:2, 5, 6, 12; 1 Peter 4:7. Self-indulgence is often condemned: Proverbs 31:3–4; Ecclesiastes 2:1–11; Isaiah 5:22; Amos 6:4; 1 Timothy 5:6; James 5:5.

one note to write,
one essay to scan,
one thought to inscribe,
Before I can measure the day and sigh it to a close.

The Body begs to sleep, but
The Mind, that traitor, awakens as it reclines,
Enlisting, as its startled ally,
Emotion, which demands to know
      why he did this
      and she said that.
Dashed hopes and old jealousies drip from the ear and soil the pillow
Defenses fall, insurrections rise, and the king stumbles.

Not to rest, not to sleep, not just yet
      one more line to scan,
      one more thought to scribe,
      one nightmare to still,
Before I can measure the day
      and sigh it, cry it, medicate it, meditate it,
      to a close.[5]

Humans don't curl up and doze off like puppies. Sleep eludes us. The exhausted laborer drops off readily, but the king, despite all his privileges, stares into the darkness. That's why the Bible calls sleep a *gift* (Ps. 127:2). As with most gifts, we need to open our hands and receive it.

I struggle with sleep when I work too late and when my problems are complex and emotional. I may try to power through my tasks by toiling past midnight, but then the day's unfinished business, its unprocessed conversations, surge in. As God's children, we know we *should* be able to sleep without worry. We can entrust ourselves to our Father, who protects us, but it's hard to turn off the mind. Psalm 127 tells us to stop our frantic labors, relax, and go to sleep:

---

5. Dan Doriani, "Sloth," *The Midwesterner*, July 8, 2013, http://www.themidwesterner
.net. Used with permission.

> It is in vain that you rise up early
> > and go late to rest,
> eating the bread of anxious toil;
> > for he gives to his beloved sleep. (Ps. 127:2 ESV)

The original of Psalm 127 is a bit uncertain. The NIV translates, "[God] grants *sleep* to those he loves" (v. 2). The NASB reads, "He gives to His beloved *even in* his sleep." That implies that we can stop working and go to sleep because God works for us *as we sleep*. Whatever the precise translation, the meaning is clear. We can sleep at night because God doesn't. We can slumber because "he who watches over Israel will neither slumber nor sleep" (Ps. 121:3–4). Since the sovereign Lord can either nullify or multiply our efforts, we ought to do our duty, then rest in him. If we trust the Lord to save us forever, we should trust our daily affairs to him and sleep, whether every task is complete or not (Matt. 6:30–34).

The Bible mentions sleep about 150 times. Sleep is often a metaphor: If a man sleeps with a woman, they are intimate. If a man sleeps in the earth, he has died. God also sends visions while people sleep (Gen. 15:12; Job 4:13; 33:15; Dan. 10:9). But usually *sleep* means physical sleep. The main idea is positive: since the Lord is sovereign, we ought to work, then rest, trusting God to watch us as we sleep. There are several more lessons.

First, *sleep is normal and good*. Both heroes and villains sleep. Men as different as Jacob (Gen. 28:11–16), the Canaanite king Sisera (Judg. 4:21–22), and the disciples sleep (Matt. 26:40–45). Jesus slept and ordinary people sleep (Deut. 24:12–13; Matt. 8:24). Sleeplessness is a misfortune. Those who suffer troubles often cannot sleep. Insomnia can strike anyone, even kings like Ahashuerus and Nebuchadnezzar (Esth. 6:1; Dan. 2:1; 6:18).

Second, *it is a blessing to sleep well*. If insomnia is a grief, sound sleep is a blessing. We aren't sharks that must keep moving or die. We sleep well when we feel safe. God says the wise sleep better: "When you lie down, you will not be afraid; when you lie down, your sleep will be sweet" (Prov. 3:24). In the Bible, laborers often sleep better than kings. "The sleep of a laborer is sweet, whether he eats little or much" (Eccl. 5:12). Honest labor brings honest sleep. As practical counsel, if we can't sleep, we may need more exercise, since the human body is made for it.

Third, *we must control our sleep*. Excessive sleeping is sloth. To sleep at the wrong time shows a lack of vigilance. Israel's sentinels must not sleep (1 Sam. 26:12; Isa. 56:10; cf. Judg. 16:14–20). At times, Jesus prayed through the night (Matt. 14:23–25). Tragically, the disciples slept on the eve of Jesus' betrayal, even though he asked them to watch and pray with him (Matt. 26:40–45). Paul tells us to wake up when there is work to do: "For you are all . . . children of the day. . . . So then let us not sleep, as others do, but let us keep awake and be sober" (1 Thess. 5:5–6 ESV).

Fourth, *too much sleep is a sign of laziness*. "As a door turns on its hinges, so a sluggard turns on his bed. The sluggard buries his hand in the dish; he is too lazy to bring it back to his mouth" (Prov. 26:14–15). The result will be disaster: "How long will you lie there, O sluggard? . . . A little sleep, a little slumber, a little folding of the hands to rest, and poverty will come upon you like a robber, and want [or scarcity] like an armed man" (Prov. 6:9–11 ESV). A farmer earns disgrace if he sleeps during the harvest, when there is work to be done (Prov. 10:5; 20:13).

Fifth, *control of sleep is a sign of dedication*. King David vowed, "I will allow no sleep to my eyes" until he completed a task God appointed (Ps. 132:1–5). Uriah, a captain in David's army, refused to sleep in his own bed while his troops were in the field. By contrast, David took a nap at the wrong time and awoke to a temptation he couldn't resist (2 Sam. 11:2–13). The apostle Paul's work brought him sleepless nights (2 Cor. 6:5; 11:27). Once he spoke all night to a group of leaders that he would never see again (Acts 20:7–12).

Sixth, *to go to sleep can be an act of faith*. If the Lord has redeemed us eternally, we can trust him with the details of life.

Then we can say, "I will lie down and sleep in peace, for you alone, O LORD, make me dwell in safety" (Ps. 4:8).

Restful sleep is a gift. Solomon promised, "Your sleep will be sweet," if we embrace God's wisdom (Prov. 3:24). After God made great promises to Jeremiah as he slumbered, he said, "At this I awoke. . . . My sleep had been pleasant to me" (Jer. 31:26; see also Ezek. 34:25).

So the right use of the body includes the right use of sleep. We don't toil endlessly, as if we save ourselves, neither do we sleep whenever we feel a bit drowsy. There is a time to discipline our bodies and finish our work, and a time to go to sleep, even if a task is incomplete. May the Lord grant us discernment in this and every other use of our bodies.

Speaking of the right use of sleep, it's 12:30 a.m. just now, and the jet lag from Singapore is piling onto my normal weariness. I have more notes, but I need to follow my own advice. I've written enough and I'm tired. If I failed to say something important, may the Lord lead you to whatever you need to know. When you turn the page, I'll be awake again. Till then, may he bless you as I sleep zzzzzz . . .

Discussion Questions

1. How much do you exercise? Are you strong enough and fit enough? What might you do to get (or stay) in good or better shape?
2. What can we learn about food-, drink-, and sleep-related physical gifts from the way Jesus ate, drank, and slept?
3. Surveying the teachings of Scripture on wine, how do you think you should handle wine and other alcoholic beverages?
4. How much do you sleep? How well do you sleep? How can faith in our loving and providential Lord help you sleep better?
5. The Lord created the physical body, took a physical body, and promised to redeem our bodies. How does our faith in him shape everything we do in the flesh?

| 12 |

A Man and His Play

The award-winning movie *Chariots of Fire* tells the story of two runners in the 1924 Olympics. Harold Abrahams is a serious runner. Long before it became standard, Abrahams and his coach analyzed, dissected, and reconstructed his running style to achieve a tiny advantage that would lead to victory in the 100-yard dash. When his girlfriend, who senses his joylessness in the sport, asks why he runs, he replies, "I'm more an addict. It's a compulsion, a weapon." A Jew, he runs for Britain, not from love of running, but to prove his worth and to overcome anti-Semitism. The Olympics are not fun, they are agony. In the film, hours before the Olympic finals, he tells his coach and confidant, "I have ten lonely seconds to justify my existence." In real life, just before the race, he said he felt "like a condemned man feels just before going to see the scaffold." In fact, Abrahams won his race, set a world record, and gained the social acceptance he sought. A little later, he sustained an injury and quit running. It had achieved its purpose.

The second runner, Eric Liddell, smiles and laughs as he runs, drinking in its pleasure even in fierce competition. Liddell and his sister Jenny are Scottish Christians dedicated to mission work. Jenny fears that Eric's love of running will lure him from that commitment. One blustery day they go for a walk, and Eric pledges that he *will* go to China for missions. Yet, to her dismay, he declares that he has a lot of running to do first. He explains, "Jenny, you've got to understand it. I believe that God made me for a purpose—for China. But he also made me fast. And when I run I feel his pleasure. And it's not just fun. To win is to honor him." Liddell wins too, the 400-yard dash, then returns to China as he said he would. Once there, he continued to minister and to run until his death in a World War II internment camp.[1] The story of Abrahams and Liddell illustrates both the joys and the riddles of sports, exercise, competition, and play. Games are supposed to bring joy and "recreation" (re-creation) to its participants. At best, we engage in play for the pure pleasure of it. Then God delights in our delights; our "lawful pleasures" are his.[2] Yet, for too many of us, sports and games have become a mirthless exercise. Competition brings out the best and the worst in us. As we strive to prove and improve ourselves, we subject ourselves to pressures that are too much like work.[3]

Play is more than sports and competition. Play can begin with the squirt of a water pistol and end with water hoses blasting everyone. It includes a child playing house or friends playing keep-away with a ball in a pool. It includes the silly games fathers make up for their children, like Gatekeeper, Shirt, Monkey Baby, Crab Arm, and Tickle Button to name a few.[4]

Gatekeeper (ages 2 to 7). An adult, the gatekeeper (or troll), lies down, kneels, or stands in a doorway or hallway. He tells the children, in an ominous voice, "You shall not pass." The children then try to slip past or run over the gatekeeper/troll. The gatekeeper may let the child pass easily or only after Herculean effort, according to the ability and expectations of the child. A child can opt out of the struggle and pass freely at any point by paying the fee (a Cheerio perhaps).

Shirt (ages 2 and up). A father "wears" his daughter or son like a shirt. She puts her arms around his neck as he pretends to eat ice cream or pie. Alas, he spills something on his shirt. He needs

1. Liddell features briefly and very positively in Langdon Gilkey's brilliant record of that camp, *Shantung Compound* (New York: Harper & Row, 1966).

2. Leland Ryken, *Redeeming the Time*, (Grand Rapids: Baker, 1995), 118–19; Thomas Adams, *The Works of Thomas Adams* (Edinburgh, 1861), 3:134.

3. Gary Warner, *The Competition* (Elgin, IL: David C. Cook, 1979).

4. Game possibilities are almost unlimited. In building games, children fashion visible forts that foes try to breach, or hideaways that no one can find. There are throwing games, games of food and drink, games of running, and games of being still.

to scrub or spray the stain away (ticklishly). When that fails, he has to wash his shirt, which he dumps into an imaginary washing machine. The machine sprays, tumbles, and spin-dries the shirt. After that, he hangs the shirt on a wash line, where it is buffeted by the wind. Finally, the shirt is hand-ironed, folded up, and put away.

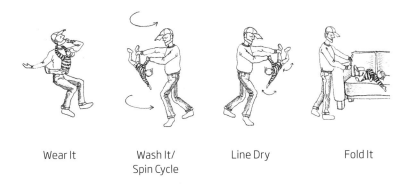

Wear It   Wash It/   Line Dry   Fold It
                       Spin Cycle

Monkey Baby (ages 3 and up). In the forest, monkeys generally don't carry their young. Instead, almost from birth, monkeys cling to their mothers as they swing through the trees. As the game begins, the father exhorts his child, "Hold on, monkey baby!" and then bounces around the house as if swinging on vines. The child holds on as long as possible, lest he fall to the floor, which is, of course, a raging, alligator-laden river. The vigor and length of the swinging vary with the age and strength of the child. The parent may become energetic to break the grip of the stronger child.

Swinging through   "Hold on,
the forest   monkey baby!"

Crab Arm (ages 4 and up). Children hide in the house as the slow-moving but fierce-visaged Crab Arm stalks them, calling out, "Claw of the crab will *pinch* you" (Crab Arm usually has a foreign accent). When Crab Arm, whose right limb and hand are frozen in a crab-like pose, finds a child, the child may run away, but Crab Arm lumbers after him, wailing, "Crab Arm is coming to pinch you."

Tickle Button (ages 3–9). This game rests on two facts: (1) children like to be tickled, and (2) there are especially ticklish spots at the knee, waist, and shoulder. It's most fun when an adult tells a child, "You have a tickle button, and I can find it—without even touching you—if you hold still." The adult then waves his hands near the child. Loaded with anticipation, the child may collapse in laughter the moment the adult finally presses his tickle button.

Play needs no justification, but lots of child play has benefits. Monkey Baby builds strength or endurance. In Wheelbarrow, father or mother holds the legs of a child, whose arms function as wheels as they go through the house. In Tree, a father's arms and legs become branches as his child slowly climbs up until she sits on his shoulders. In Bounce, a father throws a school-aged boy high in the air again and again. As the child touches down, he joins father in springing upward.

Some games teach lessons. Occasionally, after we played Monkey Baby, I said, "The game Monkey Baby is fun, but you know I would always hold on to you in real life. And Jesus holds onto us too. He never lets us go."

The Definition of Play

"Play is a *voluntary* and *absorbing* activity engaged in for the enjoyment it gives," without regard for the results.[5] *Voluntary* means we cannot *force* someone to play. The statement "I don't want to play" has a certain finality.

5. The quote is from Carmen Renee Berry, *Are You Having Fun Yet?* (Nashville: Thomas Nelson, 1992), 43, but this discussion owes more to Robert K. Johnston, *The Christian at Play* (Grand Rapids: Eerdmans, 1983), 31–49.

Enjoyment means play is an attitude. Two children can rake the same leaves, but if one frowns and rakes to finish his chores, he works. If the other smiles and heaps up foliage so he can dive into it momentarily, he plays. When we play, it's safe to make mistakes. After all, it's only a game. Play absorbs us, not because something depends on it, but because it is delightful.

Absorbing means the whole person—body, mind, and emotions—participates in play. Play offers wholeness for adults who perform mindless physical work or disembodied mental work all day. By engaging both mind and body, it refreshes and enlarges the spirit.

Without regard means that while play produces benefits, we don't play *for* those benefits. When we play "bucking bronco" at home or bocce ball with friends on the beach, we don't calculate whether the expenditure of time and effort matches the benefits. Play stands outside the normal world of clocks and calculations. Time seems suspended when we play. Sometimes we lose track of it; sometimes it stands still. It can make sense to hurry at work, but not at play. Hurrying would ruin everything. Play is meaningful in itself. It justifies and rewards itself. But play does bless us. It pushes us to explore the world and to form bonds with new people. Play offers a respite from the tyranny of work and routine. Peak performances give us a glimpse of perfection, of eternity (and pitiful performances make us yearn for perfection in a different way). Play has many lessons to teach us, but that is not why we play. We play for the fun of it.

The Purity of Play

There is nothing quite like play. Play shares features with sports, competition, and exercise. It overlaps with rest and leisure, but there is nothing exactly like play.

Yet having fun gets complicated. The wealth of Western societies should liberate leisure activity as never before, yet we feel that we have less leisure than ever. And when we do have free time, we can't decide what to do. Should we adopt the Greek

ideal, that leisure time should be dedicated to self-improvement—
ennobling music, literature, exercise, and contemplation? Or
should we adopt the Roman model and passively watch entertainments and spectacles? If so, are the critics right when they
say that mass entertainment anesthetizes us to the pain and
emptiness of daily life?

The Greek view can lead to leisure that feels a lot like work.
But the Roman view can lead to leisure that looks like waste.
And even as the Romans perverted their leisure with gladiatorial
games and other debasing entertainments, we degrade ourselves
with depraved television shows and movies, not to mention pornography. The Colosseum's masses cheered injuries in battles,
but we find ways to injure ourselves with our recreational activities, don't we?

People think about sports, competition, rest, leisure, games,
and exercise more than ever these days, but I want to focus on
play. Play is part of sports, competition, and the rest, but play
is narrower and purer. Strange as it may seem, there is serious
theoretical reflection on play. Some issues are important, but I
have put them in this chapter's "Word on the Nature of Play."
Maybe the essence is this simple: it's good to play, so good that
God built it into his creation.

God Wove Playfulness into Creation

God's creation reveals his playfulness. Frolicking otters and
puppies, colorful salamanders, and clown fish all display his
exuberance and wit. The sheer diversity of colors, sounds, and
smells shows God's playfulness. Psalm 104:26 says God created
leviathan to frolic in the sea. Wild animals play in the hills,
declares Job 40:20. But alas, sin and the fall taint everything,
even play.

The Perversion of Play

Play certainly goes wrong in many ways. Some adults don't
play enough. They are too alienated from their bodies to try

sports. They work so hard and worry so much that spontaneity drained from their lives long ago. They feel guilty when they relax, so that they work hard even at their leisure. Some are too harried by social engagements to play. Others waste their leisure, leafing through magazines, drifting across the Internet, and flipping through vapid television programs.

Some want to play all the time. Students fail in college due to video game addictions. Adults lose jobs for playing games on their computers during work. A certain kind of man plays too hard. He has to win, to prove himself. A loss is a blow to his fragile ego. Losing makes him angry and sullen. He even cheats in order to win.

We can play for the wrong reasons. People play to escape, to get away from work, to get away from home, to flee their meaningless lives. They live for the weekend. Play becomes an idol, as they find an identity in low golf scores or rock-climbing skills.

Many men only play vicariously. They play through their children, dreaming that their child can achieve the glories that eluded them. They compel their children to practice sports until the joy of childhood flees, until they injure themselves.

Some play through local teams. They feel that the star's touchdown or home run was theirs. Fanatical spectators can let passion for the achievements of a sports hero blind them to their own lack of achievement (brilliantly if painfully portrayed in the 2009 film *Big Fan*). Fans yearn to know ever more about their sports heroes but come to know ever less about themselves. Men walk around, moping and sullen, for days after someone on their football team drops a pass at a critical moment. Their soul withers and dies (temporarily) because a teenager who attends the nearby university and suffers an excess of human growth hormone misses a foul shot in the final seconds of a basketball game. Someone needs to shake these men and tell them the truth: "The players don't know you. They don't care about you. If they did know you, they would not be your friends. They aren't from around here. They live here because someone offered them money (or a scholarship) to play here. Stop worrying about the speed and musculature of strangers. Get up, dust the potato chips off your belly, go outside, and have some fun."

Spectator sports have their defenders. They point out that sports teams foster community and let unexpressive men shout for joy and weep in sorrow.[6] But surely it is better to form community around relationships than around figures on a screen. Surely it is better to express our feelings daily, not once a week during football season. Surely, if we can choose between watching and playing, we should choose play.

The follies of play are numerous, but play can be immoral, not just foolish. Play goes astray when it indulges "the flesh" with licentiousness and carousing (Gal. 5:19–21). Play offends God when it includes obscene or coarse talk (Eph. 4:29; 5:4). Such jesting degrades everyone—the speaker, the hearer, and the object of the jokes. Play can be hedonistic and self-indulgent: "Eat, drink and be merry" (Luke 12:19; see also 1 Cor. 15:32).

Ecclesiastes teaches that there is ultimately no pleasure when we live for nothing but pleasure. "I refused my heart no pleasure. . . . Yet when I surveyed all that my hands had done . . . everything was meaningless, a chasing after the wind" (Eccl. 2:1–11). Amos says the quest for pleasure leads to boredom and a vain search for distractions. In his day, prosperous Israelites lapsed into "refined and sophisticated triviality" as they stretched out on couches, sang idle songs, and drank bowls of wine (Amos 6:4–6).[7]

Sports display the fallenness of play all too often. Excess competitiveness leads to cheap shots and flared tempers. The desire to win even leads athletes to cheat. Some take performance-enhancing drugs, others bend the rules to their advantage. For example, tennis players must cover *their* side of the net when they call the lines, so they must call their opponent's shots in or out.

6. David Holmquist, "Will There Be Baseball in Heaven?" *Christianity Today,* January 10, 1994, 29–30.
7. Ryken, *Redeeming the Time,* 183–89.

Honor requires players to call the lines honestly, but sometimes the desire to win is too strong. I once played a tight doubles match with first place in a men's league on the line. After splitting the first two sets, my partner and I played a strong third set. But one player from the other team was keeping the match close by calling so many of our good shots "out" that his own partner yelled at him to quit cheating. Eventually we were ahead 5–3, with the cheater serving. My partner put away an overhead for our advantage. Now the cheater served to me with the match on the line. His serve came in hard but waist high to my forehand. I swung hard but a little late, so that the ball rifled over the net, beyond the server's reach, near the line. We held our breath, then released it, as the ball landed inside the line by about eight inches. We had won the match and headed toward the net for the traditional handshake. But after a long delay, the cheater called the ball out. We were stunned. Unable to stand another lie, I exploded "Out? That ball was in by a foot and you know it." Guilty and dumbfounded, he replied, "Well, it might have been in by a few inches, but not a foot." He practically confessed, "Yes, I cheated, but not *that* much."

Why would anyone cheat while playing a *game*? Yet most men can remember a time when they cheated because somehow they felt that they had to win. Sadly, we find more meaning in winning than playing.

So we pervert play, but the perversions are not the essence of play. To base our attitude toward play on its abuses is like basing a book about humanity on prison visits. Everything God creates is good, but open to corruption. Play is fallen, but redeemable.

The Redemption of Play

All men enjoy play, but Christians should be most free to play, for three reasons. First, as we noted in an earlier comment on frolicking animals, God the Creator has woven playfulness into his world. Second, God the Redeemer liberates us from burdens that impede play. Third, God the Provider permits play. He showers his grace on all, so everyone can play, but believers should be first to play.

After working six days, God rested one, establishing our pattern for leisure and rest. By putting a boundary on work, he censured the urge to get and spend, get and spend. It permits us to sleep, play, and worship, to find contentment in what we have.[8] The Gospels have no record of Jesus playing as a child.[9] Yet he shows his Father's commitment to rest rather than endless labor (Mark 6:30–32). Moreover, Jesus went to enough parties to be called "a glutton and a drunkard" (Matt. 11:19; Luke 7:34). We can even see playfulness in some of his teaching. In Matthew 23:24, he says the Pharisees, in their effort to keep their food pure, will "strain out a gnat but swallow a camel." The image is witty, but Jesus plays with words too. The original words were, "You strain out a gamla [gnat], but swallow a kamla [camel]."[10] It doesn't always translate well, but there is humor in the Bible.[11]

God's Grace Liberates Play

If creation encourages honest play, faith liberates it. Margaret Mead observed that "within traditional American culture . . . there runs a persistent belief that all leisure [and play] must be earned by work and good works." Further, while we can enjoy play and leisure, "it must be seen in a context of future work and good works."[12] But grace liberates us from the impulse to earn everything.

The redeemed man understands he cannot *earn* the right to rest. Indeed, the gospel says we cannot truly earn anything. But

8. Ibid., 165–67; Josef Pieper, *Leisure: The Basis of Culture* (New York: Pantheon, 1952), 51–60.

9. Apocryphal stories are shallow and demeaning to Jesus. Jesus was a normal child, so we assume he played, but we have no record of it. The Bible is the account of redemption, not the cure for curiosity.

10. Robert Stein, *The Method and Message of Jesus' Teachings* (Louisville: Westminster John Knox Press, 1994), 13; Craig Keener, *Commentary on the Gospel of Matthew* (Grand Rapids: Eerdmans, 1999), 551–52.

11. For example, when the Philistines capture the ark of the covenant, the statue of Dagon, their deity, keeps falling down (and losing body parts) as if to worship before God's ark. The Philistines have to prop him up again and again. See also the account of David feigning insanity in the court of Achish (1 Sam. 21).

12. Margaret Mead, "The Pattern of Leisure in Contemporary Culture," in *Mass Leisure*, ed. Eric Larrabee and Rolf Myersohn (Glencoe, IL: Free Press, 1958), 10–12.

when we trust in God, he gives us rest. He also gives us significance through our union with him. Neither past nor future works can make us worthy of this. All is a gift of grace. Therefore we don't play to justify our existence. Instead, when we play we feel his pleasure. For the disciple, play is celebration, not distraction. Of course, our lives can seem miserable and insignificant. But we do not deny our miseries. In the gospel, we face our sin and inability and rejoice that God overcame them for us. We do not play after *we* work, we play after *God* works.

If so, then while the Lord's Day remains first a day of worship and rest, it also becomes a good day to play. I cannot favor Sunday leagues and tournaments that eliminate corporate worship and rest, but I can support casual play. When friends or family toss a Frisbee in the backyard, no one is competing. We relax and celebrate life together. To play on Sunday is to play on the first day of the week. Most of the United States thinks we work five days, then rest and play on the weekend. But believers know we start the week with rest and worship, and even play, *before* we work. We do not earn our play with good works. Play, like rest, is a divine gift.

And like rest, play can turn our hearts toward heaven. Its pleasures foreshadow eternal pleasures at God's right hand (Ps. 16:11). Its timelessness, its absence of hurrying hints at eternity. Our lack of skill can stir a yearning for perfection. Even the decline in our skills and the aches in our bones can teach us to long for the new creation.

God's grace liberates play, but with play, as in all of Christian living, there is still a place for law, *following* grace. Grace permits play, but without law, play is impossible. The prime law is love for our neighbor, respect for our partner in play. Because players have partners, we must exercise self-restraint. We refuse to play solely for self-gratification. For example, in a playful water fight, we forbid malice and bullying. The fastest person has to *let* the slowest person douse him, too.

We embrace the rules that govern play. Sports need boundaries and procedures. Even make-believe has its ways; the play has to strive to imitate reality. Even playing tea party, a child has the right to say, "No, that's not the way you do it."

God's Providence Permits Play

Play is an activity born of abundance. When someone is starving or homeless, he can hardly play. We are free to play occasionally because we believe God will provide for us. We play freely when we feel confident that he will meet our needs.

That is why play is especially an activity of childhood. Children are free to play because someone else is working, handing them food, clothing, shelter, and affection. Perhaps beloved children understand play better than adults because the flow of parental gifts has taught them they live by gifts, not by the sweat of their brow. They know their parents are working, even when they are not. A father's gracious provision lets his children play.

After a death or a season of illness, depression, or unemployment, people need to rediscover play. Jesus promised we would face trouble, but he didn't foretell unmitigated sorrow. Our Father gives good gifts to his children. Those who have suffered long need to break free from a mindset of deprivation. We relax and play again.

Play through the Ages

For centuries, the church was wary of pleasure, so the great theologians of the past have not advocated play. Augustine recognized that the normal desire to be happy readily causes men to live for pleasure. That, says Augustine, can lead away from God, in whom we find real joy. Good things such as food, drink, music, art—even the love of a friend—become dangerous, since our love of these pleasures lets them control our souls. Whether they lead to gluttony, drunkenness, and adultery or not, they can lead to affections that substitute for love of God.[13] For Augustine, conversion to Christianity meant conversion from hedonistic self-indulgence. (He even questioned the pleasure of idle curios-

---

13. Augustine, *Confessions*, trans. Henry Chadwick (Oxford: Oxford University Press, 1998), 56–61, 196–216, chapters 4:4–7; 10:21–37.

ity, the appetite to know something for its own sake.) If every pleasure is dangerous, since it can lead us away from God, then play is dangerous. According to Augustine's worldview, if play is simply a delightful activity, it is suspect.

This line of thought persisted for over one thousand years and owes more to Greek philosophy than to Scripture. Many medieval theologians shared Augustine's concerns, but others supported festivals and celebrations. Calvin was austere, but he favored lawn bowling, even on Sundays. The Puritans have a reputation for despising sports and dancing, and they did hold a strict view of the Sabbath, but they never objected to good food or beer, and they blessed good music and exercise the other six days a week.

Today, everyone seems to love good times, yet for all the preachers who announce, "God just wants you to be happy," many Protestants still think like Augustine. We enjoy pleasure, but feel uneasy about it. So we make pleasure a reward for hard work. Or we play for refreshment before the next onslaught of deadlines. We justify our sports as a way to stay fit, release tension, make contacts, or meet unbelievers. Must we always be goal-driven? Can't we say, "I like to play."

Five Suggestions to Improve Our Play

Get out and play. Men in their thirties, forties, and fifties don't play as they once did. Bones ache and schedules tighten. We arrive home late and weary. We slump onto the sofa, devouring the news and sports in the data delivery system we judge most convenient. Resist, my brothers. Years ago, I made a commitment. If I have a choice between playing and watching others play, I will play, every time (except maybe for premium tickets to the World Series). I will not watch sports on television, if I can get up, get out, and play. Will you join me?

The key here (as we said in the chapter on friendship) is to form and cultivate *practices* that encourage play. Plan to play with your children when you come home from work or at set times in the day. Make it so regular that when you skip it, everyone feels it. Find games, formal or informal, physical or mental, that you like to play with your friends. I have friends that remind me of certain games—whether tennis, ultimate Frisbee, bocce ball, or Boggle. We've played so often that it's easy to keep it up. These are practices that help me keep playing, and I am thankful for them, especially when work is tiresome.

Lighten up. Even if we do keep playing sports, our ability declines over time. Further, men who excel at a sport are too cool to say so. Stars will concede, "I play a little." At most they offer the nonchalant oxymoron, "I'm a serious player." What does that mean? Play keeps us light on our feet and light in our hearts. When they were young, my children liked to play restaurant. They crafted colorful menus with huge decorations but few items:

Crakers $2.00
Stake $3.00
Soup $2.50

The waitress always had an accent from Germany or Scotland. After initial politeness to the customers (Gortha Flinderpotts and Sicily Syzygy), she got bossy, "What will you have, dearies? Hurry up. I can't wait here all day while you decide if you want broccoli or cauliflower!" But the menu and prices slowly became realistic. At one point, an eleven-year-old daughter and her friend designed a catalog center with such accurate images and prices that they seemed ready to start a business, if only they could find a naive venture capitalist.

As we get older, our play looks more like work. We press to win, to stay fit, to improve our skills. If we really play, it's safe to make mistakes. We don't have to prove anything. When we work, we must fulfill our duties and accomplish our tasks. But players are free. *Players* don't force themselves into grueling workouts. If we sweat, it's because we love the game enough to play hard.

Enjoy yourself. Play means skipping instead of walking, bouncing instead of standing still. Players don't put their shoes away; they try to throw them up the steps, over the staircase, and into their bedroom. They clap and dance if they succeed. It's hard to sing or play when we are sad. The Israelites couldn't sing the songs of Zion when they lived in Babylon (Ps. 137:1-4). But when they returned to their land, their "mouths were filled with laughter" and their "tongues with songs of joy" (Ps. 126:1-2). The Lord puts songs in our hearts and voices. He richly gives us all things for our enjoyment (1 Tim. 6:17-19).

Augustine and Aquinas thought Christians should never do anything—eat or kiss or play music—for pleasure, since pleasure encourages the lusts of the flesh. They were wrong. The Song of Songs praises romantic love. Ecclesiastes says it is a gift of God to find pleasure in food and drink (2:24-26; 3:12-14). Paul says everything is good if consecrated by the word of God and prayer (1 Tim. 4:4-5). "When God gives any man wealth and possessions, and enables him to enjoy them, to accept his lot and be happy in his work—this is a gift of God" (Eccl. 5:19).

Christians don't live for pleasure (Prov. 21:17; 1 Tim. 5:6), but pleasure is good in itself. Moses commanded Israel to use part of its tithes for the poor and for priests, but part for a feast in God's temple. "Buy whatever you like: cattle, sheep, wine or other fermented drink, or anything you wish. Then you and your household shall eat there in the presence of the LORD your God and rejoice" (Deut. 14:22-29). We have gone far wrong when teenagers sign up for school sports, less to play the game than to build a résumé for college applications.

Get involved, body and mind. Card games and board games like chess are mostly mental, but ideally, play engages both mind and body. This is most obvious when we play music or play charades. But for the millions whose main physical exertion at work involves tapping a keyboard, play often creates a blessed re-union with their bodies. Sadly, we can become estranged from our bodies, especially as we age. They hurt in strange places; they get lumpy and gray. They bungle familiar tasks and forget old skills. When we play, we call our bodies back into active service. If we play enough, dormant talents return. At best, play absorbs the whole man, from balding head to aching heels. Players leave ordinary space and sail into another world.

If you can't play, at least be playful. Some men retire in their fifties to perfect their golf game, but for the rest, the older we get, the less we play. Yet, as responsibilities and burdens add up, we need to play as much as ever. Part of the cure is fostering a playful spirit while we work.

If your son's music sounds like a chain saw buzzing through barbed wire, don't shout, "Turn off that noise." Give him a wink and say, "Ah, the song of the week." Professional athletes work hard at their game. Despite the risk, some insert a "love of the game" clause in contracts, saying they can play their game anytime, anywhere. Preachers have the sober responsibility of pointing out the sins of mankind. But we can condemn them from the pulpit's heights, or we can step down to laugh at ourselves occasionally. Playfulness means taking opportunities to have fun. People can be playful and productive—perhaps more productive—at work.

I once sat with friends in the bleachers at a dull baseball game. A couple of women asked, "Can you watch our seats while we go to the concession stand?" then left for about an hour. We proposed ever more extravagant explanations for their disappearance, then settled on a play on words. They had gone looking for the rarest sort of concession stand, the one that offers apologies. We wondered about the menu and prices:

I'm so sorry	$4.50
I admit that I was wrong	$6.75
It was all my fault	$9.25
All right, all right, you win	$11.00

Conclusion

We could debate whether the last conversation was play or not, but play is like that. It's hard to analyze because it's both an action and an attitude. Two athletes can run side by side, yet one is playing, the other toiling. Two lecturers can speak a room apart. One wields his dullness like a weapon, bludgeoning his stupefied audience to sleep. The other uses wit and imagination to engage his partners in a dance through a topic.

Playfulness is a way of life. It means not taking everything too seriously, not acting as if everything rides on us. Lightheartedness is never escape or denial. We know who we are—sons of a playful God. The redeemed play without guilt because we know we don't need to justify our existence by our good works. We know our heavenly Father will provide for us, so we can play, at least occasionally, like his little children.

Discussion Questions

1. How often do you play? If you don't play enough, are the obstacles external (e.g., your schedule) or internal (e.g., loss of a playful heart)? How can you restore and refresh play in your life?

2. Do you prefer to play or to watch others play? Explain and evaluate your answer.

3. Why do many men feel they must win when they play? What would you say to such a man?

4. Why do we play? Do you see play as a diversion? A reward for hard work? A reflection of God's nature? A divine gift? Does your view of play affect the way you play?

A Word on the Nature of Play

In a way, the notion of thinking hard about play seems strange. Do we need to analyze play? Who wants to think hard or read a book about play when it's sunny outside? If we form a theology of play, will it make half the readers feel self-righteous, because they do it right, and the other half feel guilty, because they do it wrong? For adults, half the joy of play is that we *stop* analyzing and do what comes naturally. Besides, didn't we master play as children and move on? Maybe we could say everything in ten words: "Go out and play. It will be good for you." But sin and the fall taint everything, even our play. To enjoy the garden of play as God intended, we need to pull the weeds that can choke it.

When we watch children, puppies, or otters at play, we realize that God wove playfulness into his creation. Although we often bury it, it can still surface in adults. As the main chapter says, play is an activity of abundance and of trust. We play when we know we have what we need to live. We thank God that he often sends us abundance and that he promises to supply what we need. That lets us play. Again, play is a voluntary and absorbing activity. We play for pleasure, for its own sake, without regard for the results. Play should be joyful and relaxed, but things get in the way, as we will see. It is vital therefore to think about work as clearly as possible, so it will be easier to play. Let's start with some distinctions.

Play is often athletic, but not all athletics is play, and not all play is athletic. Most sports probably began as play of some kind, but sport is not always playful. The desire to win, beat the clock, or defeat an opponent, easily drives the playfulness out of competitive athletics. Sometimes the exertion (think of marathons) and the business (think of salary negotiations) of sport suffocate the enjoyment. When we play, we are supposed to smile and laugh, but during competitive sports we keep our game faces on.

We usually exercise when we play, but we can play without exercising and exercise without playing. We play board games and make-believe, but neither one is exercise. On the other hand, exercise includes running, weight lifting, aerobics, martial arts, and calisthenics. Like play, they are voluntary, but we rightly call them "working out," not "playing out." Running and weight lifting are exercise and we may enjoy them, but the level of exertion makes them serious. We don't joke around while lifting weights, unless we pervert them, for example, by lifting light weights and pretending they are heavy. Unlike play, we rarely exercise for its own sake. We do it to reach a goal, to stay fit, or to recover from an injury.

Play is fun and relaxing, but not all relaxation is play. To sit by a stream is relaxing, but not play. Play is participatory. You need a partner (at least a computer program) to play. Movies and amusement park rides can be fun, but they are too passive to call them play.

Work has playful moments, but work is not play. We can be playful at work, and work can resemble play in some ways. We can have fun, get exercise, and become utterly absorbed in our work activity. But work is not play. It is good to be playful at work on occasion. It lifts the spirits from the drudgery, but if we play too much we accomplish nothing. Whoever said, "We should play at our work and work at our play," was clever, but he probably excelled at neither endeavor.

We could spin out the relation between play, competition, leisure, and games at length, but the concept is clear. Play fits under exercise, leisure, competition, and games as a narrower category of each. Any of them can be playful, if we go at them a certain way—with a light heart, engaging others, and having fun for the pleasure of it.

The Paradoxes of Play

Nothing could be simpler than play, yet play gets complicated. For example, *organized sports take the play out of the game, especially for children.* In times past, short kids played basketball and skinny kids played football because there was always a pickup game. Children play fewer pickup sports than they once did, since adult-sponsored leagues now dominate children's sports. Children know the most important condition for a good pickup game is fair teams. No child wants a game where teams are stacked so that one side inevitably wins. Yet when adults pick the sides in sports leagues, the teams can be unfair enough to yield baseball scores of 18-1 and soccer scores of 10-0. When adults organize sports, children generally have less fun. They also have less play, since there is pressure to practice and perform.[14] Referees and leagues coordinate, yet interfere with, play.

To excel at games is more fun in the short run, but less in the long run. If we excel at a sport, we taste the sweetness of accomplishment, of victory, of that "in the zone" feeling during peak performances. But if we truly excel, someone will recruit us for a competitive team. Coaches then require practices early and late, in pouring rain and burning heat, to hone techniques and gain endurance. We battle through close games, where tension runs high. For students, the bait is prestige, scholarships, possibly even a professional career in sports. But there are always more athletes than openings, so players have to work hard to reach the next level.

Play is relaxing, but too much relaxation spoils the fun. If the seeker is lazy in hide-and-seek, the hider is bored. In athletics, there is no pleasure in scoring when the opponent puts up no defense. If you care about winning too much, it spoils the fun, but if you don't care enough, that ruins it too.

Play brings liberation from the world of rules, but to play well we need rules. Play has an openness and freedom, but if we play blindman's bluff, we spoil the game if we take a peek. A rule book can't say everything about the way to play a sport, but without rules, sports are impossible. At the gym, one group may be goofing around while the other wants to start a game of basketball.

14. "Organized" sports are not the opposite of "disorganized" sports. "Organized" means organized by adults, not children.

Eventually, someone from the serious group says, "Quit horsing around; let's play basketball." The slackers are *playing*, but they aren't playing *basketball*.

Play is the opposite of work, but play can be serious business. Among children, the boy or girl who decides what everyone plays is the class leader. Among adults, if an athlete earns $4 million per year, but one more injury could end his career, is he playing ball or working ball?

The paradoxes of play and the need to distinguish between play and its cousins have led to sustained theoretical reflection on play. Psychologists propose play therapy for children, theologians ask if play illumines the human condition, and philosophical analyses turn everything upside down. Some theories are so sad and humorless that I had to wonder if the authors ever play.

Play is an opiate of the masses, says the Marxist. Manipulative rulers promote sports heroes and rivalries so the proletariat forgets its oppression. The ruling class offers up violent spectacles, from gladiatorial shows to professional football, so the underclass can burn off its aggression, misdirecting its rage onto referees or the captains of opposing teams. Play is an outlet for suppressed desires, says the Freudian. Alien moral codes can only control the dark impulses of mankind for so long. We need bursts of play, even lawless revelry, like the Mardi Gras. People need a dash of freedom so they can tolerate their routines. Play is a distraction, says the existentialist. It diverts us, so we don't notice the meaninglessness of life.[15]

Marx, Freud, and the existentialists all agree: sports and play can't be taken at face value. The critics err when they make play so complicated and subversive. Yet they are not entirely wrong. Play *can* distract us, so we don't see the hard truths of life. Men *do*

---

15. Jürgen Moltmann, *Theology of Play*, trans. Reinhard Ulrich (New York: Harper & Row, 1972), 1-14.

use play to forget the miseries of daily life. Play *can* function as a diversion that causes less trouble than alcohol or drugs.

Pastors know, furthermore, that play can become an idol. I once played tennis on a tiny, windy rooftop court ten stories above the city street. The conditions made serious competition impossible (e.g., a proper overhead meant a lost ball), nonetheless one man was lunging and diving, on asphalt, for balls at the edge of his reach. My partner whispered the explanation, "He has to win. He has nothing else to live for." When we confuse our performance and our identity, a defeat brings an identity crisis.

Like every good gift, play can be abused. Yet we want to live with the psalmist who said, "Bless the LORD, O my soul" (Ps. 103:1, 2, 22 ESV). Play lets us bless the Lord. His abundance lets us play. We can play because we have a Father who cares for us. Because we don't need to spend every minute working, we can play. Because we don't have to prove our worth by winning, we can let play remain playful, no matter how hard we go at it.

| 13 |

The Glory and the Misery of Man

Sammy Henson ended a storied wrestling career with a silver medal in the Olympics. Henson, who suffered a narrow defeat in the hard-fought gold-medal contest, took no pride in second place. When the match ended, he sprinted off the mat and emitted a primal scream of anguish. He fell to the floor, kicking and wailing. At the medal ceremony, he wept openly, then hurled his silver medal to the ground as it finished. Since childhood, Henson had dreamed of the glory of gold; anything less was misery.

The hunger for excellence, even glory, rests deep in our hearts. Even if we don't yearn for championships or the top rank, we expect the best of ourselves. Musicians count on playing the right notes, with expressive phrasing. Speakers expect to master their content and win their audience to it. Athletes view their best days as normal. After excelling, performers don't marvel at their incredible luck. They think, "That's the way it's supposed to be," and plan to do even better next time. Similarly, though managers and administrators know large projects never go smoothly, glitches still feel odd. Craftsmen expect to do the right thing, the right way, the first time. Even repairmen half-anticipate fixing things promptly and permanently. When they can't induce pipes, wires, or computer programs to run properly, they are as likely to say, "That's odd," as to say, "That's typical." Through it all, excellence seems normal and failure seems jarring.

The drive to excel testifies that God designed us for glory. He created us in his image, as the crown of creation. He designed humanity to govern the world for him. He charged us to be fruitful and multiply, to rule the earth and subdue it. He commissioned us to represent his rule, so that all things are subject to him through us (Gen. 1, 2).

Children's books like to say every little girl is a princess. But they are too modest. We are a race of kings and queens, overseeing the earth on God's behalf. God charges us to rule for him at work, at home, and at play. When we pull weeds and plant seeds, we develop creation's potential for beauty and fruit. As we govern our homes and schedules, as we develop mind and body, we become instruments honed for his use.

Perhaps this sounds grandiose. Govern the world for God? I can hardly govern my desk top. Subdue the earth? I can hardly subdue the crabgrass in my yard. When a lawn-care analyst accosts me with the ugly truth about my grass-to-weed ratio, I can say, "They may seem like weeds to you, but I'm actually fostering biodiversity." Still, the weeds remain. In some moods, we love ironic sayings like this, "Experience is a great teacher. It allows you to recognize a mistake when you make it the second time."

Self-government is even more elusive. How shall we make our minds instruments of God's rule? Do we acquire a taste for heavy reading as for gourmet coffee, a sip at a time? How can we make our bodies God's instruments if pushing cookies aside is a challenge? God knows the apparent absurdity of it all and addresses it in Hebrews.

Jesus and Our Aspirations

Hebrews provides us a proper self-understanding. But it doesn't begin by assuring us of our worth or significance. Indeed, Hebrews does not begin with mankind at all. Instead, it directs our attention to Jesus, the Son of God, the radiance of his glory. He is the creator and sustainer of creation, the Savior who made a purification for sins (1:1–5). He sits at God's right hand, ruling from his throne, until all his enemies are subject to him (vv. 8–13).

Hebrews then turns to mankind in 2:5–15, where we hear high praise from Psalm 8:4–6:[1]

> What is man that you are mindful of him,
>   the son of man that you care for him?
> You made him a little lower than the angels;
>   you crowned him with glory and honor
> and put everything under his feet. (Heb. 2:6–8)

This sort of acclaim could certainly underscore our significance and boost our self-esteem. But as we read on, Hebrews' description of human majesty begins to sound a little *too* lofty: "In putting everything under him, God left nothing that is not subject to him" (v. 8). When he says *everything* is subject and *nothing* is not subject, it clashes with our experience. So Hebrews immediately adds: "Yet at present we do not *see* everything subject to him. But we see Jesus, who was made a little lower than the angels, now crowned with glory and honor" (vv. 8–9).

So Hebrews does agree with our experience. Indeed, the physical environment and human society are in such disarray that the call to rule the world seems a joke. We can hardly govern ourselves, let alone the world. We just can't see human majesty, but, Hebrews adds, we *do* see Jesus (v. 9). Everything *is* under *his* feet. He *is* crowned with glory and honor. He fulfills God's goal for mankind.

In other words, Hebrews says, "I hear the praise of mankind in Psalm 8, but you must see that it is *most* true of Jesus, the One True Man. He was lower than the angels for a little while. Yet he is now crowned with glory and honor and rules over all things." After the fall, Psalm 8 best describes Jesus, although it is also a

---

1. Hebrews uses several Old Testament quotations to praise Christ. Passages cited from Psalms 2, 45, and 110 originally described Israel's kings. But as Hebrews quotes lines about thrones, scepters, and rule over enemies, it applies them to Jesus. Thus the highest praise of mankind is never fully true of ordinary man. Rather Jesus, the God-man, fulfills the songs that praise mankind. This is especially true of Psalm 8, which initially described Adam and Eve (mankind at creation). The grandeur of Psalm 8 is unattainable for us, after the fall, but Jesus steps in to take the role of man in glory.

fair description of believers, in our union with the Lord, for he is our representative. Jesus fulfilled the charge God gave us, to rule. Then he took us with him to the glory God planned for us. As Hebrews 2:9–10 puts it:

> Jesus . . . [is] now crowned with glory and honor because he suffered death, so that by the grace of God he might taste death for everyone. In bringing many sons to glory, it was fitting that God, for whom and through whom everything exists, should make the author of their salvation perfect through suffering.

God created mankind in his image and crowned us with glory. By rebelling, we ruined that glory. But Jesus redeemed us from our ruin, and God crowned him with glory and honor. He could have kept the glory scheduled for us to himself. But he wanted to bring "many sons to glory." That is, *he wants us to share his glory with us.* Therefore, Jesus endured a humiliation greater than ours, in order to bring us a joy that is near to his, "so that by the grace of God he might taste death for everyone" (v. 9).

To "taste death" means to experience death. On the cross, *he* experienced the consequences of *our* rebellion, that we might live with him (v. 10). In this way, Jesus solved two great problems. He removed our *subjective* misery over our lamentable behavior. He also removed our *objective* guilt before God. He felt compassion for both forms of our misery, and removed it.

Hebrews says it is "fitting" for Jesus to rescue us (v. 10). He did not have to do this, but it fits because God is gracious, loving, and good. It fits God's character to do this through Jesus, the "author" of salvation. The word *author* is unusual. The original is a compound word whose parts mean *chief* and *leader.* Jesus is our chief leader, our pioneer, trailblazer, hero, or champion. In context, *champion* is a good translation, because Jesus fought and defeated our great foe, Satan. He is also a *trailblazer* because we follow his path.

Jesus Is Mankind's Champion

Hebrews 2 calls Jesus our champion, and the concept has biblical roots. In antiquity, some wars were settled when two champions engaged in combat on behalf of their people. David and Goliath fought each other as champions of their armies. The troops were at a standoff, so they resolved the impasse by letting two champions represent them (1 Sam. 17).

The idea of champions fighting on behalf of their people is also modern. In elections, political parties put forward their champions or heroes, and whoever wins, wins for the whole party. In athletic championships, teams represent their school, city, or state. If a city's team wins, the whole city feels it has won, too.

All of us have cheered for a champion who represents us, even though the applause can sound faintly ridiculous. We hold our noses and vote for politicians with glaring flaws. We cheer for athletes who play for our teams solely because the local billionaire owner won a bidding war for the star's talents.

But Jesus is one champion who deserves our cheers. He calls himself our champion, a hero who defeats our malevolent foe. Jesus compares Satan to "a strong man, fully armed" who "guards his own house." But Jesus is stronger: "When someone stronger attacks and overpowers him, he takes away the armor in which the man trusted and divides up the spoils" (Luke 11:21–22). Jesus "binds the strong man" by casting out demons, healing disease, and proclaiming God's reign (Matt. 12:29; Mark 3:27 ESV). But above all, he "shared in [our] humanity so that by his death he might destroy . . . the devil—and free those who all their lives were held in slavery by their fear of death" (Heb. 2:14–15).

Jesus is the victor, but, paradoxically, he won by appearing to lose. He achieved victory over Satan by letting Satan's minions kill him, then rising from death. By "tasting death" *for* us, he broke Satan's quasi-legitimate hold *over* us. Satan's hold is "quasi-legitimate" because he can say we have done evil, even love evil, so that we deserve to die (Rev. 12:10). But when Jesus died in our place, Satan lost the right to accuse us. By rising,

Jesus also liberated us from fear of death. He demonstrated that resurrection, not death, is the final word.

Jesus Accepts Us

So Jesus is our champion. Unlike many heroes, however, he never despises his admirers. He is not like an entertainer who tries to escape adoring mobs, but like a politician, who wades into the crowds. But Jesus does not make contact because of an impending election (kings are not reelected). He seeks us because he loves us and is proud of us. Hebrews says, "Jesus is not ashamed to call [us] brothers" (2:11).

Of course, he *could* be ashamed of us. Almost every clan has a shameful relative—an uncle, perhaps, with no social grace, no job, missing teeth, and perhaps an indictment or two. In God's family, you and I are prime candidates to embarrass God our Father. We do plenty that might shame our older brother, Jesus. Yet, amazingly, he is not ashamed to call us brothers, nor is the Father "ashamed to be called [our] God" (Heb. 11:16).

Let me put it differently: I hesitate to put Christian bumper stickers on my car, because I wonder if my driving is up to it. I'm not a bad driver, but I don't want Jesus' reputation to be identified with every hurried decision I make on the road. I might shame him. But my hesitation is trifling, since my very life is like a car adorned with Christian stickers. You and I commit crimes, misdemeanors, and follies that could dishonor Jesus. These acts render us unworthy of Jesus' family. Nonetheless, God loves us and claims us as his children.

Many men long for this pure acceptance, and seek it in vain from their fathers.

- Our fathers said, "You will never amount to anything, you will never do anything right." But God declares, "These are the good works I prepared for you to do" (see Eph. 2:10).
- Our fathers said, "You weakling." But Jesus whispers, "I empathize with your weakness."

- Our parents hissed, "You should be ashamed of yourself." But Jesus calls us his brothers and shares his glory with us. Paul says that we "with unveiled faces all reflect the Lord's glory [and] are being transformed into his likeness with ever-increasing glory" (2 Cor. 3:18).

Jesus is like a man proudly introducing two beloved friends to each other. He presents God the Father to us and presents us to the Father. He declares the Father's excellence to us: "In the presence of the congregation I will sing your praises" (Heb. 2:12). But he also presents us, his brothers, to God. Jesus says, "Here am I, and the children God has given men" (2:13).

How amazing, how liberating! There is, deep in every man, a feeling that he must prove himself. Of course, many give up and decide to do barely enough to get by. Still, most men want to prove themselves by performing notable deeds. Yet we all have multiple flaws, so we doubt that we have proven ourselves. Whatever we achieve, it is never enough, until we are number one. But even if we become number one, we have to stay there, which is another uncertain proposition. Jesus bids us to quit the performance game. He accepts us as family just as we are.

Of course, struggles continue even after God accepts us. If Jesus, our big brother, "tasted death," though crowned with glory and honor, we ought to expect adversity, too. God announced his pleasure with Jesus from the beginning, but he still brought Jesus to maturity through suffering (Heb. 5:8). Jesus is our elder brother, and younger brothers should expect our lives to echo his, in both suffering and glory (Heb. 2:11–13; 1 Peter 1:11; 4:13–14; 5:1).

Jesus and Our Failure

We now have the elements for a sober self-concept: We enjoyed grandeur at creation. We fell into misery through sin. Then we returned to grandeur in Christ. The grandeur-misery-grandeur pattern is our condition. A realistic self-concept makes us expect to succeed, but also to fail, and feel miserable over it.

The thought, "I should be doing better," is fundamentally true. We belong to a great family, a family of champions. God made us for something better than failure, whether "failure" means sin or poor performance. Since we belong to God's excellent family, we can handle disappointment. But first, recall some fruitless strategies we use to manage failure:

- We indulge in self-pity: "I'm a wretched, miserable failure. No one is worse than me."
- We wallow in self-recrimination: "I failed myself, I failed those who love and trust me. People should stay away from me, and I wish I could get away from myself."
- We shift blame and get angry at others: "I failed, but it's really *his* fault."
- We resolve, with grim determination to do better next time—and forever: "I'll never commit *that* mistake again."
- We brush it off, pretending we didn't fail or don't care. Or, like the fans who once attended the games of a dreadful football team with bags over their heads, we create ironic detachment from ourselves.
- We berate ourselves, calling ourselves idiots or dummies and cursing ourselves.

But because we possess a secure identity in Christ, because God loves and accepts us despite our blunders, we have better ways to respond to failure. If we do our best, but our performance falls short, we can accept it, saying, "I did my best, but it wasn't God's will to bless my labors just now." If we sin, we count reproof as a blessing (Prov. 9:9). We say, "I failed because I erred" or "I failed because I was not diligent." We hope to learn a lesson, but we know better than to vow "never again." We probably *will* sin or commit our sins again—and there will be mercy that day, too.

If we can't detect why we faltered, other options remain. If we "fail" in a good cause, we can view it as experimental scientists do. Edison tried dozens of substances before finding one that worked as the filament for his light bulb. But for Edison, the flameouts were minor successes. Each one taught him one more way *not* to do it. Above all, let us recall that God loves us and calls us his own, however we may fail.

If we know who we are, it is easier to accept disappointments. I think of the American poet Billy Collins, whose brilliant, witty word pictures will never succeed, if "success" means winning a mass audience, because *there is no mass audience* for poetry in the United States. I think of Kierkegaard, his writings neglected for a century, and recall a Christian bookseller, commenting acidly on a new monograph, "It will never sell; it's too good." But what if God calls you to write poetry? What if you are a musician who fits no marketing niche? An inventor who is too far ahead of the times? Know this: human taste is fallible. God prizes faithfulness, not success. If we please him, believing *his* appraisal matters most, we can "fail" without fear.

Heroism Today

I believe Christians can secure their identity, in part, by knowing Jesus as the hero who accepts us. But this idea is hard to grasp because our culture has lost its sense of the heroic. Materialism reduces mankind to "an accidental collocation of atoms." How can an arrangement of atoms be "heroic"? Freudian psychology explains great achievements as the expression of suppressed desires. Freud reduced the heroic accomplishments of Leonardo da Vinci to the outworking of a sublimated homosexuality. Behaviorism and economic materialists claim that every human action seeks a reward. All behavior, they assume, attempts to meet a need or desire. Therefore, they allege, Mother Teresa did not give herself to the poorest of India because she *cared* about them; she did it to meet her ego needs, to prove her worth or make a name for herself. Economists observe that every good deed can reap a reward, and propose that everyone is so motivated. In these ways, every sacrifice is explained away. Cynicism rules.

Of course, we still have heroes, but they are one-dimensional. Athletes are mighty men of the slam dunk, the sixty-yard touchdown pass, or the home-run blast. Rock stars play blistering guitars, and opera divas have three-octave ranges. Actors' perfectly sculpted faces mimic every human emotion on camera. Once the media bestow celebrity status on them, children can hang their posters on the wall, and adults can read their intimate interviews.[2]

But don't look too closely at their personal lives. After they throw, swing, sing, or act, they have less ideas about the good life than you. Charles Barkley, the Hall of Fame NBA forward, was also a barroom brawler who was known to step on opponents and even spit at fans. Asked about his chaotic personal life one day, Barkley thundered the awful truth, "I am not a role model!"[3]

But the loss of role models cannot occur without lament. We need to recapture our sense of the heroic, because role models can outline the good life. We need true heroes. Willard McMillan was one of my heroes for years. Willard was sixty-two when I joined his Bible department at Geneva College in 1986. At 5'10" and 135 pounds, with a bald pate, a raspy voice, and imperfect posture, his physical persona was unimpressive. But Willard was my hero. Hard-working and intelligent, he was a captivating speaker and a witty conversationalist. Endlessly cheerful, he welcomed everyone who crossed his path. He spoke sparingly at meetings, but with such timing, gravity, and zeal for truth that his minimal words had maximum effect. Willard and I taught required Bible survey classes together. With three hundred students, some, inevitably, were displeased with their grades. When they complained to me, my insecurity as a new professor sometimes led to defensiveness. Not Willard. No matter how students grumbled when they entered his office,

---

2. See Dick Keyes, *True Heroism in a World of Celebrity Counterfeits* (Colorado Springs: NavPress, 1995).

3. Barkley went on to make the valid point that parents should be role models for their children and that physical prowess alone should not make anyone a role model.

they always smiled as they exited. I eavesdropped to discover his secret: he let them talk themselves out, then equipped them to grade themselves, then suggested methods to improve. This became one of many wisdom-of-Willard proverbs, distilled as I watched him live out his insights.

Heroism and Christian Living

My impulse to imitate Willard was instinctive. Later, I realized that the New Testament often commands us to imitate the wise and godly. About twelve times the Bible invites us to imitate God (e.g., Eph. 4:32; 5:1). More frequently, Scripture bids us imitate an apostle or another leader (e.g., Phil. 4:9; 2 Thess. 3:7–9; Heb. 13:7). Both commands astonish me. It would approach blasphemy for puny men to dare to imitate God, if he did not solicit it. And it would approach folly for one sinful man to imitate another, if God did not command it.

Why, then, does God command it? Because humans are imitators. When John says, "Do not imitate evil but imitate good," he *assumes* we will imitate someone (3 John 11 ESV). Some want to imitate rebellion and vice. Others strive to imitate God. Still others follow the wise, who display their insight by their excellent life (James 3:13).

Heroes *model* greatness. Their example supplies a vision of maturity that captures our imagination and inspires us. We think, "I want to be like that." We need *models* of excellence because many Christians think rule keeping is the essence of Christianity.

Some years ago, I met with a group of twenty-five leading Christian youths, aged sixteen to twenty, from an excellent church. I asked them, "How many of you would say the *essence* of your Christian life is this: First, you don't do certain things other students do, like drinking alcohol, smoking cigarettes or marijuana, or experimenting sexually. Second, you do some things they don't—you go to church, read the Bible, and seek Christian friends. Raise your hand if you think these two are the essence of your faith." All but one raised a hand. Their *doing* was the core of their faith.

Perhaps young Christians are especially susceptible to such thinking. But adults can succumb to "soft" legalism, too (see chapter 1). We think, "If I just do these things, I will please God." But the essence of Christian living is knowing God, trusting him, and conforming to him, not rule keeping.[4] Christian conduct flows from who we *are*. When God renews our minds and spirits, we do good deeds spontaneously and naturally, just as healthy apple trees naturally bear apples. We cannot change ourselves by resolving to keep external regulations.

God delivers us from legalism, but we also avoid legalism by finding heroes and accepting them as models. Good models inspire us. They give a vision of a godly life and help us live by patterns of godliness, not just legal codes. Sometimes heroic believers who have gone before us supply the model (Heb. 11). But Jesus is the best pattern we could imitate. He teaches morals, but his life offers a model of excellence that captures the imagination. He makes us say, "I want to be like that."

Think, for example, of Jesus' relational style. He moved in every circle, dining with aristocrats and fishermen, with Pharisees and tax collectors. He engaged Jews, Gentiles, and Samaritans in conversation. He ministered in city and countryside, with disciples and opponents. He treated all with dignity, yet if someone had a faulty agenda, he shifted it. If someone asked an unhelpful question, he modified it so he could answer what he or she should have asked. He feared nothing—not rejection, not death, not contamination by contact with unholy people. He knew they would catch his purity long before he caught their pollution.

Jesus is our hero because he *shares* our humanity, yet *surpasses* it. In times of trouble, we may say, "Misery loves company." True, but it is more true to say, "Misery loves relief." Jesus provides

4. See Daniel Doriani, *Putting the Truth to Work* (Phillipsburg, NJ: P&R, 2001), chapter 1.

relief. He shares our weaknesses, to lead us out of them. He is our hero, yet he humbled himself so he can empathize with us. He knows our weaknesses and loves us still. Our empathetic hero invites us to a heroic life, like his own.

The Absence of Heroism: Our Shame and Jesus' Cure

We often misconstrue Paul's famous statement, "All have sinned and fall short of the glory of God" (Rom. 3:23). We tend to think Paul says the same thing twice—we are sinners, sinners! But Paul makes two distinct points. First, we *sin*. That is, we violate God's law, transgress his standards, and so become guilty. Second, we *fall short of glory*. That is, we lack greatness. We fail to reflect the divine majesty, as Adam and Eve once did, so that we are ashamed of ourselves.

Jesus solves the twin problems of sin, which creates guilt, and lack of glory, which creates shame. He cures our guilt by atoning for our sins. He kept the law for us and gave his righteousness to us. Thus, when we stand before God, the Judge, he will declare us "not guilty." Jesus' atonement grants us good legal standing with God (Rom. 3:24–5:21). We are justified. Jesus also cures our shame by adopting us and assuring us of his love (Rom. 8:12–39).

Shame is a complicated phenomenon. People ought to be ashamed of some things, such as sin. Indeed, to have no shame is to be oblivious to God's standards. Shamelessness is a sign of a defective conscience (Jer. 6:15; 8:12).[5] On the other hand, we can also become ashamed when there is no guilt. If our bodies are too large or too small, too lean or too fleshy, we can be ashamed of them. Facial blemishes, hair loss, and a weak voice can all induce feelings of shame. If we have less money than our peers, if our clothes or cars fall short of social norms, we can feel ashamed. If we lack a skill, if we are clumsy or technologically illiterate, or halt of speech, we may be ashamed. A chart may clarify the idea.

---

5. Consciences become defective when (1) someone commits a sin repeatedly (especially if they are not caught), (2) the entire culture denies that an evil act is indeed wicked, and (3) they deny that the law binds them.

Moral sphere: Our doing	Personal sphere: Our being
Keep rules ⟶ Righteousness	Display greatness ⟶ Glory
Break rules ⟶ Sin, guilt	Display deviance ⟶ Shame
Solution for guilt: Atonement	Solution for shame: Acceptance, achievement

It is easy to neglect an element of the guilt-shame relationship. Secular people deny the existence of a transcendent, moral God. If there is no God, there are no absolute moral standards, hence there is no objective guilt. People may *feel* guilty for falling short of local standards, but friends and therapists can help them overcome their feelings. Christians, meanwhile, focus on guilt and neglect shame, except as a feeling that follows any exposure of misdeeds. But guilt and shame are both valid categories.[6] We can describe their relationship this way:

The Experience of Christians (Romans 3:23)

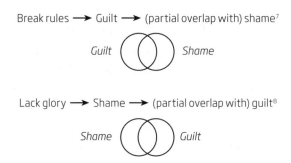

Break rules ⟶ Guilt ⟶ (partial overlap with) shame[7]

Guilt   Shame

Lack glory ⟶ Shame ⟶ (partial overlap with) guilt[8]

Shame   Guilt

---

6. See David Wells' analysis of guilt and shame in *Losing Our Virtue* (Grand Rapids: Eerdmans, 1999), 129–41; see also Brene Brown, *The Gifts of Imperfection* (Center City, MN: Hazelden, 2010).

7. It is normal to feel shame when we are guilty, but if one's moral compass fails, they may not feel it.

8. It is common to feel shame for lack of glory, but lack of glory can be guiltless, as when we spill food on ourselves, or guilty, as when we sin.

We know Jesus removes our guilt, but he also erases our shame and starts us toward glory. First, if we are ashamed due to guilt, our guilt must be covered or removed. Jesus removed our guilt by "tasting death" in our place (Heb. 2:9). Second, our shame dissolves if we know we are beloved and accepted despite our failures. Jesus loves and accepts us. He is proud that we joined his family. Though we do much that might embarrass him, "Jesus is not ashamed to call [us] brothers" (v. 11). Third, we overcome shame if we do something great or significant. If an athlete's mistake costs his team a victory, he feels ashamed, but if his stellar performance wins the next two games, he is exonerated. Likewise, after Jesus covers our guilt, he empowers us to do notable deeds. We perform the good works he prepared for us. We begin to undo the effects of the curse. We *can* govern the earth for God.

The Quest for Excellence Revisited

It is good to know that Jesus forgives and accepts us. Important practical implications follow:

Understand your desire to excel. There is nothing wrong with a passion to excel. It is right to apply our God-given energies to make the most of our abilities. The desire for excellence is natural, and it is honest to admit it.[9] The wrestler Sammy Henson showed that we are bound for anguish if our identity depends on our performance. But God designed us to reflect his glory. We have lost much of it, but it is proper to seek its restoration.

Help others excel. There is nothing wrong with aspiring for greatness, but to attain glory by squashing or dominating or ignoring others is another matter. God created mankind for glory. Therefore, godly men yearn to take others with them to restored grandeur. We instinctively nurture and develop the potential of our children. But we can neglect our wives, though God destined them for glory too. So let us sacrifice some of our development to foster theirs. "Every marriage moves either towards enhancing one

9. Ernest Becker, *The Denial of Death* (New York: Free Press, 1973), 4.

another's glory or toward degrading each other." We should draw our wives toward their glory and let them do the same for us.[10]

We should enlist members of our communities to remove the curse and to seek God-pleasing glory. People set their sights so low. "I hope to make it to the weekend," they sigh. "I'm a survivor," they say. A plague on such pitifully small goals! Let us aspire for grandeur, together.

Let your excellence enlighten others. Like it or not, every decent man is someone's hero, someone's refuge from the storm (Isa. 32:1–4). Fathers are heroes to sons and daughters. Teachers and leaders set standards. Therefore, guard yourselves, for people do imitate you. The way you treat your body and your friends; the way you control or indulge your emotions, words, and calendar—it all functions as someone's model.

Conclusion

We aspire to grandeur because God designed mankind to partake of his glory and to govern creation for him. But we rebelled and lost both our grandeur and our sense of direction. We sin and feel guilty, we fail and feel ashamed. We retain some glory, yet it hurts to know that God scheduled us for more. Jesus cures us. He removes our guilt and restores our honor. He accepts us into his family. He reinstates our rank and strength. He resets our moral compass. His life models the greatness we seek. Our Lord has rescued us from our misery and restored us to glory. Let us live like it.

Discussion Questions

1. How large is the gap between your aspirations to glory and your achievements? How painful is the gap? Restate this chapter's answer to your misery.

2. How do you handle failure now? How would your response to failure change if you could fully rest in the providence and loving acceptance of God?

---

10. Dan Allender and Tremper Longman, *Intimate Allies* (Carol Stream, IL: Tyndale, 1995).

3. Describe one or two of your chief heroes. What have you learned from them?
4. Do you think of Jesus as your hero? What could you gain from meditating on his life pattern?
5. How is your conscience functioning? Does it rightly lead you through the shame-guilt maze?

Epilogue

Someone once said, "No one ever finishes a book, they just stop writing." Just so, I now stop, though unfinished business remains. I see questions left unanswered: Does virtue have a gender? Is the godliness of men different from the godliness of women? (Does 90 percent of this book hold for women too?) What are the other principles for discipline, after "proportional justice" and "quantity time yields quality time"? Then there are questions about the way our culture affects our efforts to live biblically. How can men be rich toward God when the culture urges us to plow all excess into investment plans and retirement savings? What are the effects of working in a market economy where people will sell *anything*—silk, marble, spices, wine, cattle, and even the "bodies and souls of men" (Rev. 18:11–13)? Don't we make and sell things, to this day, that harm both the buyer and the seller, because there is a profit in it?

But I don't fret over the unfinished business. Other teachers and authors can address them. Much more, my confidence rests in God's work in you, by both the external means of Scripture and the internal means of his Spirit. Because I believe in the power of the Word, I spent more time on Bible exposition than most books of this type: for companionship, Genesis 2; for romance, Proverbs 5; for fatherhood, Exodus 34; for friendship, Ecclesiastes 4; for leadership, 1 Timothy 3; for money, Luke 12 and Matthew 6; for identity, Hebrews 2. I hope my words faithfully explored the Word.

Still more important is God's secret work in the hearts of men. He enlightens us and draws us to himself. The last chapter argued that noble heroes can capture the imagination and effect positive change. The Lord himself is the godly man's ultimate hero, of course. As we love him and behold him, we will grow into his likeness, as he has promised.

This thought leads to the core of all this book has explored. As I close, I want to rehearse again the roots and branches of godly manhood. The first root is the knowledge that no man becomes good (1) by resolving to change, or (2) by adopting multistep plans for success in marriage, parenting, work, and play. The second root is the knowledge that God himself is the source and the paradigm of godly manhood. Godly husbands love their wives as Christ loves the church. Godly fathers act like the heavenly Father, echoing his love, justice, faithfulness, and discipline. Godly friends act as God has acted with his friends: they disclose themselves and they are present to help. Godly workers love to create because the creator God made us in his image. When we finish our tasks, we resemble Jesus who exulted, "It is finished." Even in play, we imitate the playful deeds and words of God. He organized time to promote rest and play among his children, who know how to stop working and rest in him.

May it be so for us. Let us rest first in the work of Christ our Savior, who has reconciled us to himself, whatever our failures and demerits. Then let us rest in him. As we behold his face, may we be transformed into his likeness and glory, into men with a heart for God.

Index of Subjects and Names